Peace, Non-violence and Gandhian Concerns

Peace, Non-violence and Gandhian Concerns

EDITED BY

VIDYA JAIN

RAWAT PUBLICATIONS

Jaipur • New Delhi • Bangalore • Hyderabad • Guwahati

ISBN 978-81-316-0457-1

Published by
Prem Rawat for **Rawat Publications**
Satyam Apts, Sector 3, Jawahar Nagar, Jaipur 302 004 (India)
Phone: 0141 265 1748/7006 Fax: 0141 265 1748
E-mail: info@rawatbooks.com
Website: www.rawatbooks.com

New Delhi Office
4858/24, Ansari Road, Daryaganj, New Delhi 110 002
Phone: 011 2326 3290

Also at *Bangalore, Hyderabad* and *Guwahati*

Typeset by Rawat Computers, Jaipur
Printed at Chaman Enterprises, New Delhi

Dedicated to
two great protagonist of East and West

D.R. Mehta and **Glenn D. Paige**

the world needs people like them …

Contents

Acknowledgement

The present work traces its inception to International Peace Research Association (IPRA), Sydney, Australia, 2010. Meeting with the legendary Johan Galtung motivated me to move ahead with peace research. I feel fulfilled that the inception of this book was in IPRA and the culmination will be in the Asia Pacific Peace Research Association (APPRA), Kyoto, Japan, 2011. I am pleased that the volume has special emphasis on Asia Pacific region, a region which is still relatively neglected. I am very happy that I could get contributions from renowned peace scholars across the globe. I am deeply indebted to all of them. I was fortunate in persuading Prof. G.D. Paige, A.T. Ariyaratne, Prof. N. Radhakrishnan, Prof. Ralph Summy, Prof. T.K.N. Unnithan and Prof. Sudarshan Iyengar to make their invaluable contribution.

I would like to acknowledge and thank all those who have helped me in this endeavour. First of all, I would like to thank Padmbhushan Shri D.R. Mehta who has dedicated his life to the selfless service of mankind. A special mention of thanks is due to Prof. Glenn D. Paige whose in-depth understanding of non-killing world has always inspired me. I also acknowledge the support of Dr. Akihiko Kimijima, Secretary General, APPRA.

On this occasion I remember my late father Shri Mohan Punamia who inculcated in me the values of humility and compassion for the exploited. Whatever little I can pursue in life is due to the unfailing support and encouragement of my husband

Dr. L.C. Dhoka. I also acknowledge the intense love and concern of my sons Dr. Nishit and Nikhil and my daughter-in-law Dr. Shikha. I acknowledge the support of my dear students Mr. Jitendra Kumar Soni, IAS and Mrs. Savita Beniwal in completing the work.

I want to thank the faculty, students and staff of Gandhi Bhawan of the University of Rajasthan, Jaipur for creating congenial atmosphere of study and research. I am indebted to Rawat Publications for their meticulous editing and firm commitment to bring the book out in time and in perfect form.

Vidya Jain
Centre for Gandhian Studies
University of Rajasthan
Jaipur

Contributors

Glenn D. Paige, Professor Emeritus of Political Science, University of Hawaii (USA), is also founder and chair of the Center for Global Nonkilling. Author of *Nonkilling Global Political Science* (2002; 3rd ed. 2009) being translated into 40 languages, including Hindi, Urdu, Tamil and Malayalam, he was very much inspired by Gandhian non-violence during a study visit to Gandhigram Rural Institute in 1975.

N. Radhakrishnan, a scholar-turned activist, is presently Chairman, Indian Council of Gandhian Studies, New Delhi and leads the National Himsamukt Bharat. Author of over 70 books, he is also Professor Emeritus and Visiting Scholar in over 30 universities around the world. He was Director of Centre of Gandhian Studies; Director of Gandhi Smriti and Darshan Samiti, New Delhi and leader of Indian delegation of artists to Unesco during Gandhi's 125th birth anniversary. He has to his credit several awards and honours including Gandhi-King Ikeda Community Builders Award, Rajiv Gandhi National Sadbhavana Award, Soka Award for Excellence and MKK Award for Social Change.

Ralph Summy has been a peace scholar, peace educator and peace activist for over 50 years. His latest book *Nonviolence: An Alternative for Defeating Global Terror(ism)* (2008) was a co-edited work with Senthil Ram. A co-founder of *Social Alternatives* in 1977, he is a member of its Advisory Board. His other main institutional tie-up is with the University of Sydney's Centre for Peace & Conflict Studies to which he recently was appointed as an adjunct Associate Professor. Though officially retired, he continues his writing, but with sets of tennis in between.

Sudarshan Iyengar is at present Vice Chancellor of Gujarat Vidyapith, founded by Mahatma Gandhi. He is trained formally in economics and subsequently worked on rural development and planning. He is a keen student of Gandhian thought. He has worked with ICCSR research institutes in Gujarat and has a wide ranging experience in field research. He has contributed articles to journals and books and is also the co-author of seven books and monographs.

T.K. Narayanan Unnithan (b.1927, Kerala, India) has had his early education in India, later in Cambridge and obtained D.Litt and Ph.D from the Netherlands on a research study which later published as *Gandhi and Free India*. Initially taught at Delhi School of Economics, but mostly at the University of Rajasthan, where he was the founder head of the Department of Sociology and founder director of the Gandhi Bhavan. He has published extensively on Gandhian thought, non-violence and peace studies in India and abroad. He has also attended the IPRA conferences in the sixties and seventies and also organized a summer institute on Peace and Development in Calgary. Dr. Unnithan's other interests have been in human ecology, value education and *sarvodaya* as a political strategy. He was twice Vice-Chancellor of the University of Rajasthan.

Balwant Bhaneja, a former Canadian diplomat, was Senior Research Fellow (2003-2008) at University of Ottawa. He has been a key figure in the civil society movement to establish a Federal Department of Peace in Canada. He is also author of the book, *Quest for Gandhi: A Nonkilling Journey* (2010), co-published by the Center for Global Nonkilling, Honolulu and the International Gandhian Institute for Nonviolence and Peace, Madurai.

R.S. Yadav is Chairman, Department of Political Science and Director, Gandhian Study Centre, Kurukshetra University,

Kurukshetra, Haryana. Earlier, he has also worked as Director, Academic Staff College from 2003 to 2005. He has to his credit six books and sixty research papers published in reputed Indian and foreign journals and edited volumes. He is member of Board of Studies and has been Visiting Professor/ Visiting Fellow in a number of universities.

Manish Sharma is Senior Assistant Professor of Gandhian Studies at Panjab University, Chandigarh. He is a young scholar having interest in non-violence, peace research, Gandhian thought, Buddhist studies, rural development and Panchayati Raj in India.

A.T. Ariyaratne founded the Sarvodaya Shramadana Movement in Sri Lanka, aimed at spreading Buddha's teachings for sustainable development and peace. He has authored several books including eight volumes of collected works. He has trained volunteers from other countries in Sarvodaya as well. He is also winner of many awards and honours including Magsaysay Award for community development.

Vidya Jain is Professor of Political Science and Director, Centre for Gandhian Studies, University of Rajasthan, Jaipur. She has also held many important positions such as the Deputy Secretary General of APPRA (Asia-Pacific Peace Research Association), member of Non-Violence Commission and Global Political Economic Commission of IPRA and the Non-killing Political Science Research Committee, Hawaii (USA). A widely travelled scholar, she has over thirty research publications and has made presentations at many international forums. Her areas of research interest are Gandhian studies, peace, non-violence and gender studies.

Akihiko Kimijima is Professor of Constitutional Law and Peace Studies at the College of International Relations at Ritsumeikan University in Kyoto, Japan. He has also held many important positions including board member of the Peace Studies Association of Japan and the International Association of Lawyers Against Nuclear Arms, co-chair of Nonviolent Peaceforce, Japan and Secretary General of Asia-Pacific Peace Research Association (APPRA).

Selvarajah Senthan is a freelance journalist and a writer. He is currently pursuing research in the area of 'Peace Journalism' at the Swansea University, UK. He was attached to the Centre for the Study of Human Rights, University of Colombo, Sri Lanka as a Research and Publications Officer. He has over two years of experience in media and conflict research (2005-07) at the Foundation for Co-Existence (FCE), Colombo.

Nand Kishore Acharya is an eminent poet, playwright, thinker, historian and a widely travelled scholar. Author of over sixty books, he is currently member of Sahitya Academy and Professor of Eminence at IIIT, Hyderabad.

Ramjee Singh, a former parliamentarian, has also been Director of Gandhian Institute of Studies, Varanasi and Vice-Chancellor of Jain Vishwa Bharati, Ladnun (Rajasthan). He is a widely travelled scholar, prolific author, philosopher and a grassroots Bhoodan and Sarvodaya worker.

Bernedette Muthien directs an NGO, Engender, which works in the intersectional areas of gender and sexualities, human rights, justice and peace. She has published widely, written for diverse audiences, and believes in accessible research and writing. Over the last two decades she has produced more than 160 publications and conference presentations in all the six continents.

John Synott is an adjunct professor at the Centre for Peace and Conflict Studies, University of Sydney, Australia. Widely travelled peace scholar and a prolific writer, he has also been APPRA's Secretary General.

Nishikant Kolge is Assistant Professor at the Department of History, Tripura University, India. His areas of specialization include Gandhian philosophy, environment, deep ecology and dalit studies. He has also presented papers in both national and international seminars and conferences.

Sreekumar Nellickappilly is Associate Professor of Philosophy at the Department of Humanities and Social Sciences, IIT, Madras. His areas of expertise include Hermeneutics, Bioethics, Gandhian Philosophy and Indian Philosophy. He has published widely in national and international journals and delivered lectures. He is also an Associate of the Indian Institute of Advanced Study, Shimla.

Introduction

VIDYA JAIN

The twentieth century is the bloodiest century in history with two world wars and endless conflicts. The last decades have put the world on the path of globalisation where phenomena of intolerance, terrorism and wars are inherent. If we look at the balance sheet of development and human well-being, of power and poverty, of hegemony and equilibrium and of global village and fractured civilisation, a disastrous picture of the new world (dis)order emerges. The basic nature of world cosmos (i.e., truth, beauty and goodness) is shattered.

The liberalisation of trade has led the way to enslavement of people. The industrial technological development, military supremacy, cultural hegemony and dehumanising competition have endangered the very existence of human souls and mother nature. The world today is composed of autonomous, solitary individuals and big markets. This is a world without families, neighbourhood, ethnic communities, cities, towns and even nations.

The contemporary world is witnessing a continuing struggle between the forces of violence and the compulsions of non-violence. While violence seems to be getting a grip on the thinking and behaviour of man, it is also leading to the emergence of increasing revulsion against itself.

There is thus a need to create some sensitivity about the growing incidence of violence and new challenges to non-violence in different countries as also developing an understanding of how to move to a peaceful world order of Gandhian vision. Today, Gandhi is relevant as he was never before. There is a strong need to understand Gandhi in this complex context of globalised world.

Gandhi is an apostle of peace, a man who lived and died for peace and non-violence. To quote Gandhi, "Non-violence is the greatest force at the disposal of mankind. It is mightier than the mightiest weapon of destruction devised by the ingenuity of man. Destruction is not the law of humans. Man lives freely by his readiness to die, if need be, at the hands of his brother, never by killing him. The first condition of non-violence is justice all round in every department of life. Perhaps, it is too much to expect of human nature. I do not, however, think so. No one should dogmatise about the capacity of human nature of generation or exaltation."

The more one learns of the legacy of non-violence, the more he or she can be confident of its future. Alternatives to violence exist and many individuals and groups have conducted creative reflections on non-violence and engaged in creative non-violent action. It implies active and dynamic love, respect and reverence for all living beings that inhabit this planet.

The world is not just a world of conflicts and wars, of greed and hatred, of possession and waste. More people live in peace and harmony. More people care for others than self. More people follows the dictum of 'simple living and high thinking' than those who lead luxurious lifestyle.

An effort to harmonise ecology, society, polity, economy, religion and technology with what Gandhi calls a law of life is essential. The present volume, therefore, attempts to share international understanding which will enable us to re-live the legacy of non-violence and peace. The essays contained in this volume are inspired by a commitment to establish a culture of peace and strengthening the forces of non-violence throughout the globe. Each contributor has made in-depth analysis of theoretical understanding of Gandhian paradigm and empirical reality of different societies. The fact that contributors are drawn from different countries indicate that non-violence has now become a global concern.

The volume has been divided into three sections. The first section, mainly dealing with the Gandhian perspective on non-violence, begins with an article "Gandhi's Contribution to Global Non-violent Awakening" by Glenn D. Paige. According to Paige, Gandhi might summarise the problems of today's global village pointing to the fingers of his left hand, "peace and disarmaments, economic justice, human rights, preservation of the environment and realization of problem-solving cooperation among all the people of the earth". Then pointing to his wrist he might add, "this is non-violence, the way we must go about solving these problems".

N. Radhakrishnan in his scholarly discourse warns us about the threats and challenges of grinding poverty, frightening environmental degradation and questions of human survival and security. The present century is an era of war and violence though the growth of science and technologies has reached an all-time high. But Gandhi's prophetic assertion is the silver lining in this dark horizon is the recognition by the humanity that violence cannot be countered by violence and the answers to the various questions and problems facing humanity could be found only through non-violence.

Ralph Summy in his article "Gandhi's Non-violent Power Perspective: A Comparative Study" examines the revolution of 'Ramrajya' (the Kingdom of Heaven on Earth). The author brings a sharp contrast between the Gandhian template and the way power relations are envisaged by most political scientists.

Sudarshan Iyengar argues that the Gandhian model of self-regulated individual has greater potential to move towards sustainable and non-violent societies. Gandhi's macro-model of society is consistent with the micro-model he sets for an individual. It is interesting to note that a set of self-regulated individuals not only feel liberated, but also simultaneously help build a sustainable society that requires least governance and equally takes care of ecological questions.

T.K.N. Unnithan's article "Mahatma Gandhi's Non-violence: The Only Way to Peace" examines the efficacy of Gandhian non-violence in creating social harmony and developing a qualitatively better social order. The greater will be the predominance of non-violence power, the greater will be the progress and vice versa. By accumulating the forces of moral voluntaristic power, positive values of life are activated and the normative structures altered and societies taken to higher realms of existence which are characterised by qualitative differences in human life.

Balwant Bhaneja tries to analyse the unique contribution of Gandhi to establish a link between the moral qualities of non-violence (founded in the religious practices of Jainism,

Buddhism and Hinduism) and the techniques of a social and political action in the course of national movement.

The thrust of R.S. Yadav's paper is three-fold: to highlight the conceptual parameters of Gandhian vision about the world, to make an effort to examine as to how this could be put into operational use and finally, relevance of this model in the contemporary, polarised post-cold war is sought.

In the last article in section one, Manish Sharma examines the Gandhi's approach of conflict resolution through non-cooperation, passive resistance, civil disobedience and satyagraha (holding on to truth)

The second section deals with the experiences of Asia-Pacific region. A.T. Ariyaratne is of the view that victim of violence today can be a small micro organism to the planet itself. Sometimes it is difficult to identify between 'imposer of violence' and the 'victim' and quite often they happen to be subject and object of violence. This demands a reappraisal of the Sarvodaya and Gandhian approach to counter violence and to disseminate new thinking, techniques and technologies. In this context, the author analyses the situation in Sri Lanka and efforts done by Sarvodaya Shramadan Movement to establish peace within human communities and between human beings and nature itself.

Vidya Jain examines the most critical issues of poverty, unemployment and social discrimination in the globalising India and offers study of Gandhian techniques of non-violent action, especially Swadeshi Movement. The hegemonistic paradigm of globalisation has sought to undermine not only the normative-centric social values and economic justice but also tends to dehumanise the world web. In this context non-violent action is the imperative of time in order to realise social justice for marginalised sections of society.

While presenting theoretical and conceptual description about constitution and pacifism, Akihiko Kimijima analyses the practice of pacifism in Japanese society in the historical perspective. In addition to highlighting the accomplishments of the Japanese society in attaining peace and constitutional system, he also underlines Japanese contribution in containing and regulating American military power through constitutional and peaceful means.

Senthan's article attempts to discuss the emergence of new media and its potentiality of providing power to the transnational non-violent politics of diasporic communities of ethnic minority groups in Sri Lanka. The emergence of new media in the globalising world has become a complementary tool to enhance the power of the transnational non-violent politics of the Tamil diasporic community.

The final section of the book focuses on the understanding of non-violence in dealing with several issues of social relevance.

Nand Kishore Acharya deliberates on the basic text of Gandhi's philosophy of Hind Swaraj. The dream of an exploitation-oppression-free society can only be realised if we initiate an alternative methodology or a non-violent discourse which Gandhi propounds in Hind Swaraj.

Ramjee Singh feels that we must desist to applaud acts of terrorism even when employed for a noble cause, because means and ends are inseparable. Instead we should concentrate on peace research and try to perfect the science of Satyagraha. Peace demands a new civilisation, a new asceticism and a new attitude. Man and money power spent over terrorism, if channelised towards Satyagraha, can yield better results and create a happier life.

Bernedette Muthien critically interrogates constructions of security generically and human security specifically in relation to women and women's security. She argues that state-centred security concerns are specifically gendered and neglect issues relevant to women.

John Synott explains that tokenism of putting Gandhi's statues and using Gandhi as a "brand India" is against the authentic soul of Gandhi's path advocated towards the achievement of humanistic, non-violent egalitarian societies in India specifically and the world at large.

Nishikant Kolge and N. Sreekumar try to draw a parallel line between the Gandhian and the ecologist critiques of the modern European understanding of modernity, in order to highlight the basic axioms of this understanding which are responsible for the creation of the modern structures of exploitation and tyranny. Both Gandhi and ecologists problematise some of the fundamental assumptions of modernity on which both the social and political lives of men and their relationships with the non-human world are organised in the contemporary world.

Section I

Revisiting Non-violence: Gandhian Way

1

Gandhi's Contribution to Global Non-violent Awakening

GLENN D. PAIGE

In this essay, I wish to explore the subject of Gandhi's contribution to global non-violent awakening. This is of immediate importance and will be of perennial interest in the future development of world civilisation.

In the course of this exploration we will touch upon many subjects only lightly. Also, these subjects may not be presented in as orderly a fashion as one might prefer. Furthermore, the variation of the English language, that is, my native tongue – and that must be used because of my inability to communicate in Hindi or other Indian languages – may not be easily understandable to all. Nevertheless, it is hoped that the reader would find this paper simple in structure and practical in content. We will begin with the fingers of the left hand, then proceed to the fingers of the right, and finally bring both hands together.

It is said that when Gandhi spoke to villagers, he frequently pointed to the fingers of his left hand to represent five great calls for problem-solving action that confronted India in the struggle for independence: spinning, removal of untouchability, improvement in the status of women, abstinence from drugs and alcohol, and achievement of Hindu-Muslim harmony. Then, it is said, he would point to his wrist and say something like "this is non-violence."[1]

If we had the joy of his presence today, Gandhi might summarise the pressing problems confronting our global village in a similar way. Pointing to the fingers of his left hand, he might say: "Here are the problems we must solve – peace and disarmament, economic justice, human rights, preservation of the environment, and realisation of problem-solving cooperation among all the peoples of the earth." Then, pointing to his wrist, he might add, "this is non-violence, the way we must go about solving these problems."

I do not intend to be labour with another detailed recitation of these crucial threats to the survival and well-being of humankind: the threat of war with weapons of increasingly suicidal lethality – and the need for disarmament; the unspeakable impoverishment of vast masses of our fellow human beings contrasted with the opulence of other – and the need to ensure the welfare of all; the massive violations of human dignity deriving from discrimination on the basis of religion, colour, gender, class, caste, nationality, ideology, and other pretexts for oppression – and the need for mutual recognition of common humanity; the threats to the life-sustaining capacity of the biosphere (land, sea, and air) posed by ignorance, greed, and noxious technologies – and the need for all to respect the life of the planet; and finally, the divisiveness among nations and classes, rich and poor, strong and weak, exploiter and exploited – and the need for cooperation among all to realise global *sarvodaya*.

Gradually, an awareness of these problems, both individually and collectively, is beginning to enter the consciousness of humankind. This is coming about as the result of dedicated actions by many individuals, voluntary organisations, some governments, and inter-governmental organisations such as the United Nations, as well as by performing artists and the mass media.

From one perspective, these threats are being perceived as global problems requiring global solutions. From another, they are problems that we confront in our daily lives – individually; in our families; in our villages, towns, and cities; in our nations; and in our regions. That is, we are faced with violence, economic needs, violations of dignity, deteriorating environments, and divisiveness in each circle of our lives from the individual to the global.

As we confront these problems, many of us are gradually becoming aware that our continued acceptance of violence – our willingness to kill – while not the only causal factor, is nevertheless a major cause of these increasing threats to human survival and well-being. Our historic readiness to kill for security and revolutionary change has brought us to a mental and technological state in which no one on earth is safe from destruction. We are now able to kill more people, more quickly, in more ways, and with more far-reaching consequences than in any other age. As ancient wisdom warned us, and as Gandhi taught us, violence begets violence, and we are faced with prospects of infinite ingenuity in discovering new ways to destroy each other.

Our willingness to kill contributes to economic deprivation in many ways. It directly diverts morality, intellect, science, labour, capital, resources, and technology from service to human needs. Our gigantic global military establishment and its deadly opponents also contribute to economic death and destruction by preventing the need-responsive structural changes among nations and classes that will be required to realise the material well-being of all. The gun in service to power, greed, hatred and ignorance – as well as to more lofty aims such as peace, freedom, and justice – kills by impoverishment as well as by force.

Our commitment to violence in pursuit of human rights places them in eternal jeopardy. The violent freedom and justice fighter of today becomes tomorrow's deadly threat. One righteous atrocity evokes another and hate-filled grievances echo across the centuries. No individual, family, group, organisation, community, religion, culture, or nation can be safe in freedom and justice as long as right depends on might.

And, the more human needs such as for cultural identity, material adequacy and freedom of expression are suppressed by violence, the more the counter-violence that can be expected. Because such needs are common to all, the poor and the rich, the strong and the weak, the use of violence to assert human rights leaves each and all in perpetual fearfulness.

Furthermore, our continued commitment to violence threatens to kill the life-sustaining capabilities of Mother Earth. We kill directly by employment and testing of nuclear, biochemical and other weapons of mass destruction that threaten the land, sea and air upon which all things depend for life. The vast military consumption of fossil fuels and the wastes produced by nuclear power contributes to present and long-range environmental contamination. The resource depletion and toxic wastes produced by industries that are deemed necessary to produce weapons and services for modern warfare further contribute to environmental devastation. So great is the environmental destructiveness of global militarisation and associated disrespect for ecological vitality that environmentalist Barry Commoner has recently warned us that we are in suicidal "war with the planet" and that the planet inevitably will win. He warns that "survival depends equally on ending the war with nature and on ending wars among ourselves .... To make peace with the planet we must make peace with the peoples who live in it."[2]

Finally, our commitment to violence divides us into armoured states that resist cooperation to solve problems in the interest of all. Militarised nationalism absolves us of responsibility for the welfare of others. With soldiers, ships and aircraft we sub-divide planetary space-forgetting that sun, wind, earth and oceans, as well as plants and animals – have no citizenship. Every expert on global hunger tells us that the basic obstacle is not capability to produce food but the politics of inequitable distribution within and among nation-states.

Furthermore, the problems of war, human rights and environmental pollution cannot be solved solely within national boundaries. Like economic justice, they require the life-respecting cooperation of entire humanity.

Increasingly we are coming to understand that these five problems are both interrelated as well as derivative from the cultural acceptance of violence. Militarisation, for example, increases insecurity, exacerbates poverty, suppresses human rights, harms environment and divides humankind. Fearfully selfish divisiveness in turn leads to economic deprivation, lack of respect for human rights, inability to cooperate for environmental protection, and to militarisation. Economic injustice incites violence, violates human rights, despoils environment, divides communities, and so on.

As we awaken to the threat to global survival posed by customary violence-accepting cultures, we simultaneously search for sources of non-violent inspiration and problem-solving alternatives. This leads inevitably to the discovery of Gandhi, his life and message, of India, the society that nurtured and tested him, and of his successors in India and elsewhere as they seek to carry forward the spirit and substance of his work. Without any doubt, Gandhi, as supported by those who made his work possible, is the principal contributor to global non-violent awakening in the 20th century. Of course, when we turn to Gandhi, we do not discover him alone, but also Kasturba Gandhi, Sarojini Naidu, Sucheta Kripalani, Sushila Nayyar, Ganga Behn, and other courageous women, as well as Vinoba Bhave, Jayaprakash Narayan, Abdul Ghaffar Khan, Maulana Azad, C.F. Andrews, Horace Alexander and many others. Additionally, when we turn to India, we discover not only Gandhian non-violence but the principled non-violence of other great spiritual and practical leaders such as that of Acharya Tulsi of the Terapanth Jains, his anuvrat (small vow) movement, and its associated institutions.

Without doubt, the influence of Gandhi's non-violence can be expected to increase in world affairs in the 21st century. Despite the darkness of the past and of the present moment, the lights of non-violence being lit throughout the world provide signs of great hope.

So, let us turn from the violent problems of the fingers of the left hand to the non-violent promise of the fingers of the right. What are the key elements of the non-violent legacy that Gandhi has bequeathed to all who seek guidance in contributing to non-violent global transformation? There are, of course, many – but to continue the imagery of the hand, let us emphasise five.

First is Gandhi's insistence that non-violence is profoundly spiritual. The word is spiritual, not sectarian. In insisting that non-violence must be based on a living faith in God – defined as truth and love – Gandhi calls upon us to root our work for non-violence solidly in the principal teachings of all the spiritual faiths – great and small – that have inspired the development of human civilisation. Surely, the voice of God, the Creator, or the divine presence in life, however conceived, has not been calling upon humankind to go out and kill our fellow human beings and to destroy our planetary home. Rather, this voice has been calling upon us to love one another, to respect life, and to care for the gift of nature into which we are born.

The proof of this assertion is that there are now and have been non-violent adherents of every faith drawing inspiration from deep within the wellsprings of their tradition. This includes non-violent adherents of indigenous spiritual traditions (such as Hawaiians), non-violent Baha' is, non-violent Buddhists, non-violent Christians (Catholic and Protestant), non-violent Hindus, non-violent Jews, non-violent Muslims, non-violent Quakers, and non-violent believers in many other traditions. It includes also those non-violent humanists who disavow adherence to any religious faith but who express profound respect for life in all its forms.

In thus rooting himself deeply in non-violent spiritual ground, Gandhi makes it possible for adherents of all spiritual, religious and humanist faiths to share that ground as a basis from which to work for non-violent global change, however much they may differ in other matters. Gandhi's first legacy is undoubtedly tolerant spiritual commitment.

A second legacy is respect for science. But this is meant an experimental attitude, as illustrated by his autobiography and subsequent campaigns, in which the validity of non-violent approaches to problem-solving is open to lessons to be gained from practical experience. By extension this opens up the possibility of pursuing non-violent global transformation as a subject for modern interdisciplinary scientific investigation – engaging the natural sciences, social sciences and the humanities.

Undoubtedly, Gandhi would have been among the first to appreciate and to recognise the importance of carrying on the scientific work set forth in the 16 May 1986 "Seville Statement on Violence." In this statement, twenty distinguished scientists in fields such as anthropology, ethology and psychology with support of "the representatives of the Spanish UNESCO" met in Seville, Spain, to declare the following:

> First, "It is scientifically incorrect to say that we have inherited a tendency to make war from our animal ancestors ..."
>
> Second, "It is scientifically incorrect to say that war or any other violent behaviour is genetically programmed into our human nature ..."
>
> Third, "It is scientifically incorrect to say that in the course of human evolution there has been a selection for aggressive behaviour more than for other kinds of behaviour ..."
>
> Fourth, "It is scientifically incorrect to say that humans have a violent brain ..."
>
> Fifth, "It is scientifically incorrect to say that war is caused by 'instinct' or any single motivation ..."
>
> "We conclude," they explain,
>
> that biology does not condemn humanity to war, and that humanity can be freed from the bondage of biological pessimism and empowered with confidence to undertake the transformative

> tasks needed in this International Year of Peace and in the years to come. Although these tasks are mainly institutional and collective, they also rest upon the consciousness of individual participants for whom optimism and pessimism are crucial factors. Just as "wars begin in the minds of men," peace also begins in our minds. The same species who invented war is capable of inventing peace. The responsibility lies with each of us.

In sum, these scientists have declared that war and violence are not made inevitable by our nature, by our genes, by aggressive nature selection, by our brains, or by our instincts.

Therefore, to spiritual faith in non-violence as the law of life can be added the vast resources of scientific imagination and discovery that can contribute to a non-violent world. As Albert Einstein has reminded us: "Science itself is not a liberator. It creates means, not goals ... . We should remember that the fate of mankind (humankind) hinges entirely on man's (human) moral development."[3] In short, Gandhi's non-violent spiritual vision, combined with commitment to discovery to perfect a science of *satyagraha*, provides both moral and scientific direction towards the non-violent transformation of global civilisation.[4]

But spirit and science alone are not enough. This leads to the third important legacy of Gandhi that is contributing to non-violent global awakening. This is his insistence upon the importance of both individual and mass action. This is illustrated by his view that even a single individual, if perfectly non-violent, could free India from the mighty British Empire. But this must be combined with his assertion that several tens of thousands of Englishmen could not rule India if 300 million Indians non-violently refused their cooperation. These keen insights into the importance of individual and mass action help to explain why individual dissenters are considered such threats by authoritarian regimes. They explain why large-scale peaceful withdrawal of obedience can lead to the collapse of seemingly unassailable regimes, as we have recently witnessed in several countries around the world, including Europe. Two scholars who merit enormous credit for extending the theoretical and practical relevance of these Gandhian insights are Krishnalal Shridharani, for his book *War Without Violence*[5] and Professor Gene Sharp, for his classic work *The Politics of Non-violent Action*[6] which continues to diffuse throughout the world among non-violent activists seeking to liberate humankind from suffering and oppression.

This leads us to a fourth component of the Gandhian legacy which can be termed *compassionate constructiveness.* Gandhi's advice that we should always hold in mind's eye "the face of the poorest and most helpless" human being we have ever seen and judge all our actions as to how they will benefit and empower that person will forever stir action to remove economic and other injustices wherever they occur. Gandhi's personal example of identification with the oppressed combined with positive action to improve their condition remains to challenge the apathy of the comfortable and the inertness of the comfortless.

A regrettably little known but highly significant example of Gandhi's contribution to awakening humankind to non-violent action to remove economic suffering is provided by the manifesto on the global "holocaust" of hunger and underdevelopment that was issued by 53 Nobel Prize recipients in 1981.[7] They first declare: "All of those who denounce and combat this holocaust are unanimous in maintaining that the causes of this tragedy are political." They next call upon all the established authorities, national and international, including politicians, voters, parliaments and governments to enact the laws and carry out the policies that will end this holocaust. Finally, and most significantly, they appeal to the Gandhian legacy of non-violent transformative action:

> Although the powerful of this earth bear the greatest responsibility, they are not alone. If the helpless take their fate into their own hands, if increasing numbers refuse to obey any law other than the fundamental human rights, the most basic of which is the right to life, if the weak organize themselves and use the few but powerful weapons (means) available to them – non-violent actions exemplified by Gandhi, adopting and imposing objectives which are limited and suitable – if these things happen it is certain that an end could be put to this catastrophe in our time.

The Nobel Prize recipients' manifesto illustrates yet another aspect of the Gandhian legacy of compassionate constructiveness. It encompasses the powerful and the weak, the rich and the poor, the oppressors and the oppressed, men and women, within the same circle of humanity. Whereas violence divides for the well-being of some, non-violence unites for the well-being of all.

A fifth aspect of Gandhi's non-violent legacy is *creative courage*. Gandhi recognised that it requires a lot of creativity to be violent. As evidence, witness the creative investment of intellect that has produced the incredible killing capability of modern military forces on land, sea, and in the air. But Gandhi clearly recognised that it will take even more creativity to be non-violent. This is clearly recognised by all those who seek to discover and implement non-violent alternatives in every aspect of life. These range from efforts to provide non-violent personal, national and international security – through provision of non-violent alternatives to violence-based economies – to evocation of non-violent expressions in science, language, art and culture. In this regard, the midwife-inspired educational work cf Danilo Dolci in Sicily to bring forth latent creativity in children is a direct contribution to a fundamental global need.

Courage is connected with creativity. It takes courage to stand alone or with others, sometimes at the risk of life itself, to make needed changes. Gandhi calls upon us to be "truthful, gentle and fearless". Many in India and throughout the world have responded to that call and will continue to do so. Those deserving of honour are numberless. To mention only one way of illustration: Brian Willson in California, who refused to move from a non-violent action on railroad tracks to block a train carrying United States weapons for use in El Salvador – and had both legs cut off as a result.

If we now bring the hand of the Gandhian legacy (spirit, science, individual and mass action, compassionate constructiveness and creative courage) to bear upon the hand of global problems (peace and disarmament, economic justice, human rights, environmental preservation and achievement of human cooperation), what are the grounds for confidence that non-violent transformative action eventually can prevail?

The first is the recognition that non-violence is the fundamental condition in which all the great spiritual teachers have called upon humanity to live. The second is the fact, noted by Gandhi, that non-violence is the law of human life. Of the more than five billion humans living now, and of all those who have ever lived, only a small minority has ever directly killed anyone. And, since roughly half of humankind are women, since women traditionally have not been warriors, and since usually only a minority of men have served as soldiers, we can have confidence that a non-violent world is not beyond human attainment.

Further evidence of global non-violent human capability is shown by the fact that 39 nations have abolished the death penalty for all times, 27 nations legally accept some form of conscientious objection to military service, while another 25 nations have no armies at all.

Since we have these important general indicators of non-violent human potential, what is needed is to develop and extend non-violent capabilities into those areas of life now dominated or plagued by violence.

Let us now briefly examine the five problem areas for signs of non-violent problem-solving actions, institutions and resources. Although we are honouring Gandhi and will recognise his contributions, we must avoid placing responsibility for non-violent global transformation exclusively upon his shoulders. In all world areas there are non-violent cultural resources and traditions that have their own contributions to make. Gandhi's example can serve as a powerful stimulus to evoke them, as illustrated by his influence upon the Afro-American non-violent civil rights movement in the United States. There, Dr Martin Luther King, Jr. served as a main focus for inspired leadership by many other men and women, young and old, that reached out to all Americans. But that movement also had its own roots in Christianity and in the Black American experience. Similarly, Leo Tolstoy provided a source of inspiration and example in Russia that contributed to Gandhi's work which in turn was creatively rooted in Gandhi's understanding of both Indian and British cultures.[8]

Among non-violent world leaders of distinction, although Gandhi himself incredibly never received Nobel Peace Prize recognition, several Nobel peace laureates since his assassination have clearly drawn non-violent inspiration from him. Among these are: Dr Martin Luther King, Jr. (1964), Mairead Corrigan and Betty Williams (1976), Amnesty International (1977), Mother Teresa (1979). Adolfo Perez Esquivel (1980), Bishop Desmond Tutu (1984) and the Dalai Lama (1989). Other peace laureates, although not so clearly expressive of principle non-violence, have nevertheless shown great respect for non-violence as a compass to guide development of world civilisation. One of these is Mikhail S. Gorbachev (1990) whose participation with former Prime Minister Rajiv Gandhi in the Delhi Declaration of Principles for a Nuclear Weapon-free and Non-violent World on 27 November 1986 constituted a very significant symbolic act to encourage emergence of non-violent global political leadership.

In addition to these outstanding individuals and countless others who remain unknown, many dedicated institutions are working towards non-violent solutions for global problems. Each in its own way resonates to and reflects the teaching and example of Mahatma Gandhi. Each also tends to work not solely on one kind of problem, but to extend its work to make changes that will bring about a non-violent society as a whole in which people can live happy, creative and productive lives.

We will mention here only a few examples of beautiful and dedicated non-violent global problem-solving resources. For *peace and disarmament,* we note the War Resisters' International and Peace Brigades International to which the distinguished Gandhian worker Narayan Desai has made such an important contribution. We note also the courageous resistance to nuclear weapons sustained over many years by the Women's Peace Camp at Greenham Common Air Base in England. We note too the new movement to abolish armies that is beginning to spread internationally after initiation by the Swiss group, "Switzerland Without Army" that succeeded in gaining the support of some one million Swiss voters in a spring 1990 referendum.

For *economic justice,* we note the Sarvodaya movement in India and the Bhoodan-Gramdan legacy of Vinoba Bhave and Jayaprakash Narayan; the Buddhist-based Sarvodaya movement in the village of Sri Lanka under the dedicated guidance of A.T. Ariyaratne; as well as the non-violent United Farm Workers' Union in California guided by Cesar Chavez; the efforts in the United States (Jobs With Peace) and in England (Lucas Aerospace Workers) to shift skills and resources from military to civilian needs; and institutions that provide non-military, need-responsive capital investment services such as the Calvert Social Fund and the Pax World Fund.

For *human rights,* we note the universally respected Amnesty International Working Science 1961 to abolish the death penalty, to end torture and to gain freedom for all non-violent prisoners of conscience throughout the world. We note also the complementary work of Humanities International founded by the non-violent folk singer Joan Baize to support victims of political, economic, social and cultural oppression in many countries. In Latin America, we note the work of the major international political, social and economic human rights organisation Pazy Justicia, guided by Nobel laureate Adolfo Perez Esquivel, that grow out of the courageous protests of Argentinian women against the violent "disappearance" of their children under a military regime. For *environmental protection,* we note the non-violent direct action efforts of Green Peace International not only in defence of dolphins and whales but also to remove all threats to a life-supporting environment on land, sea, and in the air. A source of worldwide inspiration for such actions has been the Chipko ("hug the trees") movement in India to which a senior village woman, Gaura Devi, contributed so much: "This forest is like our mother. You will have to shoot me before you can cut it down."[9]

For development of peaceful relations and *problem-solving cooperation* based upon non-violent principles, we note such institutions as the 70-year old International Fellowship of Reconciliation, the Jewish Peace Fellowship, the International Network of Engaged Buddhists guided by Sulak Sivaraksa of Thailand, the Soka Gakkai International inspired by Daisaku Ikeda ("life is the most precious thing"), the American Friends Service Committee, and the venerable Friends World Committee for Consultation. The work of all these, resonating with the Gandhian legacy as well as being rooted in their own spiritual and historical traditions, refuses to accept power-striving, greed, hatred and ignorance as eternal obstacles to prevent worldwide cooperation for the well-being and happiness of all.

A further evidence of resources for overall non-violent global problem-solving that springs at least in part from Gandhian inspiration can be mentioned briefly four. They stand out in the fields of political leadership, non-violent training, non-violent research and non-violent education.

Since 1980 the fastest growing political party movement in the world has been the creation, electoral competition and electoral success of Green parties, the original example of which arose in West Germany. In just ten years these parties have spread over Western, Eastern and Southern Europe, and they are well represented in the European Parliament. They have emerged also in Australia, Brazil, Canada, Ireland, Japan, Kenya, the United States, and other countries. Green parties show every sign of continued diffusion throughout the world. According to a member of the small group who founded the original German Green Party, Petra Kelly, whom history will recognise as one of the most significant non-violent political figures of the 20th century, the original Greens very explicitly drew inspiration from both Gandhi and Martin Luther King, Jr. Although members of Green parties and movements differ in their degree of acceptance of the principle of "non-violence" as a way to cope with all instances of violence, it is customarily included with other Green values such as ecology, feminism and grassroots (rice roots) democracy as goals of Green political action. Even if somewhat qualified, the emergence of electoral parties at the end of the 20th century prepared to espouse "non-violence" as among their basic political values is of great historical significance. One reason for this is that it shifts the burden of advocacy of non-violent change from the shoulders of the victimised outside the chambers of established power so that it can be voiced by representatives within them.

Another significant institutional sign of non-violent change is the New York State Martin Luther King, Jr. Institute for Non-violence unanimously approved by the Assembly (legislature) of the State of New York and signed into law by Governor Mario M. Cuomo on 1 August 1988. The first of its kind in the United States, the purposes of this Institute are to carry out training, research and public outreach to help the citizens of New York State find non-violent means to change the very serious conditions of violence that threaten their lives. The unanimity of its approval and the substantial tax-derived support given to it testify to the seriousness of that threat as perceived by New York's political leaders of every persuasion.

The chief training adviser to the New York State Institute for Non-violence is Dr Bernard Lafayette, Jr., has developed a very effective seven-point summary of Dr King's methods: (i) define the problem, (ii) conduct research, (iii) educate all involved, (iv) negotiate until untruthfulness becomes apparent, (v) withdraw to engage in self-purification, (vi) conduct non-violent direct action, and (vii) unite in reconciliation. Internationally, of course, the tribute is richly merited by the devotedly effective training for non-violent action that has been given by Jean and Hildegard Goss-Mayr under the auspices of the International Fellowship of Reconciliation. They made an important contribution to non-violent political change in the Philippines in 1986 and continue to train non-violent problem-solvers in other areas plagued by violence such as Cambodia.

In the field of research to understand causes of success and failure in non-violent political action, a principal locus of innovation is The Albert Einstein Institution in Cambridge, Massachusetts, directed by Dr Gene Sharp, whose seminal book *The Politics of Non-violent Action* has already been mentioned. The main emphasis of this Institute is to promote "research, policy studies and education concerning the nature and potential of non-violent sanctions, in comparison with violent ones, for solving the problems of aggression, dictatorship, genocide and oppression". The importance of this research programme is that until it is conclusively shown that effective non-violent alternatives are available for coping with the most serious cases of political violence, both governments and citizens are unlikely to relinquish their attachment to violence.

A fourth major global resource in the field of non-violence is Gandhigram Rural Institute (deemed university), which is located in the Madurai district of Tamil Nadu State, India. Founded by the inspired, brilliant and dedicated Gandhian educator Dr G. Ramachandran – himself a devoted student both of Gandhi and of Rabindranath Tagore, whose qualities he combines – the Gandhigram Rural University is of global significance for at least two reasons. First, it offers us the example of an effort to base a whole university (natural sciences, social sciences, arts, humanities and professions) on principles of non-violence. That includes the effort to have the entire university respond to the needs of all who live in its surrounding areas through cooperative planning and implementation of constructive service programme.

The Shanti Sena (Peace Brigade) of Gandhigram Rural University provides an alternative to violent military training that gradually should be creatively adopted by every college and university in the world as an important source of leadership to assist transition to a non-violent global community. Some important features of the training provided are instruction in the spirit and principles of non-violence, tolerance, discipline, fearlessness, conflict resolution, selfless work with those in need to improve their condition, and joyful recreational and artistic expression. The first pledge of the Gandhigram Shanti Sainik stands before us all as a challenging living memorial to Gandhi's life and message: "I shall work for peace and if need be to lay down my life for it."

The world will always be indebted to Dr Ramachandran, the founder of Gandhigram University and of its Shanti Sena, and to Professor N. Radhakrishnan, beloved of students, who joyfully and creatively served as its chief organiser for many years, drawing upon the wisdom of senior colleagues who were veterans of Gandhian campaigns.

In this calling attention to a few non-violent problem-solvers and to these four special contributors to global awakening in the fields of political leadership, training, research and education, I equally wish to celebrate the existence of all institutions/organs in India and throughout the world that are dedicated to non-violence. These include the Gujarat Vidyapith, the Gandhian Institute of Studies, the centre for Gandhian Studies and Peace Research, the Gandhi Foundation, the Kasturba Gandhi Trust, the Self-Employed Women's Association, the Jamnalal Bajaj Foundation, the Navajivan Trust, the Gandhian publication projects of the Government of India, *Gandhi Marg,* the famous journal for the stimulation of non-violent thought throughout the world, and others. Some of these institutions are known to me but of many I am ignorant. My impression is that the number of non-violent individuals, projects and institutions is increasing virtually everywhere. It will take a major research effort to identify all of them as a basis for globally supportive action.

This brings me to the final observation to be offered for the consideration of the reader. If we are to bring the hand of Gandhi's non-violent legacy to bear upon the hand of violent global problems, in the process of global non-violent awakening, we need the assistance of an institution with global vision. Just as there are maps of world military deployments or of world energy and food resources, we need a map of global violence overlaid with a map of non-violent resources for solving global problems.

I believe that it is within the reach of human capability to bring about a non-violent global community. Such a community will have no killing and no threats to kill, no weapons specifically designed to kill, and no conditions of society that depend for maintenance or change upon the threat or use of killing force.

But to realise such a community we must identify, bring together, and advance the non-violent spiritual, scientific, leadership-followership, compassionately constructive and creatively courageous resources that are needed to bring it about. An analogy is provided by the contemporary achievement of placing a human being on the moon. Long considered an impossible dream, it rapidly became a reality when vision, will, skill, science, technology, human organisation, training, resources, and public support were combined to make it possible. Something similar can happen in non-violent global transformation as the historical preconditions for it begin to converge and to interact with future vision.

I believe, as our brief survey has shown, that there is already in existence substantial non-violent knowledge and experience which, if acted upon by individuals and translated into policy by private and public institutions, can assist significant non-violent change throughout the world. Furthermore, I believe that an institution to accomplish this is not a luxury but a necessity, as illustrated partly by the New York State Assembly's unanimous response to violence within their society – the creation of an institute to promote non-violence. The same logic is applicable on a global scale.

A non-violent global institution should be inter – spiritual, interdisciplinary and international in composition. Its purpose should be to advance and to combine vision, knowledge, education – training, and action to assist humankind to replace conditions of violence with life-respecting conditions of non-violence. In structure, the non-violent global institution should be patterned somewhat after the United Nations University located in Tokyo. That is, with an international guiding council, based upon substantial endowment resources, the institution should carry out its work by assisting individuals and organisations throughout the world to advance knowledge, education and action for non-violence. It should devise means to be responsive to the needs of non-violent workers everywhere. At the same time, it should help to encourage and support research at the highest reaches of spiritual, poetic and scientific imagination. Like many previous scourges that have afflicted suffering humanity, the ancient terror of violence is not likely to subside by prayer and commonsense alone, although both are indispensable for its removal.

A ten-year start-up programme for a global non-violence institution can readily be envisioned. For one thing we need a series of exploratory seminars to begin discovery of past roots, present manifestations and future prospects of non-violence in every country and region of the world. For another, we need a series of advanced research seminars to explore what we know and what we need to know on subjects such as the following: (i) non-violence in religious and philosophical traditions; (ii) brain studies and non-violence; (iii) non-violent gender relationships; (iv) non-violent economics; (v) the role of the military in non-violent global transformation; (vi) high technologies for non-violence; (vii) non-violence and the environment; (viii) problems of leadership in non-violent movements; (ix) non-violence in the arts; (x) non-violent training and education; (xi) non-violent communications; (xi) non-violence in the professions; and (xii) the formulation and evaluation of non-violent public policies.

The results of such explorations, research inventories and discoveries should be brought together in forms suitable for informing humankind of its non-violent heritage. From the basis, research, education, and policy development can be raised to higher levels of consciousness and effectiveness on a global scale. With such awareness, non-violent knowledge, leadership and skill can be focused more precisely and diffused more widely to solve specific problems of violence.

Some will say that a non-violent world is impossible and that therefore a non-violent global institution is unnecessary. But for those of us who have witnessed the incredible changes taking place throughout the world over the past two years, the wisdom of Gandhi's insight into possibilities of human change shines a new: "We are daily witnessing the phenomenon of the impossible of yesterday becoming the possible of today."[10]

Therefore, let us be confident that the seemingly impossible dream of establishing a Centre for Global Non-violence to help bring the legacy of Gandhi and other non-violent resources to bear in global *satyagraha* (non-violent action based on truth and love) for global *sarvodaya* (non-violent well-being of all) may yet become a reality. And let us also be confident that with or without such a Centre, Gandhi's contribution to global non-violent awakening will continue to resonate throughout the world.

Notes

1. Geoffery Ash (1968) *Gandhi*, New York: Stein and Day, p. 243.
2. Barry Commoner (1990) *Making Peace with the Planet*, New York: Pantheon Books, p. 243.
3. Otto Natham and Heinz Nordon (eds.) (1968) *Einstein on Peace*, New York: Schocken Books, p. 312.
4. A.T. Hingorani (ed.) (1957) *The Science of Satyagraha*, Bombay: Bharatiya Vidya Bhavan.
5. Krishnalal Shridharani (1962) *War without Violence*, Bombay: Bharatiya Vidya Bhavan.
6. Gene Sharp (1973) *The Politics of Non-violent Action*, Boston: Porter Sargent.

7. "Manifesto of Nobel Prize Winners", *FDA Dossier*, 25, September-October 1981.
8. See Bikhu Parekh (1989) *Colonialism, Tradition and Reform: An Analysis of Gandhi's Political Discourse*, New Delhi/London: Sage Publications.
9. Mark Shepard (1987) *Gandhi Today: A Report on Mahatma Gandhi's Successors*, Arcata, California: Simple Productions.
10. *Collected Works of Mahatma Gandhi*, New Delhi: Publications Division, Ministry of Information and Broadcasting, Vol. 26, p. 68.

2

Towards a Non-violent, Non-killing and Peaceful World

Lessons from Gandhi

NEELAKANTA RADHAKRISHNAN

Perhaps never before in history has there been so much speculation and anxiety about the future of humanity as is today. Will our world always remain a theatre of violence? Will there always be poverty, starvation and misery? Are we going to have a firmer and wider belief in religion, or are we going to see a godless world? If there is to be a great transformation in society, how will that transformation be brought about? By war, or revolution? Or, will it come about peacefully as Gandhi had wished?

What Jonathan Schell, the author of landmark books like *The Fate of Earth*, *The Gift of Time*, and *The Case of Nuclear Abolition Now*, points out could be of great use to us in our understanding of the present human predicament, that too on an occasion like October 2, which the United Nations thoughtfully declared International Day of Non-violence in deference to the contribution Mahatma Gandhi made to humanity:

> "Two paths lie before us. One leads to death, the other to life. If we choose the first path – if we humbly refuse to acknowledge the nearness of extinction, all, while increasing our preparations to bring it about – then we in effect become allies of death, and in everything we do our attachment to life will weaken our vision blinded to the abyss that has opened at our feet, will dim and grow confused; our will, discouraged by the thought of trying to

> build on such a precarious foundation anything that is meant to last, will slacken, and we will sink into stupefaction, as though we were gradually leaning ourselves from life in preparation for the end. On the other hand, if we project our doom and bend our efforts towards survival – if we arouse ourselves to the peril and act to forestall it, making ourselves the allies of life – then, the anaesthetic fog will lift: our vision, no longer straining not to see the obvious, will sharpen: our will, finding secure ground to build on, will be restored and we will take full and clear possession of life again. One day – and it is hard to believe that will not be soon – we will make our choice."

In spite of such hope and wishful thinking, there are dark clouds all over threatening a heavy downpour at any moment. It appears there is no respite for humanity. If anybody believed that the Cold War era has ended and humanity could live henceforth in peace, justice and happiness, those hopes have been completely belied in the face of raging violence and senseless killings in various parts of the world. Notwithstanding all high-sounding assurances on arms reduction and cuts in military expenditure, we see only an alarming escalation in the production of lethal weapons. It is estimated that there is an annual worldwide expenditure of one trillion US dollars on arms alone. Even one-sixth of this huge amount is sufficient to remove world hunger within the next six years.

Grinding Poverty and Frightening Environmental Degradation

How can anyone forget the fact that over a billion human beings are now living on an average annual income of less than two hundred dollars! More frightening than this is the revelation that, by 2000 AD, the world population has already crossed the six billion mark. Ecological degradation and the callous manner in which precious non-renewable energy resources are being squandered in the name of progress have started sending shockwaves at least in some sensitive souls.

It is imperative to remember the warning given to humanity of the impending danger by Dr Daisaku Ikeda (President of Soka Gakkai) and Josef Derbolav, in their dialogue, *Search for a New Humanity*. The authors argue that further technological progress should be undertaken only after a careful analysis of the present situation and humanity should not allow the condition to go out of its control.

The nagging question is "what is the contribution of the last century to the alleviation of human suffering?" Planners and administrators do not seem to be worried about unemployment, absence of basic education facilities, large-scale infant mortality, hunger, malnutrition and dearth of safe drinking water, endured by millions of people who live in those veritable hells called urban slums or shanty towns. Most people do not realise that while the nations of the world spend two billion dollars per day on military preparations, thousands of people are daily starving to death and millions more living on the verge of starvation. Every second, somewhere in the world a child dies or is permanently scarred by the diseases incumbent on poverty. At the same second, mankind spends $23,000 on enhancing military strength.

The former US President Dwight D. Eisenhower had realised the enormity of the problem. When he addressed the American Society of Newspaper Editors, on 16 April 1953, he stressed the following:

> "Every gun that is made, every warship launched, every rocket fired, signifies, in the final sense, a theft from those who hunger and are not fed, those who are cold and not clothed. This world in arms is not spending money alone. It is spending the sweat of its labourers, the genius of its scientists, the hopes of its children .... This is not a way of life at all, in any true sense. Under the color of threatening war, it is humanity hanging from a cross of iron."

What We Must Know?

Let us know, and constantly remember, the following facts:

- That enough classrooms could be constructed for 30,000 children for the price of only one military tank.
- That one jet fighter costs as much as 40,000 village pharmacies.
- That half a day's military expenditure would be enough to eliminate once and for all, one of humanity's greatest foes – Malaria.
- That a half per cent of the military expenditure being incurred today would be enough to pay for all the machines and equipments required to help the Third World countries in attaining an adequate level of food production.

The Hijacked Humanity

Most of the nations are guided by greed, suspicion and intolerance even though faint noises are heard about laudable goals such as a global village, a warless century, and a world without boundaries. Noble sentiments apart, the one question that troubles all those who care for human survival and security is: Should we not envision alternative concepts of the future as against the violent structures that had an unprecedented growth, respectability and to some extent consolidation of its hold on the harassed, threatened and starving humanity?

The present century as a worthy successor to the 20th century continues to be an era of war and violence though the growth of science and technology has reached an all-time high.

The one and only silver lining on the otherwise dark horizon is the belated recognition by the humanity that violence cannot be countered by violence and that the answers to the various questions and problems facing humanity could be found only through non-violence.

Mahatma Gandhi's prophetic assertion in this regard seems to have created appreciative resonances all around:

> "We have to make truth and non-violence, not matters for mere individual practice, but for practice by groups and communities and nations. That at any rate is my dream. I shall live and die in trying to realise it. My faith helps me to discover new truth every day. Ahimsa is the attribute of the soul, and therefore to be practiced by everybody in all affairs of life."

This statement of Gandhi, read along with two other brief messages he gave, one to a journalist and the other to his disciples in the government, reveal the essential Gandhi. To the journalist he said, "My life is my message". To the new rulers of India he gave this unfailing advice:

> "Recall the face of the poorest and the weakest man whom you may have seen, and ask yourself if the step you contemplate is going to be of any use to him. Will he gain anything by it? Will it restore him to a control over his own destiny?
>
> In other words, will it lead to Swaraj for the hungry and spiritually starving millions?"

Unpleasant but Crucial Facts

Whenever we discuss peace, we do not forget to mention Hiroshima, Nagasaki, the Holocaust, the world wars and some of the major and minor conflict zones and killing fields in different parts of the world. But how many of us think even for a moment about the hunger and starvation endured by millions of human beings?

It is desirable that we constantly keep in mind the following unpleasant but crucial facts:

- More people have died from hunger in the past two years than were killed in World War I and World War II combined.
- Every year 13 to 18 million people die of hunger and starvation in this world.
- More than one billion people are always chronically hungry.
- Every 24 hours, 35,000 human beings die as a result of hunger and starvation (24 every minute), 75 per cent of whom are children under the age of five.
- No other disaster is comparable to the devastation of hunger.
- The number of people who die every 48 hours out of hunger and starvation is equivalent to the number of those who were instantly killed by the Hiroshima bomb.
- The worst earthquake in modern history – in China in 1976 – killed 24,200 people. Hunger kills many more people every day.

The Shadow of September 11

The insane destruction of the World Trade Centre, New York on September 11, besides altering the course of human history, has also revealed how fragile our castles and glass houses of progress are. The deadly efficiency of genocidal weapons to inflict crushing defeat on enemies has also been unmistakably established. Nuclear weapons or war, though they still haunt humanity, are no longer the deadliest deterrents. In human hands any new toy of this scientific era could become deadly and fatal. Hence, our perception of peace as the mere absence of war and violence needs to be reviewed.

Gandhian Assertion of Peace Through Peaceful Means

Humanity has witnessed several wars and revolutions. Occasionally it has also seen great changes being effected through gentle and peaceful means.

Non-violence as an Alternative to War and Violence

Gandhi demonstrated the irresistible power of 'Ahimsa' as a political weapon and instrument of liberation. He also emphasised and successfully demonstrated it in his various campaigns both in South Africa during the close of the 19th century, and later in India during the early decades of the 20th century. Since then, it has made its mark on the world and has come to stay as an effective weapon and strategy in the hands of those who believe in the supremacy of soul-force and moral law.

While the general contemporary interest in non-violence is largely due to Gandhi's relentless fight for the adoption of a non-violent alternative. It cannot be said that Gandhi is the progenitor of all that goes along with the concept and practice of non-violence. On the contrary, the history of the idea of non-violence as a religious or philosophical doctrine can be traced to the ancient Upanishads, the hoary Indian pearls of philosophical insights and intuition. *The Chandogya Upanishad* as well as the Chinese Tao-Te-Chim of the 6th century B.C. glorified non-violence both as personal virtue and as a desirable societal goal. The New Testament of the Bible also upholds the virtue of non-violence for the edification of mankind. Gautama Buddha, who was a rebel against the gory and corrupt practices of religion, was an apostle of gentleness, non-violence and compassion and he laid the foundation for a modern outlook and emphasised the need for developing social awareness based on respect for all living beings.

Gandhi as a Trendsetter

Plato had advocated truth and goodness, and he gave a vague sort of advice to overcome evil by good deeds. But with Gandhi (and later with Martin Luther King Jr.) non-violence became a creative, challenging and eloquent force symbolising man's inalienable right to live in peace and harmony and to help himself and his fellow beings to reach out towards their Creator.

The tragedy of Hiroshima and Nagasaki, the rampant colonial exploitation which was no less dehumanising than the reality of mass murder, and the capitalist injustice, prevalent all around, have now brought non-violence to the centre stage. Those who apparently control human destiny may still find it as an inconvenient irritant, that would go against their selfish worldly interests, particularly the economics of exploitation that they have developed.

The Gandhian perspective on non-violent human transformation is slowly but steadily receiving extensive attention in varying degrees in almost all parts of the world. A considerable number of social activists, freedom fighters, human rights activists, thinkers, political leaders and even, to some extent, those to whom acceptance of non-violence would hurt their national economics, which are based on military hardware, and those who encourage and engineer troubles and conflicts globally so that their armaments could be sold – have demonstrated their conviction that the non-violent option as advocated by Gandhi needs serious attention. Thanks to this positive development, humanity is assured of a re-examination of the Bismarckian approach of treating war as a wholesome therapy that strengthens human nature, when civilisation becomes too soft and frail.

The protagonists of the Bismarckian notion had propagated the obnoxious theory that aggressiveness is healthier than gentleness, waging war invigorates mankind, and it is genuinely positive to be vigorous, and offensive.

At one stroke, Gandhi demolished this myth – though the significance of the Gandhian initiative was not immediately understood all around. Let it be remembered that at first the industrialised West as well as the developing world did not take Gandhi seriously, though they were aware of what he was advocating. At that time, the difference in the cultural context in which Gandhi worked and the difficulty of many leaders to see beyond their noses were important factors which prevented the international community from realising the supreme importance of the Gandhian strategy. But gradually the situation changed.

Humanity learnt a few lessons from the experience of the world wars. Thereafter, Martin Luther King proclaimed the efficacy of the Gandhian strategy of non-violent resistance in these words: "... The Christian doctrine of Love, operating through the Gandhian method of non-violence is perhaps, one of the most potent weapons available to the oppressed people in their struggle for freedom."

But, still, the international community took the Gandhian initiative as expounded by Martin Luther King only as a freak development for some more time.

Non-violence as an Effective Strategy

As we have already entered the 21st century, a few major developments stand out as one thinks of non-violence as an effective strategy not only to counter violence, but to bring about peace in human lives. In all continents, and in almost all countries, several motivated groups of individuals who firmly believe in non-violence have sprung up. However, it has not yet become as mainstream strategy. The pace of non-violent collective action along Gandhian lines, initiated by Martin Luther King, was continued with conviction and courage by various activists of civil liberty movements all over the world. Kenneth Kaunda, Albert Luthuli, Desmond Tutu, Julius Nyerere, Nelson Mandela, Ho Chi Min, Aung San Suu Kyi and Maired Maguire are only a few of the most illustrious names which come to mind in this context.

The acceptance of Gandhian tactics for non-violent transformation by "the Greens", notably by Petra Kelly, has led to the propagation of a new dimension of ecological and sustainable developmental model as envisioned by Gandhi to various countries of Eastern Europe. 'The Quakers' then adopted Gandhian non-violence as their ideology. This was another hopeful sign and it led to a resurgent collective action for justice and freedom in many Western nations. The impact of their initiatives, notably in the Latin American nations, is quite substantial and extensive.

Several motivated scholars who developed strong faith in the efficacy of non-violence in the service of mankind such as Glenn D. Paige, Gene Sharp and Johan Galtung through their dedicated efforts and sustained critical interest added new and valuable inputs to the concept and practice of non-violence as a strategy for human survival.

Professor Glenn D. Paige is one of those scholars, who have been instrumental in bringing into the scene a whole generation of young researchers and peace activists by offering them an appropriate framework to understand, scrutinise and analyse the various aspects of non-violence. The herculean efforts of Professor Paige to develop a wholesome critique of Non-violent Political Science is an important phase in modern history. Professor Paige has also made a significant contribution in enthusing several young scholars of international repute to adopt 'non-violent political action' as their area of specialisation.

Ahimsa as a Moral Counterpart to Wars

Can Ahimsa and Sathyagraha be moral counterparts to wars and other violent conflicts that corrode human character and jeopardise human survival? It is claimed by both Western and Indian scholars that Ahimsa and Sathyagraha can be resorted to in any given situation involving injustice. In their view, even in those situations where armed resistance is impossible, Sathyagraha and Ahimsa can be resorted to as ultimate instruments of justice. This assertion happens to be partially ambiguous. Horsbough has stated that the prospects of non-violence in the sphere of international conflicts are brighter than what is commonly supposed even though people still believe in the efficacy of armed forces.

As Gandhi had advocated, and demonstrated, a conscientious effort to make Ahimsa a way of life, and not a curious creed, is the need of the hour. Gandhi says, "Man either progresses towards Ahimsa, or rushes to his Doom".

Analysed against the background of all that the great preachers and prophets of humanity and votaries of Ahimsa have instructed throughout the centuries, Gandhi's contribution to the cause is most outstanding and crucial. Incredible optimist that he was, Gandhi believed in the essential goodness of all.

As in Gandhi's own time, his concept of non-violence continues to be diversely understood, interpreted and discussed in different parts of the world. While to some it is an ideal that all men should cherish, to an overwhelming number of others it is a moral principle which can guide thought and action. Many people view it as a policy which can be adopted and made effective only in certain given circumstances. A large number of people all over the world find in it a practical tool which can be used in certain situations according to the capabilities of the user. Some others view it as a technique suggesting one range of actions which may at times be supplemented or even substituted by other techniques as and when the situation demands. Each one of these different interpretations is usually upheld with the support of quotations from Gandhi's own words and citing Gandhi's own actions.

Hubert Humphrey, Rev. Jesse Jackson, Senator Diakno, Johan Galtung, Gene Sharp, Erik Erikson and Richard Keyes have found in Gandhi's concept of non-violence a great opportunity for humanity which enables mankind to take a fresh look at the various problems man has created for man, disregarding the laws of nature. France Huthchins and several others find Gandhi's approach towards non-violence as absolutist. To them Gandhi's view of non-violence explicitly or implicitly includes motive as well as action, so that Ahimsa or non-violence is both psychic and corporal.

Thomas Clark and several others also find great scope for the practical application of the principle of non-violence. William Robert Miller, James E. Bristor, William Stuart Nelson, A.J. Maste, Ted Duncan, Willock Michael, W. Sonneleitner and many other scholars and pacifists find in Gandhian non-violence a force and a method of action that can well become the basis for the 21st century man to adopt and practice. Dr Daisaku Ikeda, SGI President, and one of the most profound thinkers of our time, regards Gandhian non-violence as a potent force and an effective instrument to secure justice and peace.

Non-violent Struggles After Gandhi

A cursory glance reveals that during the last six decades since the assassination of Gandhi, a considerable degree of intellectual efforts have gone into the appreciation and understanding of the concept of non-violence in different parts of the world. This ranges from deep sociological analysis of the dimension of the conflict to the policy implications of the Gandhian mode. Many see, in the Gandhian non-violence, clues to ways of dealing with national problems of tensions, conflict, arms race and war. What most of the analysts, critics, followers and admirers have seen in Gandhi, is a "challenge rather than a stereotype". It is natural that different levels of perception developed as the Gandhian approach expanded globally. Since Gandhi represented a model value system, it is quite natural that people viewed the Mahatma from different social, political and territorial perspectives. Klaus Scuts, Mayor of Berlin, was categorical in his assertion when he says, "Non-violence does not mean passivity or political vegetarianism". It is an active attitude, it permits fight for justice, challenges the opponent to declare himself.

The Gandhian concept of non-violence never visualised surrender to evil or injustice, but pitting of one's soul against the will of the tyrant. The philosophy of soul-force visualises three kinds of persons. The first category is that of the coward who supinely submits to injustice in order to save his skin; while the second category is that of the brave man who is eager to redeem justice by person, the Sathyagrahi, the believer in and practitioner of non-violence, who in the fullness of his strength using the natural force method, forgives the evil doer and attempts to persuade one to adopt right doing through non-violence and love.

Gandhi's Early Laboratory

South Africa was the laboratory of Gandhi. The twenty-one years that Gandhi spent in South Africa witnessed great changes both in his private and public life. Much of what Gandhi did later in India had been tempered by the South African experiments. Gandhi's ascetic ashram life had its beginning in the Phoenix Ashram in South Africa. Non-violent resistance, simple living, Charkha spinning, insistence on simplicity and moderation – all had their origin there. In fact, Gandhi had already become a Mahatma in the making by the time he left South Africa for India. His was a heroic struggle, involving several millions of people over a long period.

Gandhi's Influence on South Africa's Fight Against Apartheid

The votaries of peace and non-violence all over the world would find it inspiring to realise that the epoch-making changes in South Africa, signalling the extinction of apartheid, owe their inspiration to Gandhi's heroic struggles in that country. Nelson Mandela openly acknowledges this truth.

Gandhi who proceeded to South Africa as a lawyer to fight a court case, found on his arrival, a situation highly mortifying and humiliating and too harsh for any human being to tolerate. He was already aware of the inhuman segregation known as untouchability which a section of Indians were enduring back home in his own country. But what Gandhi had to face in South Africa was beyond his understanding. The strange experience of man being segregated in the name of the colour of his skin and getting his basic rights denied came to him as a rude shock. In South Africa millions of the local black population and the Indian settlers (most of them indentured labourers) were languishing in inhuman conditions. Gandhi himself became a victim of this dehumanising practice not once or twice but several times.

On June 7 of 1893, a few months after his arrival in South Africa, Gandhi while travelling by a train in a first class compartment was thrown out of the train at the Petermauritzburg station. The charge against Gandhi was only that he was black in colour. The blacks of South Africa were not permitted to travel in the first class compartment. On another occasion Gandhi was denied travel in a coach along with white passengers. Once he was denied hotel accommodation because of his colour. Taking pity on him, a kind individual then offered him accommodation in the hotel on the specific condition that he would not come down to the dining hall, but remain closeted in his own room throughout his stay. On another occasion, he was pushed down by the guards for having walked along a road in the vicinity of the residence of a highly-placed white official. Later Gandhi came to know that the blacks and the coolies were not allowed to walk along that road.

Gandhi also found that the children of the blacks were not allowed to study in schools along with the white children.

These were only some of the visible symptoms of the dreaded practice of apartheid which had many more humiliating aspects, the foundations of which were too strongly entrenched and defied all attempts of uprooting. The fact that a satisfactory solution to this vexed issue was finally found in the year 1993 which marked the centenary of the beginning of Gandhi's struggle in South Africa, is a matter of rejoicing for all Gandhian peace activists all over the world.

It is interesting to note how the local blacks responded to Gandhi. By and large, Gandhi was fighting against the inhuman and discriminatory laws enacted by the Pretoria regime. But he was equally opposing a system that was perpetuating racial discrimination in the name of colour and nationality. The general condition faced by the blacks in South Africa was not much different from what the Indian settlers were confronting. It would be naive to believe that the black population was insensitive to what was happening in South Africa under the leadership of Gandhi. Though he was concentrating on the Indian settlers there, the principle he was fighting for had importance far beyond what the Indians in South Africa were endeavouring to secure. But it cannot be claimed that Gandhi had great influence on them when the Gandhian struggle was actually taking place in Natal, Pretoria Mini and other places.

The law of nature teaches us that the seeds of change always take time to sprout. In South Africa, the Gandhian variety of non-violent struggle had to wait until Nelson Mandela appeared on the scene. No one can deny that the ANC was considerably influenced by Gandhi. The ANC movement drew strength and vigour largely from the inspiration of Gandhi. The basic question that arises is whether it was the brute force of the white minority which kept the blacks at bay or whether the blacks themselves by their own quiet surrender were responsible for their plight.

The fact remains that from their own experiences, they have developed a different notion of non-violence as a creed and a strategy. It was conceived as creative and positive and in their own way the black majority tried to give it a fair trial. The ANC leadership in general and Nelson Mandela in particular seemed to be familiar with and appreciative of Gandhi's work and the success of his campaign. Mandela's speech after two days of his release from jail on 11 February 1990 was significant, since apart from referring to his indebtedness to Gandhi, he said:

> "Another strand in the struggle against oppression began with the formation, right here in Natal, of the Indian Congress founded in 1884, a tradition of extra parliamentary protest that continues with the present. The next decade saw the increasing radicalization of Indian politics under the leadership of Mahatma Gandhi .... In 1906 – when Bambatha led sections of Africans in a war to abolish the poll tax – our brothers who descended from India, led by Mahatma Gandhi, fought against the oppression of the British Government."

Mandela had quoted a passage from Jawahar Lal Nehru before his arrest:

> "There is no easy walkover to freedom anywhere and many of us will have to pass through the shadow again and again before we reach the mountain tops of our desires."

This also indicates that Mandela studied the Gandhian option carefully. Though the release from jail of Mandela and the legalising of ANC cannot be viewed as concessions, they gave definite indication of the superior wisdom and statesmanship of President De Clerk, which none of his predecessors had displayed. Of course, there were other ground realities which prompted De Clerk to adopt an attitude of reconciliation ignoring the stout opposition from the die-hard whites.

There was resurgence in the people's movement despite the imposition of emergency in 1985 and the banning of the UDF and other organisations. The upsurge of 1989 and the open defiance of the segregation laws, made it practically impossible for De Clark to govern South Africa which had almost become an untouchable among the comity of nations. Further, the nation's economy was showing signs of a total collapse following the strikes by COATSU and the mine workers. The sanctions imposed by the international community also shattered the economy. The so-called military supremacy of South Africa proved to be a myth when Angola gave a hard knock to its military might. There were many hurdles to be crossed. Yet there was the silver lining as was revealed from the manner in which both the government and the ANC denounced criminality, and violence. Despite several setbacks, the ANC and the government moved closer. The lifting of emergency, except in the Natal province, also helped large number of refugees to return.

The signing of the 'Pretoria Minutes' augured well for the future. The repeal of discriminatory legislations, the release of political prisoners and the acceptance of the principle of 'one man one vote' were very central to the transfer of power and the restoration of peace.

The deep scars of apartheid and the legacy of distrust, the cynical attempts made by the apologists of apartheid, the growing internecine war among the blacks and the stridency of the neo-Nazi groups made the process of change painfully slow. But, the final victory as reflected in the triumphal emergence of South Africa as a free democratic nation under Nelson Mandela recreated visions of non-violence as a matchless life force.

Significance of Truth and Reconciliation Commission

As the dismantling of apartheid proclaimed the humanistic side of non-violence in political arena, the wisdom shown by Nelson Mandela in the setting up of the Truth and Reconciliation Commission under the leadership of the much-revered Bishop Desmond Tutu revealed unparalleled creative non-violent leadership. Their adherence to non-violence enabled the new leaders to proclaim firmly that "there is no future without forgiveness".

Gandhi's Influence on Martin Luther King Junior

In his own way, Martin Luther King Junior added new dimensions to Gandhian non-violence in the 1960s in order to make it an effective instrument of his fight against evil. When the fight derives its strength from the moral and spiritual caliber of the victim and depends on the quality of his suffering, it takes quite a long time to effect what we call the 'change of heart' of the oppressor which is the goal of a non-violent struggle as opposed to 'victory'. In an armed conflict, victory is not assured to either of the parties involved. The racial violence which broke out in Los Angeles and some other parts of the USA speaks volumes regarding how fragile our modern civilisation is. It is actually an ominous portent and a disturbing reminder of what has been simmering underneath the surging welter of modernity and progress.

These events also reveal how skin-deep is our pretension of adherence to the equality of human beings. It is surprising to see that such racial disturbance should occur in the land of Abraham Lincoln, Thoreau, Emerson, Walt Whitman, Kennedy and Martin

Luther King; and that too several decades after the eradication of the demon of racial discrimination. Gandhi warned humanity as early as 1909 when he published his book, *Hind Swaraj*, that a civilisation bereft of human considerations is 'Satanic'.

Even from his school days Martin Luther King was greatly influenced by the teachings of Mahatma Gandhi. Therefore, it was only natural that he adopted the Gandhian doctrine of non-violence as the most effective weapon at his command to fight racial segregation in the US. He once said in explaining his philosophy: "I believe in a militant, non-violent approach in which the individual stands up against an unjust system, using sit-ins, legal action, boycotts, votes and everything except violence or hate."

Acknowledging his indebtedness to Gandhi, Dr King said: "... from my background I gained Christian ideals; from Gandhi I learned my operational technique."

In another context, Dr King acknowledged his debt to Mahatma Gandhi, while explaining the Montgomery bus boycott programme as follows: "This is a protest of passive resistance depending upon moral and spiritual forces. We will return good for evil. Christ showed us the way and Mahatma Gandhi showed us it could work."

He declared that the American Black will not resort to "more radical ways to gain civil rights", because he has full faith "that he can get justice within the frame work of the democratic set-up".

It is a fact that Gandhi continues to inspire a considerable section of American opinion even today. E. Stanly Jones, himself a renowned pacifist, had this to say about Jesus Christ and Mahatma Gandhi: "I bow to Mahatma Gandhi, but I kneel at the feet of Christ and give him my full and final allegiance." Referring to Mahatma Gandhi, Stanly Jones stated that he (Gandhi) "has taught me more of Christ than perhaps any other man in East or West".

Global Influence of Gandhi

There are quite a few among the liberal pacifists in the West who found in Gandhi the argument against the inevitability of the deterministic social order propagated by Darwin and Marx. Albert Einstein, Aldous Huxley, Oswald Garrison Villard, Roger Balwin and many others were able to see in Gandhi a reinstatement of the Renaissance faith of the perfectibility of man. In contrast to this school, there was the group of religious pacifists such as A.J. Maste,

John Nevin, Haynes Holmens, Norman Thomas who found in Gandhi "a moral equivalent of war".

There may not be a Martin Luther King now in USA, but the number of true votaries of non-violence, both as a political strategy and as a creed, substantially increased. Several internationally famous pacifists such as Johan Galtung, Homer Jack, Glenn D. Paige, Gene Sharp, Lou Ann Guanson, Barnard Laffeyette, Vance Engleman, Dr Richard Deats, Captain Charles Alphin and Richard N. Nagler are the ardent practitioners, exponents and champions of non-violence today.

The spilling of blood in both the erstwhile Yugoslavia and former Czechoslovakia and the uncertainties created by the events following the dismemberment of the USSR should be viewed as the inescapable consequence of incongruities engendered by the die-hard communist philosophy which by and large did not care about purity of means in achieving laudable ends. The validity and relevance of the Gandhian insistence on purity of means – something which the communist blocks hallways scoffed at – became obvious now. The Gandhian concept of non-violence thereafter began to attract the attention of the youth of Czechoslovakia. There arose a general belief that non-violence which is as old as the hills and which is based on the primordial instinct of man to live happily and to let others live comfortably would be an answer to the seething problems of the nation.

Four decades earlier, at the time of the Soviet invasion of Czechoslovakia in 1968, there was a Gandhian protest efficiently organised by the Czech youth. From the youth the message gradually spread to the elders also. The Czech people also organised extremely significant programmes during the Gandhi centenary. The Speaker of the National Assembly of Czechoslovakia specifically stated in a message that "Gandhi's thought is of special significance". In the crossfire of the dismemberment of the USSR and the vaulting ambition of the selfish political leaders of Czechoslovakia, the helpless people looked up to the Gandhian concept of non-violent social transformation more than ever before. In Yugoslavia also, the total collapse of the monolithic communist structure encouraged the people to think of a Gandhian alternative. The USSR, Czechoslovakia and Yugoslavia – the three main pillars of communism in Europe – faced very serious existential crisis, a crisis that called for a gentle humanitarian touch to get defused. Reports indicate that profound political thinkers and leaders seriously considered the Gandhian alternatives in these countries as means to prevent political extinction and to avoid internecine killings.

There is no doubt that the previous century was a glorious one in terms of man's continued conquest of nature including the outer space. Man has reached the very zenith of material achievements. The rapid technological strides that have changed the lifestyle of man also induced in him a new sense of hope and also insecurity. The hope lies in his ability to rise like the phoenix reconstruct life from its ruins and the indomitable spirit of 'never to yield'. The insecurity arises from the realisation that unless worldly progress is tempered with the elixir of spiritual values humanity will land itself on the desert sands of crass materialism.

In former centuries, Europe had overawed the rest of humanity with its superior military might and an intelligent harnessing of the fruits of science and technology. Asia, in the meanwhile, was enveloped in spiritual and philosophical pursuits. The appeal of the Buddha, despite the tidal wave of material progress, swept almost the whole of South East Asia while the Indian civilisation and the Chinese civilisation made feverish attempts to come to terms with the new challenges. The Asian nations were condescendingly described as 'developing' countries while the African region with its infinite natural resources and tremendous manpower was described to be the 'dark' and 'underdeveloped' continent. The fact was that it suited the colonial exploiters to keep it so. It did not escape the notice of the impartial observers that Africa is only a 'sleeping giant' who when awakened will be a formidable force to reckon with. In spite of the hangover of the centuries and the traditional old colonial exploitation which is still hampering the different countries, there is no doubt that the rejuvenated African continent which would be self-confident of its inherent strength will play a crucial role in the 21st century. Brushing aside these seething problems, Africa and Asia – that have several common features in between – would boldly challenge the West and, as and when this happens, it would mark a new phase in human history.

Daisaku Ikeda's Contribution

As Johan Galtung points out Gandhi has become a part of the world political culture and Gandhian thought is bound to influence the progress of the 21st century. Even religious and cultural organisations and movements across the world emphasise conscientiously the relevance of Gandhi's teachings in their strategies. The fast-spreading Soka Gakkai movement under the presidentship of Dr Daisaku Ikeda is a wonderful example. Dr Ikeda, an unbelievably energetic and creative leader, has always emphasised the supreme importance of the Gandhian method for achieving world peace. The SGI leadership has also shown remarkable awareness of the value of Gandhian non-violence as is evident from the thrust the SGI President Dr Ikeda gives to the propagation of Ahimsa as enunciated by Shakyamuni Buddha. Dr Ikeda strongly advocates that a world without war, which has become one of the cherished goals of humanity, can no longer be treated as a distant dream. A spiritual awakening supported by strong cultural, educational and social movements is the need of the hour.

What kind of basic change, then, are we hoping for? It cannot be anything other than a non-violent, non-exploitative, non-killing and a just society where no child, no woman, no man will die of hunger, where everyone's self-respect will get prime consideration and where no one will be segregated in the name of caste, class, colour or sex.

Are we just dreaming about an unattainable Utopia? Certainly not. Moreover, even if it is a dream, only dreams like this give hope and strength to the human race. The tragedy of the present times is that a large segment of our fellow men are still denied their dreams, hopes and opportunities of growth.

Denial of Justice and the Widening Gap between the Rich North and the Poor South

There can never be peace and happiness on earth if humanity does not address the basic problems that perpetrate inequality. Let us look at the following staggering facts provided by the World Watch Institute (State of the World, 2002, New York, 3):

- More than a billion people on earth today lack access to adequate clean water.
- Nearly three billion people do not have access to adequate sanitation facilities.
- Nations have long grappled with inequality; but never in history have the assets of the three richest individuals matched the combined national economies of the poorest 48 nations as is the case today.

- In spite of a of unprecedented economic growth that has added over 10 trillion US dollars every year to the global economy, the number of people living in poverty (at the rate of one US dollar a day) remains more than one billion, without any change.
  A billion people are being added to the human population every 15 years.
- The lack of democratic political representation and the concentration of economic and political power in a few hands have created a fundamental instability in many nations – an instability that has far-reaching consequences in the form of large-scale human migration, illegal drug exports and increasing terrorism.
- The average American uses 19 times more paper than the average person in a developing country, and most of it ends up as trash.
- Some 27 per cent of the world's coral reefs have now been irredeemably lost (whereas it was only 10 per cent in 1992). Coral reefs are second only to forests in biological wealth, and such an extensive loss of the reefs inevitably takes a great toll on many aquatic species of living beings. The goods and services obtained from reefs were valued at 375 billion US dollars in 1997.
- Global emissions of carbon have grown by an additional 400 million tonnes during the ten years it has taken to arrive at an agreement for a modest climate protocol.
- Twenty known communicable diseases – including tuberculosis (TB) malaria and cholera – which had been effectively controlled, re-emerged virulently and spread widely in the last quarter of the 20th century. At least thirty previously unknown deadly new diseases – including HIV, Hepatitis C and Ebola – have also surfaced in the same period.
- After sixty years of near-continuous decline in deaths from infectious diseases in the United States, the trend reversed in 1980 and death rates have nearly doubled since then.
- A pharmacological study made in 1999 reported that only 13 out of 1,223 medicines commercialised by multinational drug companies between 1975 and 1997 were designed to treat life-threatening tropical diseases.
- The market for drugs meant to cure minor ailments like toenail fungus, obesity, baldness, face wrinkles and impotence runs into billions of dollars.

- A third of all adults are overweight in Europe; the figure stands at 61 per cent in the United States. Obesity (the extreme condition of overweight) rose dramatically in the 1990s – by 10 to 40 per cent in most European countries and by 50 per cent in the United States.

Gandhi for Social Justice

Social justice and human rights have been the two key areas of Gandhi's concern both in South Africa and India. Gandhi predicted that unless expeditious corrective measures are taken, humanity will see more mega-death weapons proliferating among nations and there will be population explosion, more pollution and poverty, reducing our planet's life-supporting capabilities.

Gandhi insisted that social justice, distributive justice and community justice have to be woven into the matrix of social, political and community life.

Community justice is based on the dignity and equality of all persons while distributive justice guarantees the right of all men and women to have equal share of essential goods and services, material comforts and social security. Social justice should encourage citizens to engage themselves in the creation of just social and political structures which constitute genuine democracy. Truth will be the guiding principle in all of them.

In the Gandhian concept the way of peace is the way of truth.

What Jaime L. Cardinal Sin pointed out in the annual lecture series in United Nations University (1985), aptly sums up the frightening scenario:

> "Poverty in the third world or anywhere else is an indication of failure. But the subject and agent of this failure are not the poor themselves; rather, they are the victims of this failed human and technical enterprise.
>
> The responsible agents of poverty are the rich and the powerful. The agents of poverty are the economic planners who choose to import capital intensive technologies and whose victims are the jobless industrial workers. The technocrats of poverty are the educators who promoted school systems that are replicas of foreign universities. Their victims are the youth who became alienated from their own people and culture. The merchants of poverty are those unscrupulous industrialists who manipulate fragile economies and destroy their self-reliant foundations. The innumerable victims are the small farmers, fishermen and entrepreneurs whose labour and produce are brought cheaply and

whose daily rice depend on market decisions made in Chicago or Geneva. The poor are poorer because they must contend not only with the exploitative powers of local groups, but with those of an international network as well."

Seven Social Sins

Paradoxically, the emerging scenario whose defining characteristics are a kind of mad frenzy and utter contempt to all values, will have only scant regard to what are known today as the seven social sins Gandhi had reproduced in his journal (one of his admirers had categorised and sent them to him) as follows:

1. Politics without principles
2. Wealth without work
3. Pleasure without conscience
4. Knowledge without character
5. Commerce without morality
6. Science without humanity
7. Worship without sacrifice

Can we afford to ignore these principles if we care for the future of humanity? Can there be peace on earth without the realisation of these basic values?

The Pope's Prayer

The prayer of Pope John Paul II during his visit to Hiroshima reflects the anguish and agony of present-day humanity:

> To the Creator of nature and humanity, of truth and beauty, I pray:
>
> Hear my voice, for it is the voice of the victims of all wars and violence among individuals and nations;
>
> Hear my voice, for it is the voice of all children who suffer and will suffer when people put their faith in weapons and war;
>
> Hear my voice when I beg you to instill into the hearts of all human beings the wisdom of peace, the strength of justice, and the joy of fellowship;
>
> Hear my voice, for I speak for the multitudes in every country and in every history who do not want war and are ready to walk the road of peace.
>
> Hear my voice and grant insight and strength so that we may always respond to hatred with love, to injustice with total

dedication to justice, to need with the sharing of self to war with peace.

O God, hear my voice and grant unto the world your everlasting peace.

There is no doubt that in this universal prayer the Pope has summarised the philosophy of peace, love and non-violence propounded by Mahatma Gandhi. The great and indeed mind-boggling question which stares at humanity even after about six decades of the most diabolical crime perpetrated on the human race, namely, the bombing of Hiroshima and Nagasaki is: Are the bombs hurled over Hiroshima and Nagasaki the last in human history?

There are other questions as well: How is humanity going to tackle the monsters of war, violence, injustice of various types, the grinding poverty widely prevalent in large segments of human populations and what is humanity going to do to arrest the all-time high and fiercely alarming environmental degradation and spread of violence? When can humanity wake into a period where the killing instinct is kept under bay and our grandchildren will breathe the fresh air of a non-killing world which will have to be a non-violence and just world as well. Gandhi demonstrated that change is possible provided we have the will.

3

Gandhi's Non-violent Power Perspective

A Comparative Study

RALPH SUMMY

> If we become free, India is free. And in this thought you have a definition of swaraj.
>
> (*Hind Swaraj*, 1939: 73)

Most of Gandhiji's non-violent campaigns were directed at removing clearly perceived existing injustices. These struggles included the independence movement which sought to overcome colonial subjugation and restore the dignity of the Indian people. However, his ultimate goal went much further. He aimed to create a revolutionary new society – not to see an Indian raj replace the British raj. To reach that new society first required a radical change in the way power was perceived and exercised. Thus, the *sine qua non* of a preceding revolution in power prepared the path to his final social vision of *Ramarajya* (the Kingdom of Heaven on Earth).

Since Gandhiji's basic philosophy has been clearly condensed within less than one hundred pages in *Hind Swaraj*, it is to that booklet that I primarily turn in order to outline his model of power. As someone trained in political science – a discipline devoted to the study of power relations in the public arena – I cannot fail to note the sharp contrast between the Gandhian template and the way power relations are envisaged by most political scientists and proclaimed and practised by most politicians. Another group to bring into a comparative analysis would be the pragmatic strategists of non-violence influenced by the writings of Gene Sharp. The above two groupings can be clearly differentiated from Gandhiji's power perspective, as well as each other's, by inquiring into three interrelated questions that form the focus of my argument: (1) What type of power was used? (2) How was this power exercised? (3) What purpose or use was the power put to? The answers to these questions about power suggest that the Gandhian template might have some relevance to solving the major problems confronting contemporary society.

Power Paradigm of Political Science and Conventional Politics

On the basis of extensive empirical exploration and direct personal experience, I have come to the conclusion that Western political scientists are less inclined to take non-violent politics seriously than their colleagues in the other social sciences and humanities. Indeed, it is not unusual to find political scientists expressing ridicule and even hostility toward their fellow academics in other disciplines who consider non-violence a valid subject of research, that is, if the political scientists deem non-violence worthy of any comment at all. Perhaps this concealed or open animosity is not too surprising, given the fact that there is an endemic tension built into the different way non-violent and conventional politics are conducted. The difference begins in their underlying assumptions of power.

The established orthodoxy dates back to Plato, Aristotle, Thucydides and the other classical theorists and politicians. Plato's model society in *The Republic*, for instance, advanced the view that the philosopher-kings exercised their 'power to' or authority in securing societal order, but when stability weakened to the point of threatening the republic's existence, 'power over' or domination was justified in order to preserve the three-tier system of auxiliaries or military, the artisans or workers, and any rebellious faction of the philosopher-kings. Thus, from the beginning of Western civilisation there existed two types of perceived power: the 'power to' that depended on the ruler gaining sufficient authority to enjoy the loyalty and obedience of his subjects, and the 'power over' that occurred when the process of conflict resolution broke down over a putative vital interest. On such an occasion an attempt would be made to dominate the other party (domestic or external) with some type of coercion, often violence.

Such a model of power has prevailed to the present day. Highlights of this line of thinking include the 'power over' exercised in creating and maintaining the Roman Empire, and the 'power to' exercised by the papal authority during the reign of the Holy Romàn Empire. In the case of the institutional Church, when it was challenged by the forces of the Reformation, it did not hesitate to employ direct physical violence as in the Thirty Years War and the Inquisition.

Among the theorists who continue to affect the thinking of modern-day political scientists is Niccolò Machiavelli whose basic advice to his prince entailed treating everyone as a potential rival, so one acted with the cunning of a fox, but when manipulative skills proved insufficient, one should be prepared to strike with the lethality of a lion. A century later, in the mid-17th century, another renowned theorist, Thomas Hobbes, worked from the premise that the nature of humankind was "solitary, poor, nasty, brutish and short" leading to a constant state of war and insecurity. To escape this anarchic state of nature people entered into a social contract that ceded their natural rights to a sovereign who offered the protection of a secure life through a civil contract upheld by his superior power of domination. When that power waned or the sovereign abused his subjects, only under those conditions could the subjects turn to another figure of 'power over'.

Far less stark in their assessment of reality but still operating from a premise of the necessity of outright elite control (not disguised by representative democracy) were the late 19th century Italian school of conservative elite theorists: Vilfredo Pareto, Gaetano Mosca and Robert Michels. Sometimes they are referred to as the 'New Machiavellis' due to their insistence on the inevitability of political elites being set against the irrational masses. Pareto spoke in terms of a constant 'circulation of elites'. The established elite attempted to either co-opt or defeat any challengers to its power; if, however, it failed, it faced replacement by the new group that – irrespective of its original intentions – would soon become the new established elite (assuming it were not simply a factional struggle within the existing ruling elite). Mosca observed that every complex social order was ruled by an organised minority who exercised authority over the majority, and this ruling elite's power was not necessarily derived from its control of the economy as claimed by Marx and the socialists; and Michels introduced the popular phrase 'iron law of oligarchy' to describe how political parties, although professing a set of high-minded principles, soon discarded them in favour of the leadership's material competitive interests, thereby creating hierarchies. With the Italian triumvirate the key political dynamic came down to who was able to mobilise the greatest 'power over'.

The theorists of the 20th century subscribing to the paradigm of 'power to' and 'power over' represent virtually the entire discipline of political science. However, the names of a few are especially worth singling out for their influence. The sociologist Max Weber had a particularly influential impact on political scientists around the turn of the 20th century when the term 'science' was first associated with the study of politics. In a famous lecture to his students he warned them about entering the field of politics if their aim was the well-intentioned one of contributing to the creation of a better world, because politics led to the sordid business of sacrificing principles to power interests in compromise after compromise. While Weber later slightly modified this austere view of political behaviour, it was the earlier version that was universally adopted by the discipline and continued by the politicians.

When it came to international relations and strategic studies at the time of the Cold War, the power position was predicated on the bleak Hobbesian world view adopted by Hans Morgenthau in *Politics among Nations* (1961). He contended that the "elemental biopsychological drives ... to live, to propagate, and to dominate are common to all men" (ibid.: 33). On the basis of this presupposition the agents of the state act to preserve their society's peace and security against neighbours driven by the same elemental forces and goals. Each party subscribes to the Roman maxim, *Si vis pacem, para bellum* (If you want peace, prepare for war). Building up one's power sources, negotiating from strength and maintaining a balance of 'power over', mixed occasionally with astute measures of 'power to', not only bring peace and security but advance the society's various interests. Thus, the first responsibility of every state leader, whether engaged in domestic or international politics, is to operate on the principle that "all political phenomena can be reduced to one of three basic types. A political policy seeks either to keep power, to increase power, or to demonstrate power" (ibid.: 39). It was exactly this kind of grand dictum of so-called realism that brought the world to the brink of nuclear exchanges on a number of occasions.

In more recent years the austerity and bellicosity of the realist school has been somewhat mitigated and replaced by the leading school of neo-realism, headed by Kenneth Waltz (*Theory of International Politics*, 1979). The neo-realists place far more emphasis on structural and cultural factors, and – influenced at the time by the flowering postmodernism movement – reject the essentialism of the realists (e.g., their stark view of human nature as a starting point). Political actors, it is contended, have their own particular concept of national interests. In striving to advance national interests in an anarchic international system, effective state leaders are compelled to take note of the structures, societal values and conditions that inhibit inspirational and enlightened policy-making practices. While a greater focus is directed at the exercising of authority ('power to'), the commitment to upholding the sovereignty of the nation-state means that 'power over' or domination must always be held in abeyance for possible use or threat.

The theoretical formulation of both realists and neo-realists is based on the evidence of what they observe – an empirical method. Hence, their responses to creative initiatives that call for more experimental and dissenting approaches to how power is exercised are rejected out of hand. They are usually seen as 'naive' and 'utopian'. This is the fate that non-violence encounters in dealing with political elites or autocrats, and it poses the questions whether the different power paradigms can ever be bridged, and, if so, how?

Power Paradigm of Gene Sharp and Non-violent Political Action

Gene Sharp is generally acknowledged for elevating the theory and dynamics of non-violent political action to the level of a finely tuned science. He starts from the proposition that no ruler or elite can rule without the consent of the ruled. Gandhiji would agree. If the ruled collectively and non-violently withdraw their support in large enough numbers – that is, refuse to accept an unjust law, policy or direction – the ruler will in all probability be compelled to concede on the issue or else attempt to intimidate the resisters with violence. The violent option ultimately depends on the loyalty of police and military troops to exercise force and even fire on well-disciplined resisters, an order that may not be obeyed. Furthermore, when this kind of extreme 'power over' is exercised – providing the brutality is widely known within and outside the society – it will often prove counter-productive. Such an action, as

Hannah Arendt has pointed out, is indicative of weakness. "Power and violence," she notes, "are opposites: where the one rules absolutely, the other is absent … . Violence can destroy power; it is utterly incapable of creating it" (*On Violence*, 1969: 56).

The only way the desperate ruler will create power is if the ruled submit to his violence. However, as Sharp and other non-violent exponents have shown, there are multiple non-violent ways to circumvent and counter the violence without needless human sacrifice. Sharp noted in his three-volume seminal work of *Politics of Non-violent Political Action* (1973) that there were some 198 non-violent methods to draw upon, and he has subsequently been informed of about at least another two hundred.

In most cases the non-violent votaries do not represent a majority of the ruled. If this minority is lacking the power to make the ruler dependent on its support, its members are at the mercy of the ruler who can either ignore their pleas for justice or punish them at will. However, the resisters' non-violent response may evoke sympathy from other sections of the society that are able to take 'power from' the ruler through disobedience. Sharp has called this process political ju-jitsu since the power of the ruler has rebounded against himself.

Another way in which seemingly powerless minorities can take 'power from' an unjust ruler is by appealing to a third party that does have the ability to evoke a dependency relationship with the ruler. The third party can be induced to act on behalf of the powerless minority, because the latter does hold a dependency relationship with the former, either in the form of a material interest or moral compassion. The well-known peace researcher Johan Galtung has referred to this process as the 'great chain of non-violence'. It may be possible to extend the process through fourth, fifth or even more parties.

The power formula behind successful non-violent action is for the aggrieved party to undermine the opponent's human and material sources of power (taking 'power from' him), while simultaneously engaging in 'power with' – that is, building up the strength of the non-violent forces. Strengthening a movement entails such actions as fostering solidarity, maintaining morale, developing non-violent discipline, creating affinity group structures, and promoting an independent culture through music, theatre, art, dance, novels and comedy. Thus, the strategic aim of the non-violent actors is to increase the ruler's dependency on them ('power from'), while at the same time increasing their independence ('power with'). If one carefully studies Gandhiji's campaigns (and others), their successful or failed outcome is directly related to one or a combination of these factors.

Despite recognising the important contribution of the Sharpians to the development of non-violent strategy, the more radically inclined advocates of principled non-violence – like the Gandhians – are often critical of what they consider the limited and short-term pragmatism that Sharp and his adherents promote. While this criticism may be valid about some of the Sharpians, it fails to account for the nuances and wide ranging canvas of Sharp's own position.

In his third book, *Social Power and Political Freedom,* published in 1980, Sharp's analysis went well beyond the pragmatics of non-violent political action. He noted four major problems that needed to be resolved before one should even begin to think about designing an ideal world. These were dictatorship, genocide, war, and systems of social oppression. Thoughtful questions needed to be posed that "might give us new insights into them (the problems), or might lead us to other helpful questions, facts or interrelationships" (ibid.: 14). He then proceeded to set out a list of questions for each problem, followed by an appeal to rethink our politics and the unexamined postulates that lie behind it. The next step, he argues, is:

> to develop new approaches to politics and new programs of social change – in short, to create a new kind of politics ... . We must develop concrete steps which will, stage by stage, make significant progress toward a more humane society and world (ibid.: 20)

Like Gandhiji, Sharp has a vision that comes into play with his concept of power.

Gandhiji's Power Paradigm as Primarily Enunciated in *Hind Swaraj*

Having examined how power is wielded in the world of conventional politics by Sharp and his followers, it is now proposed to make a comparison with Gandhiji's perspective of power on the basis of the three interrelated questions posed in the beginning: (1) What type of power did he use? (2) How was this power exercised? (3) What purpose or use was the power put to?

First, Gandhiji's template of power begins with a 'power within' and radiates outward as a 'power through' to all the other forms of power. Thus, he subscribes to a 'totality of power', encapsulating Sharp's 'power from' and 'power with', and the political scientists'/politicians' 'power to' and even 'power over'. The character of the 'power over', of course, excludes physical violence, and contains some other characteristics that differentiate it from the other two groupings (as will be explained later).

Second, the way in which Gandhiji exercises his power is different from the other two groupings. As already suggested, Sharp and Gandhiji (the latter whose principled perspective is premised on the four cardinal virtues of truth, love, non-violence, and sacrifice of self) stand directly in opposition to each other on the means/end debate. For Gandhiji and the *satyagrahi,* the means shape the end, so it becomes critical if one is striving for an enduring and long-term goal to ensure that the two converge. As Gandhiji expresses the point in *Hind Swaraj,* "There is just the same inviolable connection between the means and the end as there is between the seed and the tree … . We reap exactly as we sow" (1939: 64).

Gandhiji is also adamant about showing courage and fearlessness. The *satyagrahi* must be prepared to sacrifice his/her life, "walking into the face of a cannon if need be." Since the English triumphed in India due to the people's fear, their slavery can only end by rising up with the strength of fearlessness. "What is granted in fear can be retained only so long as the fear lasts" (ibid.: 62). Mental and moral commitment will prove decisive over bodily force, because, "(s)trength," he reminds his reader, "lies in absence of fear, not in the quantity of flesh and muscle we may have on our bodies" (ibid.: 40).

His point was subsequently driven home when well trained and disciplined *satyagrahi* marched courageously in wave after wave on the Dharasana Salt Works. When one wave was beaten back mercilessly with the *lathi* sticks of the police, another wave would take its place to receive the same fate. The bloody massacre was witnessed and telegraphed to the *Chicago Tribune* by its news reporter, so that soon the British excessive response to the *satyagraha* protest was known throughout most of the western world. The process of the great chain of non-violence had gone into operation, so that the opponent ended up suffering a grave moral defeat for having repeatedly struck down unarmed passive resisters.

The charge is often levelled at Gandhiji that he did not hesitate to resort to 'power over'. His willingness to use coercion not only marked most of his campaigns but was frequently featured in his speeches. For instance, he openly informed the British in *Hind Swaraj:*

> If you do not concede to our demand, we shall be no longer your petitioners. You can govern us only so long as we remain the governed. We shall no longer have any dealings with you. (ibid.: 67–68)

While Gandhiji called this soul force or truth force (popularly at the time referred to as passive resistance), the British interpreted such language as coercive threats. For someone like Sharp, throwing down the non-violent gauntlet at the opponent did not raise any logical inconsistency. He made no pretense at linking means to end. However, with Gandhiji's philosophical position, there was an "inviolable connection". To circumvent the apparent contradiction between his philosophy and action, Gandhiji argued that in the long run the ultimate result would be a win-win for both parties, and that he would never undertake an action that humiliated an opponent and stripped him of his dignity. He also insisted that his primary purpose in submitting an opponent to 'power over' involved bringing him to the negotiating table where the issue at stake could be discussed in the civilised manner of a dialectic, with persuasion replacing coercion or disintegration of the regime. Whether these were justifiable explanations I leave to the readers' consideration.

It needs to also be remembered that Gandhiji was not opposed to the building of defense and police forces to protect the citizenry of the state. If it is attacked, he claimed that it is sometimes necessary to resort to the violence of 'power over' on the grounds that security and stability are essential in creating and maintaining the just, non-violent society – what he called *Ramarajya.* Had he been around at the time non-offensive defense (NOD) was launched by Bjorn Moller and Anders Boserup in 1985, lie would have, in all probability, incorporated its major provisions into his vision along the path of truth.[1]

The third factor to consider about Gandhiji's power perspective is the purpose to which the power is put. This is unequivocally stated in *Hind Swaraj* in a series of specific negatives as to what India should not do. It should not follow Western civilisation down the path of "mak(ing) bodily welfare the object of life" (ibid.: 32); it should not emulate the institution of parliament, for it "does not serve the interests of general population" (ibid.: 29). "Parliaments are really emblems of slavery" (ibid.: 34). They represent the apogee of Western civilisation's folly. India should not use the instrument of education to advance its knowledge of liberal arts. Its focus should center on that which enables us to do our moral duty" (ibid.: 77–82). For the peasant this meant an education appropriate to his basic needs – one that eschewed most machinery because it detracted from his moral welfare. As for the workers in the mills of Bombay, especially the women, machinery turned them into slaves, whereas formerly there were no mills, these women were not starving. "If," he predicted, "the machinery craze grows in our country, it will become an unhappy land" (ibid.: 83).

Eliminating the negatives was for Gandhiji the *sine qua non* of creating the new society. He knew what it would look like and gave it a name, *Ramarajya* – the kingdom of God on earth. It would feature the spiritual and moral principles of soul-force, love-force, truth-force and non-violence. Human relations would prevail over surplus material wants. This was the purpose to which power should be positively put.

On a number of occasions Gandhiji emphasised the importance of linking *Ramarajya* to the goal of the Indian independence movement, explaining:

> Independence of my conception means nothing less than the realization of the 'Kingdom of God' within you and on this earth. I would rather work for and die in the pursuit of this dream, though it may never be realised. That means infinite patience and perseverance. (*The Selected Works of Mahatma Gandhi,* Vol. VI, ed. Shriman Narayan, Ahmedabad: Navajivan Publishing House, 1968, p. 446)

The above appeared in the *Hindustan Standard* in early 1940. A few years later (1946), when writing an editorial for *Harijan* on the topic of 'Independence', Gandhiji commented:

> Friends have repeatedly challenged me to define independence. At the risk of repetition, I must say that independence of my dream means Rama-Raja, i.e., the Kingdom of God on earth. I do not know what it will be like in heaven. I have no desire to know the distant scene. If the present is attractive enough, the future cannot be very unlike. (cited in Budhadeva Bhattacharyya, *Evolution of the Political Philosophy of Gandhi,* Calcutta: Calcutta Book House, 1969, p. 472)

Piecing together the many comments of Gandhiji to explain *Ramarajya*, one can discern at least seven characteristics that stand out:

1. *Purna swaraj* or complete self-rule. Gandhiji maintained "that political self-government ... is no better than individual self-government" (*Selected Works*, Vol. VI. pp. 440–41).

   Continuing the explanation, he asserted:

   > The outward freedom that we shall attain will only be in exact proportion to the inward freedom to which we may have grown at a given moment. And if this is the correct view of freedom, our chief energy must be concentrated upon achieving reform from within. (ibid., p. 441)

2. *Swadeshi*, interpreted by Gandhiji as self-reliance or self-sufficiency. One should work with what is available in the local community and eschew the material temptations that lie beyond in order to "feel freer men than you are now" (ibid., p. 138).
3. *Panchayats* or sovereign village communities were to be the focal point of real political and economic decision-making. As Gandhiji described the *panchayat:* "... (I)t is a complete republic, independent of its neighbors for its own vital needs and yet interdependent for many others in which dependence is a necessity" (*Harijan*, 26 July 1942, p. 238). Each village will be committed to producing its own food and cotton for its cloth. The villagers will graze their cattle on a commons, and in the event of any surplus land it can be used to grow healthy money crops for export to other villages or nations. "Any village," he declared, "can become such a republic today" (ibid.).

   The village governing body or *panchayat raj* would comprise five members elected annually by adult males and females, with no preferential treatment given to members of the higher ranking castes. The *panchayat raj* would serve as an integral legislature, judiciary and executive for one year before turning over the governmental reins to a newly elected group of five. Gandhiji considered this "pure democracy". True democracy cannot be worked by twenty men sitting at the centre. It has to be worked from below by the people of every village (Gandhi, *Selected Works*, Vol. VI, p. 450).

   Interdependence, while maintaining the independence of the village, is the keynote of Gandhiji's approach to village life.

4. *Oceanic Circles*: Towards the end of his life Gandhiji was enthralled with his discovery of an apt metaphor to explain the general structure of his power system. Overriding the conceptual centrality of the *panchayat,* he advanced the metaphor of oceanic circles:

   In this structure of innumerable villages there will be ever-widening, never ascending circles. Life will not be a pyramid with the apex sustained by the bottom ... (I)t will be an oceanic circle whose centre will be the individual always ready to perish for the village, the latter ready to perish for the circle of the villages, till at last the whole becomes one life composed of individuals, never aggressive in their arrogance but ever humble, sharing the majesty of the oceanic circle of which they are integral units. Therefore, the outmost circumference will not wield power to crush the inner circle, but will give strength to all within and derive its own strength from it (*Harijan*, 28 July 1946, p. 236).

   The metaphor graphically demonstrated Gandhiji's desire to assemble an ever widening collective, one that transcended nation and became universal, yet still depended on and enhanced the individual. Gandhiji had long endorsed the view that all power belonged to the individual and that it should also emanate from the individuals operating at the centre of the multiple oceanic circles.

   Davis George has summed up the Gandhian model in the following way: While the dynamo of power in a country like India should be the village, the village was to be "a knot in a system of oceanic circles" in which the remotest circle derived its strength from the center, i.e., the individual. This would mean that sovereignty was not to remain concentrated at any one level. It was to be diffused among units rising horizontally till they reached the national level. In terms of political science, the residuary power remained with the village and the center was there to co-ordinate the work. For Gandhiji, each individual and each nation needed to look within. The power was found at the hub, that is, the many dedicated individuals who generated the just and truthful society reaching out to the ever expanding oceanic circles. They, in turn, generated power back to the center (*Hind Swaraj and Gandhi's Search for the Conquest of Power* Chapter 1).

5. *Enlightened anarchy* was the type of political system that Gandhiji ascribed to *Ramarajya*. "There is ... a state of enlightened anarchy. In such a state everyone is his own ruler ('Power Not an End,' *Collected Works*, Vol. XLVII, p. 91). The combination of *Purna Swaraj, Panchayat Raj,* and the oceanic circles created a decentralised polity of enlightened anarchy. With such a set up any institution predisposed to centralised control would automatically disintegrate (*Selected Works*, Vol. VI, p. 436).
6. *Stages of Life and Divisions of Society:* Gandhi endorsed for India the continuation of its traditional four stages of human life (*Ashrama*), and its four divisions of society or castes (*Varna*) (*Selected Works*, Vol. VI, p. 474–75). However, he introduced important modifications that he insisted on. Strict obligations were imposed on the individual to be true to the prescriptions set down at each of the four life stages: the *Brahmachari* or student, the *Grihastha* or householder, the *Vanaprastha* or retiree, and the *Sannyasi* who renounces 'worldly pleasures' and lives detached from the material world in pursuit of a higher level of knowledge. Gandhiji acknowledged that this renunciate fourth stage might be too demanding for some people.

   Society was also divided into four major groupings: the *Brahman* or those involved primarily in advancing spiritual pursuits, the *Kshatriya* who were committed to political and military affairs, the *Vaishya* who produced the society's goods and provided its services, and finally the *Shudra* who were engaged in work for some form of remuneration. While these are the four major castes or what Gandhiji called "universal occupations," he did endorse the view of fluidity between the castes based on an individual's ability and commitment to improve his position in life (*Selected Works*, Vol. VI, p. 479).
7. At the most outer oceanic circle, *Ramarajya* aimed for a world federation. Not long after effectively assuming the leadership of the independence movement in the early 1920s, Gandhiji believed that the time had arrived for states to give up a vital aspect of their national sovereignty. As he observed:

   > The better mind of the world desires today not absolutely independent States warring one against another, but a federation of friendly interdependent States ... . I see nothing grand or impossible about our readiness for universal interdependence

> rather than independence. (*Collected Works*, Vol. XXV, pp. 481–82)

> The goal of interdependence at the global level was essential to the survival of humanity (*Harijan*, 26 July 1942). Moreover, the credibility of such a goal conformed to his belief in the "basic unity of the human family" (*Selected Works*, Vol. VI, p. 249). For Gandhiji, as outlined by Indian scholar, Anthony J. Parel, the state's power is limited to maintaining internal order and external security; it does not extend to achieving domination over other states. The state is a member of a community of independent and interdependent states … . In doing so, it has changed the very notion of political power from one that seeks to expand limitlessly to one that limits itself to the requirements of internal order, world peace, interdependence and universal *dharma* ('Gandhi and the Emergence of the Modern Indian Political Canon,' *Vidyajyoti Journal of Theological Reflection*, Vol. 73, No. 9, September 2009, p. 668).

While the nature of what the new society of *Ramarajya* would look like was sufficiently adumbrated to serve as a vague inspiration, it was never clearly and convincingly shown how the grand vision would be reached. By adherence to a set of vows that Gandhiji laid down and a willingness to suffer in the name of self-purification and truth, the new society would emerge in the process of struggling to replace the old. Beyond that minimal suggestion he offered no definitive strategy for effecting a revolutionary transformation of India's institutions and culture nurtured under the British raj. That momentous task was left to his successors after his death who chiefly turned out to be Vinoba Bhave (*Bhoodan* and *Gramdan*) and Jayaprakash Narayan (4 vols of *Towards Total Revolution* and leadership of the Janata Party). Instead, over the last decade of his life, Gandhiji's full attention and energies were caught up in the quotidian demands of the 'Quit India Campaign' and the subsequent communal riots that besieged the two new nation-states.

Shortly before his assassination, however, he was led to reflect that his life had been a failure. *Ramarajya* did not appear to be part of the vision held by India's masses, preoccupied as they were with their daily survival; nor was it incorporated into the thinking of many members of his inner circle, including his beloved associates, Pandit Jawaharlal Nehru, Sardar Vallabhbhai

Patel and Rajendra Prasad. Nevertheless, Gandhiji's perennial faith in humankind would have probably assured him that once events stabilised, the job of building the new society of *Ramarajya* – spear-headed by the philosophy and method of *satyagraha* – could commence and would be successful. A new India would be a guiding light to the other nations of the world, especially those emerging from colonial subjugation.

To the very end of his life he advised inquirers into his moral and political philosophy to consult *Hind Swaraj*. Therefore, it might be fitting to cite the succinct summary that his secretary, Mahadev Desai, gave to the central theme of Gandhiji's philosophy – namely, how non-violence (as both the means and end) was to be integrated into Indian Home Rule:

> It will take long to standardize the meaning and content of this term (non-violence). But the means thereof is self-purification and more self-purification. What Western thinkers often lose sight of is that the fundamental condition of non-violence is love, and pure unselfish love is impossible without unsullied purity of mind and body (Preface to the New Edition, 1938 (1990), p. 7).

Thus, Gandhiji was calling for a total transformation to a non-violent society, and to achieve that goal it was necessary for a critical mass of the society's members to go through a process of self-purification. With the society's institutions and norms then reinforcing the self-purification process, a mutuality of radical conversion would be generated between the society and the individual. This was the closest Gandhiji came to setting out what could be called a macro-strategy. Certainly, as already noted, no details were provided.

Relevance of *Ramarajya* to Contemporary India and Beyond

Is the Gandhian vision spelled out in *Hind Swaraj* and the writings on *Ramarajya* relevant to contemporary societies? Is the call for the self-purification of a critical mass a realistic possibility in today's increasingly globalised society? Gandhiji may well be revered on the public platform, but his ideas are constantly ignored by those same self-proclaimed idolaters when they set their public agenda.

Ironically, India is a prime example of a nation moving away from Gandhian principles. Politicians, with their eyes on electoral returns, know that the discipline and sacrifice that Gandhiji called for contravene the priorities in most people's lives. Even if potential *satyagrahi* could be found who were not seduced by the global media's siren-song to constantly acquire more and more wealth as the road to ever greater happiness, many people are committed to other interests. Some have family obligations that take precedence over any other endeavour. Others find purpose in life through fulfilment in pursuits that provide little time for building the non-violent society of *Ramarajya*.

Despite Gandhi's great charisma and his dedication to uplifting the Indian peasants and workers, neither he nor any of his successors were able to make significant and lasting inroads into improving their condition. Indeed, were he alive today, Gandhiji would be appalled at how westernised India has become. *The Economist* (31 October 2009) reported some startling economic figures at the end of the century's first decade:

> India is steadily becoming more financially stitched in to the rest of the world. Its foreign assets and liabilities add up to over 60 per cent of GDP. In the 1990s that ratio was only about 40 per cent ... . In March 2009 India's stock of direct investment abroad was worth over $67 billion, more than twice the figure in March 2007.

As more big Indian firms like Tata Steel and Bharti Airtel apply pressures to buy and merge with companies abroad, counter moves by the Reserve Bank of India and the politicians to contain overseas economic investment will most likely fail. Thus, not only has the Indian raj replaced the British raj, but the former's throne is now being threatened by a global raj – the very worst scenario Gandhiji could have imagined.

As pointed out in the preceding section, Gandhiji expressed unmitigated aversion to the idea that India should emulate the British form of government as well as the values and practices of Western civilisation. Today's Gandhians are confronted with an even greater problem. The non-moral and non-spiritual Western society that Gandhiji so deplored is now becoming the global society, and India is joining it.

Nevertheless, despite Indian society's rejection of the moral and spiritual life for the accumulation of wealth and unlimited 'power to' and 'power over', some progress continues to be made in alleviating the oppression and suffering of a small minority of Indian farmers. Yet, unfortunately, as heroic and determined as the modern-day Gandhian workers may be in eliminating pockets of the ongoing poverty cycle, they have only managed to introduce self-sufficient measures into a very small proportion of India's half million villages. The task required to reach larger numbers – an effort that would be necessary in order to register a national impact – beggars one's imagination in the current political and economic climate.

Back in the sixties and seventies there might have been some promising signs. Vinoba (spiritual) and J.P. (political) were performing what appeared to be Gandhian miracles. Two westerners, E.F. Schumacher (*Small Is Beautiful*) and Ivan Illych (*The De-Schooling Society and Tools for Conviviality*) were engaged in research along the lines espoused by Gandhiji. They came to the Gandhian Institute for Peace at Varanasi, a research centre set up by J.P. under the directorship of Sugata Dasputa, to inquire scientifically into the issues entailed in creating a non-violent society. The success of their books and the world-wide popularity of their ideas, however, did not translate into the type of communities they were advocating. The impetus for radical change on a grand scale awaits a new era.

Hope was one quality that Gandhiji had in abundance. He would have known that macro-economics is riddled with uncertainty; the discipline lies beyond exact human prediction. Perhaps a charismatic leader (or leaders) will miraculously appear to arrest the drift to the 'bodily' attractions of a Westernised global society, and a critical mass of Indian society will be converted to *satyagraha* principles. In the end, India's renowned ability to co-opt and absorb new values into the status quo will take place. This scenario is possible but not likely. It is difficult to justify such a Gandhi-like article of faith. Indeed, to most political scientists and politicians, the proposition does not even merit consideration. Sharpians, while more sympathetic, would also be inclined to take a negative view, opting for the stance that "half a loaf is better than none".

Another question to consider (a topic discussed in the previous section): Is it empirically the case that Gandhiji's use of the full complement of power techniques produces results different from those of other groupings, simply because he has inserted the vision of *Ramarajya* and the values of *satyagraha* into the equation? When exercising 'power over', as in the Quit India Campaign, his humane outreach did not melt the hearts of most of the English elite. General Smuts of South Africa and Lord and Lady Mountbatten of Great Britain represent notable exceptions. At the time of Indian independence British opinion was more representative of that of Prime Minister Clement Atlee. He commented on the way India was draining the British purse rather than acknowledging the virtue of ceding independence to the 'jewel of the empire'. In other words, a mixed reaction from his opponent meant there was no win-win outcome. Only later did more cordial tributes ensue about Gandhiji and the gaining of independence.

Critics have not hesitated to point to numerous inconsistencies in his reasoning and actions. A glaring example is how he advocated greater involvement and control at the distant global level of world federation while calling for decentralisation at the state level and placing power in the *panchayats,* which, in turn, are dependent on the individual fulfilling his/her *dharma.* In his defense Gandhiji never denied his inconsistencies and proudly pointed to the 'virtue of flexibility' based on a higher goal. What mattered was meeting human needs of security and general welfare. The *satyagraha* that permeated the entire range of his politics was based on striving for the highest relative truth in terms of a particular situation and its moment. In that way, as Joan Bondurant has pointed out, an ethical humanism was to be achieved (*Conquest of Violence*, 1965: 31–32). The concept of a 'world federation' met both the humanist and relative truth criteria, and therefore, as far as Gandhi was concerned, did not gainsay his philosophy of localism and individualism. While from the perspective of Western rationalism it may be difficult to reconcile the apparent contradiction, there can be no question about the deeply felt humanism that lies at the core of his *Ramarajya* and the concept of the oceanic circles.

Also beyond dispute has been the acceptance of Gandhiji's skill as a masterful strategist in reaching a proximate, concrete goal – a point Gene Sharp stressed in an early book (*Gandhi as a Political Strategist*, 1979) and recently confirmed in an informal discussion with the author.

Gandhiji's shrewd strategic timing in leading the most populous colony to independence has been acknowledged and emulated by virtually every great non-violent practitioner. He represents the font of non-violent knowledge and experience to which they have all deferred from every corner of the world: Martin Luther King, Desmond Tutu, the Dalai Lama, Danilo Dolci, Ken Saro-Wiwa, Petra Kelly, Thomas Merton, Cesar Chavez, Dorothy Day, Aung San Suu Kyi, Helder Camara, A.J. Muste – to name just a few. As an inspiring symbol of non-violence, Gandhiji has no equal. His name and picture are instantly and universally recognisable. From the well-spring of his teachings and campaigns have emerged new teachings and many more campaigns. Today, when people feel unjustly treated and the path to righting the injustice is barred through conventional politics, they are no longer confined to the limited options of violence or submission. A third option of non-violence is available – a political method that has been tried, tested and often proven successful, but never on a more self-conscious, more dramatic and larger scale than in the independence campaign that Gandhiji led.

Gandhiji also left a legacy that reminds us of the importance of love in all our human relations, and the futility and unhappiness attached to the endless pursuit of material wealth. Many people have found his philosophy of truth attractive – the proposition that the individual's life can be a journey striving toward Absolute Truth which he equated with God. "Truth is God," he said.

Finally, Gandhiji exemplified through his 'experiments of life' the high value to be gained by accepting the responsibility or duty to make the existential moral choice rather than allow oneself to be buffeted aimlessly about by the winds of social/political injustice. The appeal to the moral 'power within' (the love force, etc.) to permeate the wider societal structures in oceanic circles pervades every single line of *Hind Swaraj*, and has a relevancy in today's critical times that we ignore at our peril. However, a ubiquitous problem persists. How do we take the messages that Gandhiji bequeathed to us to the next level? How do we forge the structures and culture that will create and sustain a non-violent global society? Is a world of interlocking *panchayat rajs* at the sub-state level and a federation of interdependent states on the global stage realistic choices? In the framework of oceanic circles they appear contradictory. Moreover, are the types of 'power to' and 'power over' societies that currently exist beyond the pale of fundamental change? While people like Vinoba Bhave and Jayaprakash Narayan once made inroads toward the Gandhian vision, those kinds of distant events have not recurred on the same scale, and now fade into hazy historical memories.

Conclusion

Interwoven throughout this essay emerges four themes. They are designed to look at Gandhiji's principled non-violence, as mainly, but not solely, expounded in *Hind Swaraj*, through a prism of power. The first theme seeks to explain the antipathy that political scientists, along with establishment personnel in general, have for non-violence – whether it is for the anti-elitist strategy of non-violent political action featured in the writings of Gene Sharp, or the more radical proposal of Gandhiji to effect a revolution through the creation of *Ramarajya*.

As a political scientist trained in the discipline's currency of power, I have looked at the power templates that the different parties bring to their analyses of politics to explain the antagonism. It soon became apparent that the underlying power perspectives of the non-violent votaries – particularly Gandhiji's call for the power of self-rule to foment a revolutionary cultural transformation – openly challenge the authority ('power to') and domination ('power over') by which elites function. Therefore, to make the non-violence of either the Sharpian or Gandhian kind credible to the elites of Western societies, there will have to be an inordinate shift in the way the society as a whole construes power. It raises the question of how to breakthrough the pervasive cultural hegemony of the elite ... ?

One suggestion is to operate on the premise that one is dealing with a culture steeped in pragmatism. Almost any means or method that will bring success has virtually become a global norm. Therefore widely disseminating information about the successes of non-violent political action should be a first priority. If elites become familiar with the full panoply of non-violent methods – extending from interpersonal mediation skills to political techniques of non-violent coercion – and realise the tool of non-violence is available to all parties, they might be prepared to incorporate it into their political armory. While attaining political legitimacy might be seen as a way of perpetuating elite control, substituting non-violence for violence and oppression can only be viewed as a major step forward in the written history of humankind. Indeed, for the cultural and structural chasm to close even marginally would constitute remarkable progress after approximately ten thousand years of intra-species organised physical violence.

The second theme looked at and compared how the three groupings of political scientists/politicians, Sharpians, and Gandhians exercised their power. Gandhiji and Sharp differed widely on the philosophical front. Sharp was not hesitant to use the non-violent mechanisms of coercion and disintegration. On the other hand, Gandhiji sought to justify how the 'power over' was linked to a universal humane vision and worked to the advantage of his opponent in the long run – that is, whenever he strategically deemed it was necessary to resort to these mechanisms.

The third theme noted that Gandhiji led the only grouping dedicated to a purpose that was spelled out in its actions. The other groupings might aim for a noble goal, but any means (apart from physical violence in the case of the Sharpians) that did the job would suffice. The purpose advanced by Gandhiji – namely, living in a society based on soul-force, truth-force, love-force and non-violence – could only be fashioned out of tools that bore the same mark. Every action had to be tested against an ideal. Thus, the British parliamentary system was caustically denounced and considered inappropriate for the new state that he envisaged for India. Western civilisation failed the 'true test' because it put material bodily welfare above the welfare of people relations and their spiritual and ontological needs. And, if Indians failed the fearless test or were not dedicated to self-purification, the non-violent society of *Ramarajya* would never emerge.

The fourth theme posed a series of questions. They appeared under the general rubric: do the objectives Gandhiji set forth in *Hind Swaraj* 100 years ago and subsequently outlined in *Ramarajya* have relevancy in a world of the 21st century? Many of the specifics, that he proposed and demonstrated, such as relating education to people's immediate needs, advocating celibacy to sharpen awareness, and sleeping with virgins to test one's will power, open up topics to be debated. On the other hand, his general positions and actions tend to be less debatable. His sharp criticism of materialism and the need to take seriously the quality of love not only made sense in his time but speak directly to another world 100 years later.

In conclusion, while Gandhiji's grand dream may not have been realised, on a less ambitious but very significant note, he played a key role in making people aware of the non-violent option to conflict resolution. People have taken from the Gandhian legacy what has seemed most relevant to their needs and the attaining of their dream. His proposals, although frozen in the time and place of one man's journey in relative truth, offer an extraordinary assortment of thoughts and impressions that people can choose from selectively. We choose our history, Gandhiji pointed out, as long as we reject the superstition that people should obey unjust laws, and we non-violently create just ones in their place. This call to produce justice, wherever there is injustice and the denial of basic human needs, can be considered an overarching fifth theme to be derived from *Hind Swaraj* and the social vision of *Ramarajya*.

Note

1. According to Moller, there are two main definitions of NOD: structural and functional (*Dictionary of Alternative Defense*, p. 243). The former relates to the size of a state's arsenal, type of weapons, nature of military training, logistics, doctrine, operational manuals, war games, maneuvers, and textbooks used in military academies, etc. The functional definition, instead of attempting to record the nature of a long list of military factors, focuses on broad options, e.g., "The armed forces should be seen in their totality to be capable of a credible defense, yet incapable of offense."

4

Liberty and Individualism in Gandhian Perspective[1]

Implications for Societies' Sustainability

SUDARSHAN IYENGAR

Mahatma Gandhi, as he came to be known to the world after noted Indian Nobel laureate Rabindranath Tagore gave him this name, experimented throughout his life in search of truth and made perhaps the most honest attempt on the earth in recent past to live his life according to what he realised as truth. Based on the percept and practice of truth, Gandhiji developed a set of values to regulate individual life which, according to him, if one strictly followed, had potential to improve the quality of life substantially. Such an individual would be very strong and have potential to create a just, humane and sustainable society. However, as one looks at the history of the world in the 20th century, he finds that along with the development and emergence of Gandhi's persona with a global image, the major trends in the developed and developing societies hardly reflected Gandhiji's philosophy and values. Of course, there have been some attempts – successful to an extent, but by and large the saga has been the same that had continued for centuries before, with an added dimension of substantial economic growth and profuse use of technology. Incidentally, these features in the societies are known as development.

We all are aware that when the First World War broke out in 1914, Gandhiji had already made a remarkable impact on the British Empire with his successful non-violent and peaceful struggle again racism in South Africa. He had demonstrated to the world that through a non-violent struggle it was possible to persuade a very powerful state to recognise and restore basic human rights for dignified existence. And yet at the global level contentious issues of geo-politics for establishing and strengthening economic supremacy were getting settled through full-scale wars among nations. Between 1915 and 1948 Gandhiji mobilised people in India for what has come to be known as the most massive and triumphant non-violent uprising for freedom in the known history of the world. Gandhiji created such an impact that Albert Einstein had observed that it would be difficult for the future generations to believe that one like Gandhiji had ever lived in flesh and blood. While Gandhiji was demonstrating to the world the power of mobilising people for a non-violent struggle for freedom from colonial rule, the free and growing nations continued to war against one another for geo-political and economic supremacy. The First World War was not enough to settle the scores. America had already emerged as the most powerful nation in the world and was dictating the warring groups. The alignments among nations were taking place with a clear intention of waging another bloody world war. This was despite the fact that Gandhiji was making impressions among important citizens in America and Europe. The British had already come to know about this miraculous personality who had mesmerised masses in India and millions had raised their voice for independence without violent manifestation. Romma Rollan, a well-known French litterateur, had corresponded with Gandhiji and had made Gandhiji known in France.

In an article 'Gandhi in the Mind of America', Lloyd Rudolph and Susanne Rudolph[2] write that Gandhiji was introduced to America by some prominent thinkers such as John Haynes Homes and Reinhold Niebuhr in the 1920s and 1930s and Martin Luther King in the 1950s and 1960s. In the 1920s and 1930s, Gandhiji, as I have just mentioned, led non-violent struggle with the British. On how Holmes was introducing Gandhiji in the mind of America I again quote Lloyds: "Holmes announced in April 1921 that he would deliver a sermon on 'Who is the Greatest Man in the World?' By his own introspective account, 'I climbed tremulously into my pulpit on Sunday to answer my own question.' The answer he gave was M.K. Gandhi. In the light of what was known, and not known, at that time about Gandhi here in our Western world, the audacity of his declaration, Holmes tells us 32 years later in *My Gandhi*, seems now incredible."[3] Niebuhr started with doubts and questions on Gandhiji's approach of non-violence. He wanted to meet him in London at the time of the Round Table Conference, but could not do so. He wrote about him first with a perverted view that the weak Indians and weak Negroes in America could think about Gandhiji's way of non-violent resistance, but a strong resistance would involve coercion and if necessary violence. Subsequently, he changed this view and endorsed Gandhiji's perspective. Both Holmes and Niebuhr were powerful and influential thinkers of their times in America. Yet what we see is that in 1939 Europe again indulged in the World War and America openly supported it and entered into it towards the end of the Second World War. Thus, the world politics was not even learning from Gandhiji's approach to political problems, let alone practising it significantly to resolve inter-nation power conflicts. The worst ever man-made disaster in the history of mankind happened. Nuclear weapon technology was used and atom bombs were dropped in Hiroshima and Nagasaki in Japan killing and maiming millions. Despite great admiration that Gandhiji drew world over, his approach was ignored.

In the post-Second World War period the nations changed drastically. Liberal social democracies promised fast and sound economic growth. But it did not end the conflicts. The era of Cold War began. For next forty years or so America and Europe practised capitalism in different variations giving some scope to the role of the state with socialistic flavours. Many developing countries followed the capitalistic development model. Former USSR, China and countries in Eastern Europe followed communism in various forms. Thus, the world witnessed the heights of capitalism, communism and socialism. All these systems have proved to be inadequate to create a humane and sustainable society. The emergence of new societies in recent past has caused alarm in the minds of very many scholars, scientists, leaders, social workers and others. One major issue that surfaces clear from most of these concerns is about the economic, social and ecological sustainability of human societies in the long run. Of course, there is a battalion of hopeful people who almost completely rubbish most of these concerns and believe that human specie has immense capacity to come out of intermittent crisis and survive, and survive well.[4] Allowing market mechanisms to operate freely would, according to this group of thinkers, yield best results in the human interest and help consolidate creation of sustainable societies. Socialists do not think so and Anthony Giddens,[5] a renowned scholar and Director of London School of Economics and Political Science, has written a powerful commentary wherein he has exposed the limitations of the 'Right' and the 'Left' philosophies. He discusses a 'Third Way' as possible alternative and argues that some countries were already going in that direction. Interestingly, he too does not consider Gandhiji's philosophy and approach to individual life as a possible solution to the world crisis.

It is important to understand that the worldview about human being's capacity to come out of any crisis caused by his own interaction with nature with free market mechanisms in place rests on the assumption of individual freedom. The unfettered freedom offered by the state and the civil society to an individual, constrained only by broad and general regulations curbing licentious indulgences harming others, unleashes such a powerful creativity that all adversities and problems of the material world have permanent potential for finding solutions. This could be called as extreme Right Wing percept. Gandhiji had sensed this mood right in the beginning of the 20th century and wrote strongly against it. He pointed out that unless the individuals disciplined themselves, market led just socio-economic order was always at risk. He had also strongly felt against the approach where the state completely controlled the economy and therefore the life of people. The risks involved in both these approaches are unfolding in the world today and serious doubts are being raised about the sustainability of both the Right Wing and the Left Wing philosophies. The social order that was supposed to discipline the individuals appears to have failed. The free individual in the Western society has shown clear tendencies to become licentious jeopardising the prospects of creating a just and humane social order. The threat of war has not vanished. Instead it has taken different form. Violence for political agenda within countries and among countries has killed more human beings in the post-Second World War period than that during the war. Some of the terrorists groups are so well-equipped with most modern sophisticated weapons that some developing countries' armed force artillery and weaponries appear toy collection. Whether there is a candid admission or not, most of the conflicts are for maintaining permanent control over natural and man-made resources to ensure prolonged economic prosperity reflected in very high energy use and consumption levels. Gandhiji had expressed serious reservations about such a society and had thought that the economic system based on greed would ultimately adversely affect the social health of the society. Thus, even in Gandhiji's thought, an individual is very important unit like under the libertarian scheme of thought. But Gandhiji's individual is highly disciplined by self-regulation rather than forcing regulation by the society. I propose to take a fresh look at Gandhiji's philosophy and explore whether it offers key to building socio-economic and ecologically sustainable societies. Looking at the present-day circumstances, it is appropriate to undertake this intellectual journey. I have divided rest of the lecture in four sections. In section two, I will present a review of how Gandhiji shaped his personality in his early life that helped him transform from an ordinary Mohan into a highly self-regulating citizen. In section three, I will present Gandhiji's formulation about the rules or principles to be followed by every citizen so that he/she becomes a self regulating person. In section four, I will discuss Gandhiji's worldview about a sane and civilised society that has potential to be more sustainable. In section four, I will briefly discuss the modern concept of liberty and individualism being prasticed in the Western world and it will be seen that Gandhiji's model of self-regulation has better chances of creating just, humane and sustainable societies.

II

The Growing of Mohan into a Self-regulating Individual

Mohandas Karamchand Gandhi was a rare person in the recent history of humanity who though influenced by the morals of the Hindu philosophy became a believer only after closely examining its morals and principles. He became conscious of his religion when he reached Pretoria and met Dada Abdulla's English lawyer Mr Baker, who also happened to be a staunch lay preacher.[6] Gandhiji was one of the rare persons who experimented with self all through his life. No wonder he titled his autobiography as 'The Story of My Experiments with Truth'. It is important for us to understand that Mohandas Karamchand Gandhi transformed his persona from an ordinary Mohan to such a level of self-regulation and discipline that he came to be known as *Mahatma* (the great soul). This transformation began from a very early age. Mohan's resolve not to be dishonest was firmed up in the first year of high school when he did not correct the spelling of the word 'kettle' despite being prompted by the teacher with the tip of his boot. First year high school is the time when a child is 12 or 13 years old, the beginning of teen. Some impressions become indelible and continue with us for lifetime. Young Mohan too experienced it. One such lifetime impression was created in his mind by reading a play *Shravana Pitrabhakti Natak* (Shravana's devotion to father). Coincidentally, within few days of reading the play, a travelling showman had in his bi-scope a picture of Shravana carrying his parents on pilgrimage with slings fitted to his shoulders. This left an indelible impression in the young mind of Mohan and he further resolved to serve parents. Second was the play *Harishchandra* that he watched. He was so impressed that he would have watched it several times. Gandhiji writes: "It haunted me and I must have acted Harishchandra to myself times without number … . To follow the truth and to go through all the ordeals Harishchandra went through was the one ideal it inspired in me."[7] Truth and honesty got engraved permanently on the young Mohan's mind and changed his personality completely in years to come.

At the age of 15, Mohan stole a piece of gold cut out of his brother's armlet to settle a debt that his brother had run into. This bothered Mohan very much and he resolved never to steal again. He also decided to confess. Written confession to his ailing father was another major instance where the boy resolved to be honest. It should be noted that writing a confession by Gandhiji involved three aspects in improving self. First was the acknowledgement of wrong doing. Second was repentance for the wrong act, and third was willingness to accept punishment for wrong doing. At the time of conflict these are the first steps towards reconciliation. Gandhiji not only learnt it at a young age but also practised throughout his life. He not only thought that it was possible for others to do the same, he also expected that every individual should indeed do so. Honesty is cherished as a value by all societies even today, but Gandhiji took this value beyond a personal characteristic to public arena when conflict situations arose. In 1922, when people indulged in violence in public, Gandhiji suspended the *satyagraha* – mass civil disobedience movement. It is recorded in the history of Indian freedom struggle as *Chauri-Chaura* police killing by masses. This was public acknowledgement of wrong doing by people in this case. He was sorry for this and admitted it in public and as redressal he withdrew the movement. He thought that his penance was not enough and people were not yet ready for a non-violent *satyagraha*.

At the age of 19, Mohandas left for England to become a barrister. This was not so common during the last quarter of the 19th century. Indian society was very traditional then. The world view about England and English people led the traditional Indians to believe that visiting England for studies would have very bad influence on the visitors over and above the belief that it was sinful to cross the sea. The mothers of the young men were particularly worried about negative influence on food habit, alcohol drinking and having affairs with English women. Gandhiji's mother Putlibai was no exception. She wanted assurance which the young Mohan gave, but that was not enough. Advice from a family friend, who also was a Jain monk, was sought on this matter by the mother. He administered the oath and Mohan vowed that he would not touch wine, woman and meat.[8] Most young persons of his times and age perhaps made these promises to their mothers only to break them. Most of them would also have had justification for doing so. Youth is rebellious. Some young men would have found the new world exciting and hence would have taken plunge into it. Right on the passage to London, an English passenger warned him that once the ship crossed Bay of Biscay it would be so cold that eating meat would become necessary. Later in the early days in London Dr Mehta's friend, who was teaching Gandhiji the English manners to prepare him to stay with an English family as a paying guest, got exasperated and said, "What is the value of a vow made before an illiterate mother, and in ignorance of conditions here? It is no vow at all. It would not be regarded as vow in law. It is pure superstition to stick to such a promise. And I tell you this persistence will not help you to gain anything here."[9] Young Mohandas did not budge. Later, when he moved to stay with an English family he had to starve at times but did not give up vegetarianism.

I need to stretch this point a little further because it is very important to understand the process through which the young man went through and became more and more resolute which made his personality a strong one and self-regulatory. Young Mohan was hungry on the ship; he was hungry in England where he stayed as a paying guest. He writes about his predicaments in the following words: "I could not relish boiled vegetables cooked without salt and condiments .... I always starved at lunch and dinner .... I was a good eater and had a capacious stomach; but I was ashamed to ask for more than two or three slices of bread, as it did not seem correct to do so."[10] English manners prevented him picking up more food. At a young age of nineteen a normal healthy man has good appetite and to go hungry for days can be traumatic. Young Mohandas wondered the streets of London to find vegetarian restaurant and finally when he found one his joy was expressed thus: "During these wanderings I once hit on a vegetarian restaurant in Farringdon Street. The sight of it filled me with the same joy that a child feels on getting a thing after its own heart … . This was my first hearty meal since my arrival in England."[11] The easiest way out for Mohandas was to break the vows he had made to his mother. But his resolve not to do so made him very strong and he acquired self-regulatory powers to a very significant level and it served him all though his life. *Mahatma* was already in the making in the young Mohandas.

We learn from the Gandhiji's autobiography that he was a shy person. Again at a young age of nineteen to get attracted to women is only natural. A widow, to whom he became acquainted while he was looking for vegetarian food in a restaurant in Brighton that had a Menu card in French, invited him home and introduced a young lady with whom Mohandas felt comfortable. He became used to the Sunday lunch meetings and, in fact, eagerly looked forward for them. Soon he realised that the widow was well-meaning lady and wanted a good young man such as Mohandas to marry this good young lady. Mohandas took sometime but sensed that his meetings with the lady were not so innocent. It occurred to him that he had not revealed to the women his marital status. He wrote a long letter again confessing lapse on his part in sharing the information about his marriage back home in India. He also expressed regret and asked for forgiveness. Young Mohandas could have dated the girl as we call it today and could have left it as an affair. It would have been considered normal for a young person of his age in England. Many Indian youth did indulge in this practice while in England. Once again, Mohandas not only reminded himself of his vow and acknowledged his mistake, but also confessed it boldly without any fear. In his autobiography he wrote that he thus purged himself of the canker of untruth. Mohandas again was moving towards the *Mahatma*. We should recognise that more than being determined about values such as being truthful and honest under most trying circumstances, Gandhiji was at a very young age learning successfully to regulate his behaviour by imposing self-discipline. This practice hardly failed him during rest of his life.

I should now take you further in Gandhiji's fascinating life journey. As a barrister he did not succeed in Mumbai and went back to Rajkot where his extended family lived. He earned out of writing petitions. Soon he was fed up. In the meanwhile his elder brother received an offer from a wealthy businessman from South Africa for a lawyer who could act as a mediator between the White lawyer and the Hindi businessman who did not know English. Gandhiji, then around twenty three, jumped at this offer. But before taking the South Africa incidences that further built Gandhiji's character, I would take another small, but important, instance from which again Gandhiji learnt a lifetime lesson. While at Rajkot, Gandhiji's brother requested him to meet the British Political Agent for Porbandar and put in good words for him. In fact, Gandhiji's brother was facing an allegation of having misadvised the Rana of Porbandar before the latter ascended the throne. Gandhiji was reluctant, but upon being persuaded he went and met the Political Agent. He tried to renew the acquaintance and pleaded his brother's case, but the Agent stopped him and asked him to leave. Gandhiji continued to plead and the Agent called the peon to show Gandhiji door. This was an insult and Gandhiji scribbled a chit seeking his apology and threatening to complain. He received an arrogant reply. Incidentally, Sir Firoz Shah Mehta, a renowned barrister of Mumbai, was in Rajkot and Gandhiji sought his advice for suing the Agent for defamation. Sir Mehta advised him to pocket the insult and proceed with his profession. Gandhiji resolved never to recommend anybody's case in this fashion and never ever did that in his life. I am sure many of us go through this experience and yet we do not make resolves of the kind which Gandhiji had made and stick to it lifelong. This is yet another example of regulating self that young Mohandas had taught himself.

In South Africa he became acutely aware about the racial discrimination. His historic travel from Durban to Pretoria exposed him to this experience in a rather crude and shocking manner. I do not wish to recount the famous train travel and the insult heaped on him at Maritzburg. Let us only remember again that he was only a young man of twenty four. He could have pocketed the insult as almost all Indians in South Africa did in those days and get accustomed to the discriminated treatment. Or as an angry young man turned violent and hit back. He did neither. Instead, he resolved to fight back using non-violent means or passive resistance. I would simply quote from his autobiography the emotions he passed through during the incidences of discrimination. Upon being pushed out from the train he went to waiting room with his handbag in that cold winter night and shivered. His state of mind is reflected in the following passage:

> I began to think of my duty. Should I fight for my rights or go back to India, or should I go on to Pretoria without minding the insults, and return to India after finishing the case? It would be cowardice to run back to India without fulfilling my obligation. The hardship to which I was subjected was superficial – only a symptom of the deep disease of colour prejudice. I should try, if possible, to root out the disease and suffer hardship in the process. Redress for wrongs I should seek only to the extent that would be necessary for the removal of the colour prejudice.[12]

The experience of the night at Maritzburg station was unusual indeed. Rajmohan Gandhi in a chapter titled 'Two Inner Voices' in his book *The Good Boatman* writes: "The transformation of the timid Mohan into a victor over an empire and the father of satyagraha is an oft-probed mystery generally resolved with a spotlight on the 1893 ejection at the Maritzburg railway station".[13] Rajmohan continues to argue that important writings by others and Gandhiji's own expressions at places lends credence to this incidence. He quotes C.F. Andrews thus:

> Gandhi, like Paul comes clearly under the category of the twice-born among men of religion. He experienced at a special moment in his life that tremendous convulsion of the human spirit which we call 'conversion.' ... As he journeyed from Durban and reached Maritzburg this dreadful experience came to him in its cruel nakedness ... . There all night long as he sat shivering with cold, after enduring this insult, he wrestled within himself whether to take the next steamer back to India, or to go through the bitter end, suffering what his own people had to suffer. Before morning the light came to his soul. He determined by God's grace to the play the man ... . This was the turning point form which his new life would begin.[14]

Rajmohan notes that before ten years of Gandhiji's death an American Evangelist John R. Mott had asked Gandhiji to recall 'the most creative experience of his life', Gandhiji made reference to the Maritzburg incident and said: "My active non-violence began from that date."[15] The point Rajmohan wishes to make in this chapter is that Gandhiji's strong inner voices about truth and feeling to fight for his nation was not result of any inner revolution as it apparently turns up in the scanning of his life events by himself and by others, but it evolved and one has to look for it from the beginning. Rajmohan Gandhi is right to an extent in his argument as I have also tried to trace the formation of character of *Mahatma* in Mohan from early childhood onwards, but it is also true that there were certain high points of acute realisations as a consequence of the agony and test Gandhiji passed through. In fact, soon after the acute emotional trauma at the Maritzburg railway station in the dark night, the next stretch of travel further heightened the trauma.

His woes were not over with this first leg of train travel. More hardships waited in the coach travel he was to undertake to reach Johannesburg. He had to take a coach from Charlestown where the train from Durban took him. He was asked to sit on the side of the coachbox and was not accommodated inside the coach for which he had a ticket. After sometime the coach leader (conductor was called as such) wanted to sit out and smoke and hence he took a dirty sack and asked Gandhiji to sit on the floor at his feet. Gandhiji wanted to refuse. But before he could utter those sentences that he had constructed the coach leader attacked him. In Gandhiji's own words:

> The insult was more than I could bear ... . As I was struggling through these sentences, the man came down upon me and began heavily to box my ears. He seized me by the arm and tried to drag me down. I clung to the brass rails of the coachbox and was determined to keep my hold even at the risk of breaking my wrist bones.[16]

It is clear that young Gandhi stood his ground steadfastly and did not resort to violence himself. But he resisted and this passive resistance did move other passengers inside the coach who came to his rescue. His stay in Pretoria further exposed him to racial discrimination. In Pretoria coloured people had restrictions on using public footpaths after nine in the night. Night permits were issued to Negro servants. Gandhiji's white friends did not like the idea of issuing such a permit to Gandhiji. Instead, a letter authorising him to be outdoors all the times was issued to him. However, once when he was walking through a street where the President of Pretoria lived, he was beaten up by a police petrol constable who guarded the President Street. A white friend happened to pass and intervened and upon proper identification the policeman apologised. The white friend wanted Gandhiji to sue and he promised to stand witness, but Gandhiji refused. He did not want to punish a single person for this societal problem. Even at that young age Gandhiji had already scaled good height and it is evident from his reflections that he recorded after this incident and I quote:

> The incident deepened my feeling for the Indian settlers. I discussed with them the advisability of making a test case, if it were found necessary to do so, after having seen the British Agent in the matter of these regulations. I thus made an intimate study of the hard condition of the Indian settlers, not only by reading and hearing about it, but by personal experience. I saw that South Africa was no country for self-respecting Indian, and my mind became more and more occupied with the question as to how this state of things might be improved.[17]

As we can see by the age of twenty-five years young Gandhiji had accepted and had become staunch practitioner of honesty, truth and non-violence. Even under most trying circumstances and tempting situations he resolutely steered clear of giving up truth and resorting to violence. Gandhiji firmly internalised the value of passive but firm resistance with self-suffering in the situations of injustice and exploitation rather than inflicting injury and violence to the perpetrator. It was this Gandhiji who went on to lead the South Africa Satyagraha between 1896 and 1914 and after that became the most central figure in India's fight for independence. His experiments with self-regulation continued and in 1930 he penned rules for self-regulation when he was serving a term in Yarvada Jail.

III

The *Ekadash Vrat:* Eleven Principles towards Self-disciplining and Self-regulation

In September 1930, Gandhiji was in Yervada Jail. He spent most of his time in spinning, reading and reflecting on Bhagvat Geeta, reading newspapers and the letters he received in large numbers. Among the letters were ones that were written by the Sabarmati Ashram inmates. Some of them requested Gandhiji to write some inspiring letters that would enliven the inmates with new spirit and awakening. Gandhiji responded by writing weekly letters. He suggested that in the morning of every Tuesday a sermon may be read which he would write. The practice continued and Gandhiji wrote commentary on the principles that were to be followed by the Ashram inmates. He had written about ten principles but did not write anything on *swadeshi* because he had promised the British that he would not write anything critical of Raj while in jail. But after he was released from the jail he wrote on *swadeshi* and thus completed the *Ekadash Vrat*. I shall describe each principle briefly:

1. *Satya* or truth: The word *satya* is derived from the word *sat*. It means being. Gandhiji interpreted this as nothing is there as being other than the truth. He said, "In fact it is more correct to say that Truth is God, than to say that God is Truth".[18] Gandhi insisted on truth because he strongly believed that without truth there was no true knowledge. At times truth is confused or narrowly understood as speaking truth. But for people in general, and the Ashram inmates in particular, Gandhiji's message was truth in thought, truth in action and truth in speech. The effort to seek truth has to be honest.
2. *Ahimsa* or non-violence: Gandhiji used love and non-violence interchangeably. How does one feel about others? We destroy our distracters. Should we physically do so? What about the enemy within? To live with enemies within and outside is *ahimsa*. Not to hurt any living being is no doubt non-violence. But it is not enough; it is only a part. Complete non-violence means "hurt by every evil thought, by undue haste, by lying, by hatred, by wishing ill to anybody". If the man is not able to follow this broader concept of non-violence, he cannot be a truth-seeker. Attainment of truth is impossible without following the path of *ahimsa*. It is a strong moral force which gains strength only from seeking the truth and finding truth is by following non-violence. Thus, *ahimsa* is means and truth is end.
3. *Brahmcharya* or chastity: The essence of *brahmcharya* as developed by Gandhiji in his own words is as follows: "Let us remember the root meaning of *brahmcharya* conduct adapted to the search of *brahma*, i.e., Truth. From this etymological meaning arises the special meaning, viz., control of all the senses. We must entirely forget the incomplete definition which restricts itself to the sexual aspect only."[19]
4. *Aswad* or control of the palate: Taste buds are difficult to control and regulate. Hence, Gandhiji thought that in religious

traditions and practices too, controlling the palate is treated as separate observance and it is not insisted upon. This is perhaps because the greatest of ascetics in India might have found it difficult to control the palate. Gandhiji developed it as a separate observance and insisted that control over palate helps in practising *brahmcharya*. Nutrition, taste and quantity of food to be consumed have to be carefully balanced. In controlling palate taste has to be completely sacrificed. Nutritive food has to be consumed in limited quantities.

5. *Asteya* or non-stealing: For Gandhiji, it is more mental than physical. Of course, he has insisted that any type of stealing of physical good is failure in following the path of truth. Further, acquiring or desiring to acquire something even in thought that does not belong to one is theft according to Gandhiji. Non-stealing physically and in thought is the real and complete practice of non-stealing.
6. *Aparigrha* or non-possession or poverty: Possession implies provision for future. Gandhiji, like all other saints and sufis in Asia, has abhorred materialistic possession. Gandhiji says, "God never stores for tomorrow". "The rich have superfluous store of things which they do not need, which are therefore neglected and wasted; while millions are starved to death for want of sustenance."[20] Gandhiji has quoted extensively from nature and its arrangements and argues that no other specie collects and stores possessions. Mainly it is human species that owns and possesses. He argues that even brain and mind should be non-possessive, it should have only what is required for a healthy life and discard rest. Otherwise it is not possible to maintain humility. Finally, possession and richness comes in way of seeking truth. Truth-seekers have always been voluntarily poor.
7. *Abhay* or fearlessness: Freedom from death and delusions is fearlessness according to Gandhiji. A seeker of truth is bound to become fearless. Further, one who practises non-violence cannot do so with fear. Violence is the reaction to display one's own fear of inner and external enemies. If there is universal love towards one and all and the person is a seeker of truth by non-violent means, fear cannot come near the person. Gandhi quotes from *Upanishads* and argues that one should give up attachment for things, while we enjoy them. We must be interested in them, not as proprietors, but as

trustees. *Tena Tyaktena Bhunjithaha* – Enjoy the worldly riches by renouncing them is what *Ishopanishad* has said. Gandhiji endorsed it completely.

8. *Asprushyta Nivaran* or removal of untouchability: As a seeker of truth, Gandhiji despite declaring himself as a *Sanatan Hindu*, a devout Hindu, he did not blindly accept all that is said in scriptures. He singled out untouchability and identified as shame of Hinduism as in practice. He declared untouchability as an Ashram observance. In fact, remotely it connects to *shadripu* (six enemies of soul that I will discuss shortly). *Matsar* or hatred towards another being is rejected even in pursuit of salvation in staunch practice of Hinduism. Gandhiji had very strong feelings on this issue and he said, "By treating removal of untouchability as an Ashram observance, we assert our belief, that untouchability is not only a part and parcel of Hinduism, but a plague, which is the bounden duty of every Hindu to combat."[21]
9. *Jatmehnat* or bread labour: Gandhiji acknowledges influence of two writings for evolving and firming up on this observance for Ashram inmates. Ruskin's *Unto this Last* was the first book which influenced his mind about bread labour and second was the writings of Tolstoy. The influence of Tolstoy's writings was so deep that he named one of his Ashrams in South Africa as Tolstoy Farm. Gandhiji calls bread labour principle as divine law. One who does not do bodily labour has no right to eat or should not have right to eat. Gandhiji observed that there was worldwide conflict between capital and labour. Poor, therefore, envied rich. If every person – rich or poor – worked for their bread, the distinction of ranks would disappear. There would be rich people but they will hold the capital and use it as trustee in public interest.
10. *Sarvadharmsambhav:* Although Gandhiji declared himself a *Sanatan Hindu*, he became conscious of it only after learning about other religions more deeply while he was in South Africa. He could see problems in every religion and thus rejected blind faith. For him, truth is God and seeking truth is seeking divine. That is the religion for Gandhiji. In fact, he said that all religions ultimately led to the search for Truth. On why there were many religions his explanation is interesting and I would like to quote him from the lecture he sent to Ashram inmates from Yervada prison. He says:

"The question then arises: Why should there be so many different faiths? The soul is one, but the bodies which she animates are many. We cannot reduce the number of bodies; yet we recognise the unity of soul. Even as a tree has a single trunk, but many branches and leaves, so is there one true and perfect religion, but it becomes many, as it passes through the human medium. The one Religion is beyond all speech. Imperfect men put it into such language as they command, and their words are interpreted by other men equally imperfect. Whose interpretation is to be held the right one? Everybody is right from his own standpoint, but it is not impossible that everybody is wrong. Hence, the necessity for tolerance, which does not mean indifference towards ones own faith, but a more intelligent and purer love for it."[22]

11. *Swadeshi:* It is love for neighbours and duty towards them to support them in production and consumption of goods and services. This is not charity but duty. In *swadeshi* there is no room for selfishness. If at all it is there, it is of extreme type that is one which is not different from altruism. A votary of *swadeshi* will carefully study his environment, and try to help his neighbours wherever possible, by giving preference to local manufacturers, even if they are of inferior grade or dearer in price than the things manufactured elsewhere. He will try to remedy their defects, but will not give them up in favour of outside products.

If we collapse the *Ekadash Vrat* into its basic core, they can be incorporated in truth, non-violence and nationalism. Gandhiji wanted to contextualise the existence of human being in geo-political space. His idea of nationalism was not narrow, he did believe in one world for the humanity as a whole. It was his well-known saint follower Vinoba who introduced the concept of *Vasudhaiva Kutumbakam* – Universal Family. He gave the slogan of *Jai Jagat* – Hail Humankind. But in real world there were conflicts among human beings for control over geo-political spaces. It is in this context Gandhiji had understood and introduced *swadeshi.* If the societies decentralised their production for customary consumption requirements, social and environmental externalities would be minimised. This in turn would improve the scope of sustainability of the society. Even in order to appreciate the concept of *swadeshi* one has to go back to the core values of truth and non-violence.

It is interesting that Gandhiji has held a position that he is not saying anything original. It has been there in the Indian culture for centuries. He has only reiterated it once again with practical relevance for the new times. If we examine the *Ekadash Vrat* in this light, we find that the *vrat* Gandhiji wants every human being to observe originates from the Hindu religious classics. The purpose of the human body on this earth according to Hindu religion is to attain *moksha* – salvation. The pathway laid down involves conquering the enemies which are six in number and hence they are called *shadaripu*. These six enemies are *kam* (desire), *krodh* (temper), *mada* (intoxication), *moha* (attachment), *lobha* (greed) and *matsar* (envy).

Kam is carnal desire. It is the driving force for procreation. But humanity has given a new identification to *kam*. Sexuality is not a matter of shame and repression. It is freely accepted and demonstrated. Justification is given to indulgence in carnal pleasure without any objective of begetting child. Such indulgence is a sure hindrance in achieving the salvation of soul. Gandhiji has suggested *brahmcharya* – celibacy or abstinence as *vrat* to regulate desire for *kam*. Gandhiji might have had spiritual context for his *vrat*, but more than that he had practical and this worldly concern which according my understanding was paramount. Handling one's sexuality in a rational way is the most difficult task and it affects one's behaviour and rationality in all other fields where sexuality is not required. If not tamed unbridled sexuality leads to pervert behaviour which disturbs the society at large. Gandhiji has been clear that his idea of *brahmcharya* is not restricted to abstinence from sex only; it is regulating the mind too.

Unregulated *kam* is also at the root of the other five internal enemies. The desire leads to ownership and not trusteeship. What is mine cannot be of anybody else's. If somebody wishes to take away justifiably or otherwise I become angry and it manifests in *krodh* – anger. Here the illustration Saddam Hussain in Iraq can be cited who saw scheming in US's order to check the nuclear armament with him, who again did not hold it for any peaceful purpose. He knew that US came after oil reserve in Iraq. He himself was a perpetrator of his community. But his sense of ownership, his desire (*kam)* to rule his people led him to anger and hence war. Both, the US President George Bush and Saddam Hussain, the deposed President of Iraq, perceived that they own power. It has led to *mada* – intoxication of power. Both are greedy thus suffer from *lobh* and, therefore, they have developed attachment – *moha*. If both become seeker of truth in real sense, they will have to display universal love. Non-violence would be the major way to seek truth and hence peace. It is important to note here that unless both these leaders become seeker of truth at individual level, their ability to lead the path of truth for others would not be gained. Thus, in Gandhiji's *Ekadash Vrat,* self-improvement is the primary task before any attempt is made to improve the society.

By now it should be clear to the readers that in Gandhian perspective individual's behaviour is constrained by self-regulation. The liberty is to be liberated in spiritual sense. Gandhiji considers it extremely important that an individual regulates self not only to seek his own truth and salvation, but also thereby contribute to a healthy society which is by and large devoid of *shadripu.* It should be possible for audience to understand that in a way Gandhiji has been a votary of extreme individualism wherein a person seeks his own truth which in turn leads him to non-violent and be loyal to neighbour for materialist requirements. In the Western world where an individual, fiercely fighting for his freedom and wanting to feel liberated, faces a constraint imposed by the social order that he, in pursuing his freedom, cannot come in way of any other's freedom. He can pursue anything as long as he does not impinge upon other's freedom. Gandhian perspective, which has roots in the Indian culture, does not match with the Western perspective. The individual has all the freedom to be liberated and in fact should aim at getting liberated, but mainly through disciplining oneself. Obviously, emergent socio-economic model differs in both instances.

IV

Emergent Socio-economic Model in Gandhian Perspective

We can see that Gandhiji has set a tone for building his socio-economic model that is mainly based on moral and ethical grounds. He grew as a person with his experiments with truth. He tried the non-violent and passive resistance and succeeded fairly impressively in South Africa and by the time he reached the age of 40, he was in a position to comment comprehensively on the tenets of the society he had evolved out of his percept and practice. He penned it in a small book form that was titled *Hind Swaraj* – literally meaning freedom of Hind. He was returning to South Africa from England where he had attended a number of gatherings of young Indians who had decided to fight for India's freedom through violent resistance. He was replying to these forces and the book was written in one sitting in the ship in 1908. The most characteristic feature of this commentary is his total rejection of the Western civilisation. It is perhaps an exaggeration as later his grandson Rajmohan Gandhi, a scholar in his own right, has noted in the following words:

> I for one am unable to accept the sweeping statement: "The tendency of the Indian civilisation is to elevate the moral being, that of the Western civilisation is to propagate immorality. The latter is godless; the former is based on a belief in God" (Ch.13). The torch held by Hind Swaraj's author does not throw an even light on the terrain under examination. Some portions remain in darkness while the shape of others is distorted or exaggerated. Yet no study of the historic encounter between the Indian and the Western civilisations can ignore Hind Swaraj; neither can any study of the working of Gandhi's mind.[23]

Hind Swaraj, in which Gandhiji has mainly assessed the modernisation of England and Europe and has anticipated the ill-effects of it on the Indian society if the latter tried following the former blindly. In *Hind Swaraj*, Gandhiji explains the implications of the fall in the moral standards in society following material prosperity. England was the most prosperous nation in the world when the *Hind Swaraj* was penned. The First World War was still five years away. America was already emerging as a land of great wealth. Gandhiji's reflections on modern civilisation were largely based on his observations about the conditions in England. In fact, chapter 5 in *Hind Swaraj* is titled as 'Condition of England', where Gandhiji criticises the parliament as an institution governing society. The central concern of Gandhiji was that the politicians in the British Parliament were merely given over to capturing and retaining political power and rule and they were, by and large, not worried about the welfare of the people. He had also criticised the media for not being serious and sincere in assessing people and events and act as an objective guide to help in assessing their leaders. Towards the end of the chapter, he ascribes the state of affairs in England to the modern civilisation when he says, "it is not due to any peculiar fault of the English people, but the condition is due to modern civilisation. It is a civilisation only in name. Under it the nations of Europe are becoming degraded and ruined day by day."[24]

The next chapter in *Hind Swaraj* is on civilisation. Here, Gandhiji speaks of how people thought that living in better built houses, wearing on variety of clothing, wearing shoes was all part of the civilised society. Instead of spears, people carried revolvers containing five or more chambers. Ploughing land with steam engines and make wealth was hailed as a sign of civilisation. Flying from one place to another was considered the height of civilisation. He visualises the future in the following manner:

> As men progress, they shall be able to travel in airships and reach any part of the world in a few hours. Men will not need the use of their hands and feet. They will press a button, and they will have their clothing by their side. Another button and they will have their newspaper. A third and a motorcar will be waiting for them. They will have variety of delicately dished up food .... Formerly, when people wanted to fight one another, they measured between them their bodily strength; now it is possible to take away thousands of lives by one man working behind a gun from a hill. This is civilisation.[25]

What Gandhiji saw in England during his stay made deep impressions and was reflected in the following way in the *Hind Swaraj*:

> Civilisation (read modern civilisation) seeks to increase bodily comforts, and it fails miserably even in doing so. The civilisation is irreligion, and it has taken such a hold on the people in England that those who are in it appear to be half mad. They lack real physical strength or courage. They keep up their energy by intoxication. They can hardly be happy in solitude. Women, who should be queens of households, wander in the streets, or they slave away in factories. For the sake of a pittance, half a million women in England alone are labouring under trying circumstances in factories or similar institutions.[26]

In chapter 13 of *Hind Swaraj* Gandhiji comes out with his idea of reformed or modern India. He begins by saying that India is accused of non-change and hence backward. In fact, the lack of quick change is India's strength. The Indian society after long experience has decided to keep a certain form that it deems appropriate. It should not be dubbed as backwardness. There are many calls for change, India has not responded to all of them; there lies its wisdom. Reform or modernisation is a behaviour where individual is motivated to perform duties better. That is living according to morals and ethics. The moral in performing duty lies in regulating our mind and senses and keeping them in discipline. That is to knowing oneself and that is real reform and modernisation.

Instability of mind is human nature. Mind keeps wandering. Body demands more as you give more to it. By taking more it is not satiated. Mind and body want more of more. Our forefathers realised this and wisdom dawned on to them. They thought deeply and realised that pleasure and pain are the result of working of the mind. Poor are not unhappy because they are poor, they are unhappy because they see others rich. Rich are not happy too. Thus, happiness is important, not poverty or plenty. We continued our age old systems of cultivation practices, housing and other lifestyles not because we did not know how to invent and produce machines, but our forefathers realised that if run into that runnel, there is no going back or shifting possible. Bread labour is a dignified way of living forever. Thus, they resisted urbanisation. They knew there will be some who will get very rich in this process and they will cruelly exploit the poor. They realised that ethical people were better human beings, saints and *rishis* were qualitatively superior and hence they were ranked above the kings who wielded swords to control. There were lawyers and healers in the society but they were not God players, they were subservient to the society; they were dependent on people and not vice versa. People had their own way of resolving legal problems. Customary laws ruled and communities acted with more responsibility.

Gandhiji, in a nutshell, spelt out his socio-economic model in the way I have described above. Was he unaware of the social ills of his times? Was he a blind follower of the traditional society from where he came? In the same chapter Gandhiji provides answers to these questions. According to him, the social ills reflected in child marriages, child widowhood, prostitution as religious traditions etc. were to be abhorred and corrected. They were weaknesses of the system. It did not make the entire system bad and worth discarding. In short, Gandhiji was of the opinion that there was no need to throw the baby with bathwater.

Let me reiterate that the society which Gandhiji visualised stood firmly on the assumption about particular characteristic of the human being. The man there is not the 'economic man' who emerged from the modern western civilisation. Gandhiji's 'man' is quintessentially a moral and ethical man. Let us understand that Gandhiji was firm about his 'man' because he was arguing a case for sustainable societies. According to him, when an individual acts with complete freedom and no self-regulation leads to moral decay. A self-regulated individual, according to Gandhiji, could contribute best to a sustainable society, because there would be least opportunity to govern. We should remind ourselves here that Gandhiji had always stood for 'minimum state'. Minimum state is possible in his scheme only when individuals are liberated by high degree of self-regulation and are thus disciplined. Was he contemplating about the moral decay of society out of his imagination? No, here is some evidence.

Gandhiji, wrote *Hind Swaraj* in 1909 and then on December 22, 1916, he responded to Kapildev Malaviya's invitation to speak to the members of the Mysore Central College Economics Society, Allahabad, and he delivered a lecture that was titled "Does Economic Progress Clash with Real Progress"? By real progress he had meant the sustainable society that he had portrayed in *Hind Swaraj*. The tone he had set in it continued in his 1916 lecture. He hardly changed it later with regard to this matter. The central thesis to which he adhered throughout his life was the debate about the moral progress vis-à-vis material progress and it is clear from his 1916 lecture that he considered the former to be real progress. He said, "by economic progress, I mean material progress without limit and by real progress we mean moral progress, which again is the same thing as progress of the permanent element in us."[27]

According to Gandhiji, the societies that prospered materially experienced a moral fall. The fall of Rome is a classic example of this. The *Yadavas* ruined themselves morally when they were rolling in riches. Gandhiji thought that an ordinary measure of morality is possessed by most including the very rich, but their material gains did not ensure moral richness. Sharing his long-standing observation of the society of the rich, Gandhiji said, "I observed almost invariably that the greater the possession of riches, the greater was their moral turpitude. Our rich men, to say the least, did not advance the moral struggle of passive resistance, as did the poor. The rich men's sense of self-respect was not so much injured as that of the poorest. If I were not afraid of treading on dangerous ground, I would even come nearer home and show you that possession of riches has been a hindrance to real growth."[28] Gandhiji then says that Jesus Christ was the greatest economist of his time. Quoting the dialogue between the Christ, a citizen and other disciples described by St. Mark, Gandhiji emphasises in his lecture the virtue of spending wealth in the service of the poor and the have-nots. The point he keeps reiterating is against amassing wealth. Later, as we know, he formulated *aparigrha* (non-accumulation) as one of the *Ekadash Vrat* – principles.

Gandhiji gave illustrations from the Bible may be because of the important presence of the English professors and scholars in the gathering. He appeared aware of this because he makes this point: "I have not taken the trouble of copying similar passages from the other non-Hindu scriptures and I will not insult you by quoting in support of the law stated by Jesus passages from writings and sayings of our own sages, passages stronger even if possible than the Biblical extracts have drawn your attention to. Jesus, Mohamed, Buddha, Nanak, Kabir, Chaitanya, Shankara, Dayanand, Ramakrishna were men who exercised an immense influence over and moulded the character of thousands of men … . And they were all men who deliberately embraced poverty as their lot."[29]

Gandhiji then talked about the craze for materialistic progress and argues that pursuing mere materialistic goals was a fall from idealism. He says that one cannot serve God and mammon altogether is an economic truth of the highest value. He recommends the building of a truly spiritual nation (not by boasting about the glorious past) and seeking the kingdom of God should be the basis for real economics. It can be clearly seen that his reservation was with regard to limitless material prosperity in the society.

Bodily comfort and the rush to acquire bodily comfort is what Gandhiji has criticised the most. In his December 1916 lecture he introduced the concept of 'voluntary poverty'. He then asked the Ashram inmates to practise it as one of the observances *aparigraha* or non-possession. The saints and reformers he mentions were, during their times, living examples of those who courted voluntary poverty in order to achieve high moral standards. It is clear from the *Hind Swaraj* and the lecture that material prosperity does not ensure high moral standards; instead, has brought the moral standards down and led to decay of human society. Through these thoughts Gandhiji laid the philosophical foundation of the economic order of society. According to him, limitless material progress could not be the goal of economic development in a society. Material progress was important only for very limited purposes of lifting people from abject poverty and destitution that lowered or destroyed human dignity. The production and distribution system that Gandhiji conceived and tried to implement later in India along with the freedom struggle calling it the 'Swadeshi' movement was founded on the basic tenet of ultimate moral progress combined with dignified and healthy physical survival.

We can see that Gandhiji's macro-model of the society is thus consistent with the micro-model he sets out for an individual. It is interesting to note that a set of self-regulated individuals not only feel liberated, but also simultaneously help build a sustainable society that requires least governance and eminently takes care of the ecological question that is paramount in the minds of thinkers of the modern world.

V

The Modern Individual in Western World and Issues in Societies' Sustainability

In the beginning I made a remark that Anthony Giddens does not mention Gandhiji while discussing complex problems and possible solutions for the modern society. For that matter, most mainstream intellectuals have almost dismissed Gandhiji, especially the economists. Economists are important because they influence the socio-political thinking the most. In the traditional societies, economic system was subservient to the social system. In the modern societies reverse appears to be true. Gandhian thought does not figure prominently in the development debate in the world in general and in the West in particular, because the Western thought has been polarised mainly into two ideologies. At one end, it is conservatism, which ideologically places a strong emphasis on 'the individual'. The agency to facilitate is free market which will get best out of individuals and hence best for the society. On the other end are the communism and socialism that place "a firm emphasis upon the role of the state in generating both solidarity and equality."[30] Recent changes and developments have caused turbulence at both the ends. Neither of the systems is able to fully comprehend the changes and hence is not able to cope with the problem of sustainability. I shall share some of the main points that are discussed and then we will be able to see that Gandhian way holds a reasonable promise to ensure sustainability of the societies.

The debacle of Marxian or socialist system has been very prominent. Marxian philosophy was based on the premise that communist system had the capacity to form a social system that would create more wealth and distribute it more equitably. In the post-World War II, socialism bug bit most of the countries. In the West socialism was adapted into moderate, parliamentary socialism. Welfare state, although creation of both capitalist and communist thinkers, came to be owned ultimately by the socialists. Free market thinkers were relegated to background soon after Second World War and most economies accepted the welfare state. After 1970, both communist and socialist systems started to fail. According to Giddens, "Socialism also failed to grasp the significance of markets as informational devices, providing essential data for buyers and sellers. These inadequacies only became fully revealed with intensifying processes of globalisation and technological change from the early 1970s onwards."[31] By this time another important problem that had surfaced was the ecological degradation. The communist and socialist systems did not address the ecological question at all.

Capitalistic societies with welfare state also witnessed problems. Market failure was accepted in case of public goods. Unemployment problem was to be solved with the social security. It was expected that as the economies will expand and production would boom, the state will become more equipped to provide welfare. This did not happen. Welfare states were sensitive to the ecological concerns, but found it difficult to tackle them effectively. State's presence became too prominent with weak delivery. Thus, the thesis of neo-liberal was born. Let us now understand clearly that dominant role of the state is questioned under both the systems. The state, as it was under both the systems, has failed. Communism and socialism in its pristine form appear to have vanished for ever at least in the democratic societies. Capitalistic systems with welfare state are trying to cope with the new situation with two different theses. One that appears to be more popular is the neo-liberal thesis. In this thesis government is minimal. The other thesis is where government is different. This is what Anthony Giddens calls the 'Third Way' and according to him it holds better promise. Let us first review the neo-liberal thesis.

The neo-liberal thesis has pathological aversion for the state. It also follows from the classical liberal thesis that considered superiority of market over all other agencies for economic transactions. Rational economic man is the kingpin in the system. Thus, much of the government's role is assumed by the civil society. This means that there is some assumption about the individual and the civil society. Interestingly, individual freedom and liberty has its origin in rebellion against the Catholic church.[32] The values that were put forward and accepted while the economic transformation of Europe began on the eve of industrialisation, were the Protestant values. Briefly expressed it was an honest man working hard to gain prosperity for the family in best possible way. Such honest and hardworking individuals trying to maximise their individual and family welfare would form a harmonious and prosperous society. And obviously free market was the best agency which will provide equal opportunity to all thus simultaneously determine individual and social welfare.

Neo-liberal thesis also assumes similar civil society features under the changed circumstances in the present. Giddens has quoted David Green who has listed some features thus: "The virtue of civil society, if left to its own devices, are said to include 'Good character, honesty, duty, self-sacrifice, honour, service, self-discipline, toleration, respect, justice, civility, fortitude, courage, integrity, diligence, patriotism, consideration for others, thrift and reverence."[33] It is clear that it is the individual with such virtues would make the civil society whose features are listed. I am certain that Gandhiji would have been very happy to read the list because it includes more virtues than he had prescribed for the Ashram inmates under *Ekadash Vrat* – eleven principles.

But neo-liberalism is in trouble. Giddens draws attention to the paradox that obtains in neo-liberal thesis. Traditionally, market fundamentalism has been most favoured by the conservatism. It always meant a cautious, pragmatic approach to social and economic change. The continuity of tradition is central to the idea of conservatism. Tradition contains accumulated wisdom of past and therefore supplies a guide to the future. Free market philosophy under the neo-liberal thesis is pinning its hopes for the future on unending economic growth produced by the liberation of market forces. Devotion to free market on the one hand, and to the traditional family and nation on the other, is self-contradictory. Individualism and choice are supposed to stop abruptly at the boundaries of the family and national identity, where tradition must stand intact. Although it might appear a remote connection, but repeated failures at WTO negotiation meets is indicative of this conflict between unfettered freedom, market fundamentalism and conservatism. The dynamism of market forces undermines traditional structures of authority and fractures local communities. Neo-liberalism creates new risks and uncertainties which it asks citizens simply to ignore. Staunch free-market advocate F.A. Hayek is more forthright in accepting it. In one his lectures in Adam Smith Institute he has argued that in a spontaneous order individual is free to take decision on the basis of information that market provides him and hence he alone should be responsible for the gain or loss out of an economic enterprise.

Thus, under the neo-liberal thesis, it is the individual who has undergone a metamorphosis. It is not the person necessarily with 'Protestant Ethics' and hence neo-liberalism is in trouble. I must say that even the individual under the classical liberal was in trouble. The 'rational economic man' appearing in traditional economic theories has not always been so in practice. The basic value accepted is maximisation. Maximisation is a game of 'no limit'. Hence, greed enters. It sacrifices rationality. Prof. Stanislav Menshikov, co-chairman of the Russian Economists Allied for Arms Reduction says, "All economies that are based on these principles (maximisation of utility and profits) tend to create and promote unequal conditions for the people."[34] The other argument of the market fundamentalist, according to Menshikov, is that it is the natural order of things because it proceeds from human nature in which greed and need to maximise material benefits prevail. If God has created human beings that way, how can one change? The evidence does not support this claim either. It appears that individual behaviour holds the key for the social order rather than the other way round.

Now, let me examine whether 'The Third Way' really shows the way for sustainable societies and what kind of individual appears in that scheme and how liberated and individualistic she is. To begin with the 'The Third Way', or if I rechristen it as 'neo-socialism', accepts the failure of old-style social democracy with Keynesian policies. The assumptions that old system made were: a traditional family form where husbands worked and wives looked after the children and other elders, a homogenous labour market, mass production in basic sectors, an elitist and patronising state and largely domestic economies. These assumptions no longer hold true. How does the neo-socialism respond? It responds in two ways. One, it argues for a compassion towards the weak. This has been there from the beginning and it arises out the reality that market is not indeed able to take care of those who do not fall in its sphere. Second, and as a consequence of first, one cannot argue for minimum government, but one will have to have government that works. As Giddens, chief promoter of the 'Third Way' argues, "The restructuring of the government should follow the ecological principle of 'getting more from less', understood not as downsizing, but as improving delivered value."[35] The Third Way politics assumes that the basic changes are exogenous and they are: globalisation, transformation in personal life and our relationship with nature.

Examination of transformation in personal life would lead us to search the emerging individual and his values. New individualism is being explained variously. There appears to be a rise in 'me' generation proceeding fast towards 'me first' generation. If personal liberty gains paramount importance then the problems between liberty and equality will have to be tackled *de novo*. 'Me first' society would harm the social solidarity which both the neo-liberal and the neo-socialist have to achieve. The causes attributed to this 'me first' individualism are different. Neo-liberal blame it on the new permissiveness of the 1960s and neo-socialists would blame it on the rise of the market fundamentalism. However, sufficient evidence is not available to substantiate any of the reason. The new individualism rejects traditions and traditional values. Family is not the unit, individual is the unit. This might not necessarily mean a total moral decay. New postmodern values seem to be appearing in which individual is keen to see basic human rights, ecological values and sexual freedom established. It is worth recalling here that despite the concerns the ecological problem can be tackled neither in the market fundamental environment nor in the communist or social democratic welfare state environment.

In the overall assessment, the situation is complex indeed. The individualism with 'me first' characteristics and new moral concerns can turn in any way. Neither the neo-liberal nor the 'third way' seems to be sure about the future direction. Both the systems fail to ask some fundamental questions that matter for the societies to be sustainable. The issue of sustainability is raised only in the context of environment and ecology and there too the debate does not help in taking a clear position on any side. Neither the dooms day is just at the door nor is it so far that it is never going to happen. Julian Simon might have won the bet and got paid by Ehrlich in 1990,[36] but ecological issues are far more complex than what economists are trying to grapple with. What is the way out? I have shown in sufficient details above that the perspective has to change and reach near the Gandhian perspective. Practice of *aswada* – control over palate, *asteya* – non-stealing, *aparigraha* – being trustee to wealth and accepting voluntary poverty, *jatmehnat* –

bread labour and *ahimsa* – non-violence for living and in interacting with others at micro level would answer main problems relating to insatiable aggregate demand, monopolistic practices, abnormal profit appropriation and ecological disasters. Because as I have shown Gandhian model of individual behaviour has greatest potential to bring a socio-economic order that has better potential for moving towards sustainable societies.

One wonders why the world is so hesitant to consider the 'Gandhian way'!

Notes

1. This is a revised version of the Gandhi Memorial Lecture delivered at Mahatma Gandhi Centre, Moka, Mauritius on October 2, 2006.
2. Those interested should read, Lloyd Rudolph and Susanne Hoeber Rudolph, *Post Modern Gandhi and Other Essays*, Oxford University Press, New Delhi, 2006.
3. Lloyd Rudolph and Susanne Hoeber Rudolph, op. cit., p. 99.
4. For those interested in reading on this view should refer to Julian Simon's various works and prominent among them is Julian L. Simon and Herman Kahn, *The Resourceful Earth*, Blackwell, Oxford, 1984.
5. Anthony Gidden's *The Third Way: The Renewal of Social Democracy*, Polity Press, UK and USA, Reprinted in 2005.
6. Gandhiji has devoted a chapter titled 'Religious Ferment' in his Autobiography where he concludes the chapter in the following words, "Though I took a path my Christian friends had not intended for me, I have remained for ever indebted to them for the religious quest that awakened in me." p. 128 in M.K. Gandhi, *An Autobiography or My Experiments with Truth*, Mahadev Desai (trans.), 1927 Edition, May 2006 Reprint, Navajivan Publishing House, Ahmedabad, p. 111.
7. Ibid., p. 7.
8. Ibid., p. 36.
9. Ibid., p. 43.
10. Ibid., p. 42.
11. Ibid., p. 45.
12. Ibid., p. 104.
13. Rajmohan Gandhi, *The Good Boatman*, Penguin Books, India 1995, p. 37.

14. Ibid., p. 38.
15. Ibid.
16. *An Autobiography*, op. cit., p. 106.
17. Ibid., p. 121.
18. M.K. Gandhi, 'From Yervada Mandir', Translated from original Gujarati '*Mangal Prabhat*' by Valji Govindji Desai, Navajivan Publishing House, Ahmedabad, November 2005 Reprint.
19. Ibid., p. 10.
20. Ibid., p. 15.
21. Ibid., p. 20.
22. Ibid., p. 24.
23. Rajmohan Gandhi, op. cit., p. 139.
24. Anthony J. Parel (ed.), *Gandhi: Hind Swaraj and Other Writings*, Foundation Books, New Delhi for Cambridge University Press, 1997, p. 33.
25. Ibid., p. 36.
26. Ibid., p. 37.
27. *Collected Works of Mahatma Gandhi*, Publication Division, Government of India, Vol. 15, 2000, p. 274.
28. Ibid.
29. Ibid., p. 276.
30. Anthony Giddens, op. cit., p. 34.
31. Ibid., p. 5.
32. For a brief and fascinating account on history of human liberty in western world refer Fareed Zakaria, *The Future of Freedom*, Viking, Penguin Press, Delhi, 2003.
33. Anthony Giddens, op. cit., p. 12.
34. Stansilav Menshikov's lecture in *Compassionate Economics*, Tibet House, New Delhi, 2005, p. 5.
35. Anthony Giddens, op. cit., p. 74.
36. "The economist Julian Simon struck a famous wager with environmentalist Paul Ehrlich in 1980. Simon bet that, for any set of natural resources Ehrlich might like to nominate, prices would be lower at a specified moment in the future. Ehrlich chose 1990, and selected copper, chrome, nickel and tungsten. By 1990 the prices of these materials were lower by from 24 per cent to 78 per cent than they had been ten years before. Ehrlich duly paid up". Anthony Giddens, op. cit., p. 55.

5

Mahatma Gandhi's Non-violence

The Only Way to Peace

T.K.N. UNNITHAN

Mohandas Karamchand Gandhi's first two names have become unimportant. He is popularly known as Mahatma Gandhi. 'Mahatma' means great soul. People regard him as a saint, because of his sacrifices and his identification with the underprivileged, exploited, oppressed and suffering masses, as well as for his crusade for non-violence and peace. He himself strongly objected to being called a 'Mahatma'. Albert Einstein called him, "a man who has confronted the brutality of Europe with the dignity of the simple human being and thus at all times risen superior" and maintained that, "generations to come will scare believe that such one as this ever in flesh and blood walked upon this Earth". Albert Schweitzer wrote, "Gandhi continued what Buddha began. In the Buddha the spirit of love set itself the task of creating different spiritual conditions in the world; in Gandhi it undertakes to transform all wordily conditions."[1]

The people of India also call Gandhi *'Bapu'* (father), and *'Rashtrapita'* (father of the nation). In South Africa he invited the wrath of the colonial powers; they wanted to kill him and "hang naked fakir". Surprisingly, he was also called "an agent of British imperialism" and "a servant of Indian bourgeoisie". While the British went on arresting him and putting him in jail, his crusade against colonialism – a kind of structural violence – continued with sustained vigour. Firmly believing in the principles of truth and non-violence and identifying himself with the poor and the oppressed, he mobilised the non-violent power of the Indian masses and won for India freedom from colonialism.

Justice Philip Edward Archer says, "Gandhi's struggle for the independence of India was the beginning of 'decolonization' in the twentieth century. Many colonies in Asia gained their independence from their European colonial masters. This trend spread to Africa after the end of the Second World War and then the Gold Coast under the leadership of Dr Kwame Nkrumah began its struggle for independence which the country (as the first African nation) achieved in 1957. Decolonisation did not end, but swept through the whole continent of Africa. In South Africa, Gandhi's teachings of non-violence and non-cooperation inspired anti-apartheid movements led by Archbishop Desmond Tutu to engage in peaceful demonstrations and in non-violent protests throughout the cities of South Africa. These non-violent demonstrations pricked the conscience of the die-hard apostles of apartheid. The atmosphere today in South Africa is one conducive to the abolition of racial discrimination and reconciliation between all the races. In April 1994, South Africa held its first non-racial parliamentary elections-a year that coincided with the 125th birth anniversary of Mahatma Gandhi, who began his campaign in 1893 against injustices and indignities meted out to Indians in Natal by the South African Government. A century later, in 1993, one representative each of the black majority and the white minority, Mr Nelson Mandela and Mr F.W. de Klerk, were jointly awarded the Nobel Prize for Peace, because of their strenuous efforts to abolish the obnoxious system of apartheid and to bring about a non-racial society in which all human beings will be respected as dignified human beings with equal rights."[2]

Martin Luther King Jr acknowledges how he was inspired to apply the Gandhian techniques of non-violent revolution to transform American society and to make democracy a reality for the first time for millions of Americans and inspired liberation movements all over the world. In King's own words, "Gandhi was probably the first person in history to lift the love ethic of Jesus above mere interaction between individuals to a powerful and effective social force on a large scale ... it was in this Gandhian emphasis on love and non-violence that I discovered the method for social reform that I had been seeking for so many months .... I came to feel that this was the only morally and practically sound method open to oppressed people in their struggle for freedom ...

this principle became the guiding light of our movement. Christ furnished the spirit and motivation and Gandhi furnished the method."[3]

Not only in America, India or the African countries but wherever the Gandhian non-violent technique has been tried it proved successful. Conflicts resolved through non-violent methods leave less traces of ill-will or hatred. For example, the British and Indians have the best of friendly relations. So also the relations between various ethnic groups in the USA. Gandhi's non-violent techniques and "strategies have helped to make a new South Africa in which people of all races are learning how to live together in friendship and co-operation".

Thus, the efficacy of non-violence in creating social harmony and developing a qualitatively better social orders globally is well established. Yet violence has become so ubiquitous a phenomenon in contemporary society the world over that it is almost taken for granted. An average citizen of the world is increasingly becoming conscious of the growing impact of the violent social milieu in which he/she lives and functions. The various types of personal, intergroup and intra-group and international conflicts and the destruction and killings that are resulting from such conflicts indifferent parts of the world have become so much an everyday affair that the absence of the reporting of its occurrence on any day could make one wonder as to what has gone wrong with the world! The constant reporting of violent occurrences through the communication network cannot but make us increasingly conscious of the phenomenon of galloping violence globally. India is not an exception to this. On the contrary, the Indian tragedy is even greater because India is supposed to be the inheritor of the legacy of the philosophy of non-violence, which is diametrically opposed to the cult of violence. In spite of its great tradition of non-violence, India has become one of the most violent nations in the world. Apart from the murders perpetrated by organised groups like the terrorists, violence is enveloping all aspects of Indian life. And, the escalating violence is posing a serious threat to the very fabric of Indian culture and society.

Violence Breeds Violence

Human society by its very definition is based on sociability, cooperation and mutual adjustments among the members of its groups and the community, in other words, values fundamental to non-violence. Violence destroys mutual cooperation and promotes conflicts which accelerate and give rise to more and newer forms of violence. Violence destroys every form of relationship and it brings agony to oneself and others. So, the question indeed is as to how to promote good relationships and how to promote a sense of belonging and consequently human well-being; perhaps only by eradicating violence and its root causes.

In day-to-day life violence generally means the use of physical force for destroying property or people. "Force is the exercise of physical or an intangible power or influence to effect change. Violence is the wilful application of force in such a way that it is intentionally injurious to the person or group against whom it is applied; injury includes psychological as well as physical harm"[4] "The concept of violence", as rightly pointed out by Severyn T. Bruyn and Paula Rayman, "has also begun to mean the use of physical force to maintain systems of oppression and domination. The linguistic change in the term 'violence' from its original reference to physical destruction to include now 'systems of oppression' is a sign of broadening consciousness of the social origins of physical conflict in the context of society."[5]

Thus, broadly defined, violence implies hurt or injury to the 'other' in any manner. The concept of non-violence – Ahimsa – which means non-hurting others, brings the concept of violence into an even sharper focus. Any behaviour which results in harm or injury to others could be termed as violent. Violence is not only confined to physical violence, that is, physical harm, individually or destruction of property but it also includes non-physical, namely, the psychological and institutional types of violence. Violence may be organised or spontaneous, it may be interpersonal, intra-group or inter-group, it may be physical or psychological, it may be structural or non-structural. In short, violence can be classified in a number of ways depending upon the focus of our analysis.[6] Severyn T. Bruyn makes the distinction between 'physical violence' and 'structural violence' on the basis of Johan Galtung's definition: "The concept of violence is normally understood as the destructive use of physical force against people". Galtung suggests, however, that 'structural violence' is located in the organisation of society' – poverty is an example of structural violence.[7] This is the reason why Gandhi rejected Western civilisation based on unbridled industrialisation and large-scale mechanisation. Gandhi's indictment of Western civilisation as explained in his famous book *Hind Swaraj* was based on his objection to the dehumanising-violence-generating aspect of modern industrialisation. The high speed production imposed by the worship of 'Mammon – the God of Riches' according to him is bound to destroy human dignity, degrade people into being mere cogs in the machine, contaminate the environment with poisons of many kinds thus inviting unforseen natural disasters and creating situations to institutionalise violence and injustices. That is why, Gandhi has rejected both capitalism and communism and disapproved of a world built on the principle of either of them, as both embody a high degree of exploitation and violence. According to him, both capitalism and communism are born out of unlimited industrialisation and mechanisation. Hence, he offers an alternative model of social development based on the principles of truth and non-violence. The Gandhian non-violence paradigm for social development, i.e., the Sarvodaya model, is based on the goal of welfare of all in contradiction to the welfare of the maximum.

Meaning of Non-violence

In the Gandhian sense, non-violence or Ahimsa is not a negative concept, it is not mere absence of violence, but a positive state of love; non-hurting the other in thought, word or deed and love, compassion and altruism towards all. As Joan Bondurant says, "The word ahimsa expresses an ancient Hindu, Jain and Buddhist ethical precept. The negative prefix 'a' plus 'himsa', loosely meaning 'injury' make up the word, which is usually translated as non-violence. Yet ahimsa is eminently more than a negative notion. As is characteristic of Hindu and Buddhist terminology, the negative wording implies much, which remains unexpressed. The full force of ahimsa, explicitly stated, means 'action' based on the refusal to do harm." Albert Schweitzer, in his short study on Indian thought, calls attention to this further meaning of Ahimsa. Etymologically, himsa is the desiderative form of 'ban' meaning to kill or to damage, so that himsa means to wish to kill. Ahimsa, then, means renunciation of the will to kill or to damage. Gandhi refined the meaning. In his own words, "Ahimsa is not the crude thing it has been made to appear. Not to hurt any living thing is no doubt a part of ahimsa. But it is its least expression. The principle of himsa is hurt by every evil thought, by undue haste, by lying, by hatred, by wishing ill to anybody. I accept the interpretation of ahimsa, namely that it is not merely a negative state of harmlessness but it is a positive state of love, of doing good even to the evil-doer. But It does not mean helping the evil-doer to continue the wrong or tolerating it by passive acquiescence. On the contrary, love, the active state of ahimsa, requires you to resist the wrong-doer by dissociating yourself from him even though it may offend him or injure him physically." Gandhi here identifies "ahimsa with love". Violence, no doubt, because of its negative and destructive consequences engages our attention more easily and hence appears ubiquitous. Manifestation of violence in everyday life through the display of brute force and in the commission of crimes and creation of conflicts of many kinds, including organised group violence such as war, are indicative of human preoccupation with self-preservation characterised by extreme egocentric behaviour. If we look at the functioning of society, we find a continuum of coercive and non-coercive power relations. The coercive manifestations of power have a tendency to have greater resonance effect. And therefore also have a greater impact on the human mind and consciousness. That is why, most people tend to be impressed by the effectiveness of coercive power or violence and some people believe that the most effective binding force which keeps the society going is not voluntaristic conformity to norms, but fear of social sanctions. However, it is normative voluntaristic power and not coercive power that integrates society. The most vital and fundamental of all existential principles is interdependence and the consequential social awareness that results in reciprocity. The societal aspects of human aggregation is based on moral voluntaristic cooperative social processes. Coercive power, violence and conflicts do not explain a major part of societal existence. Therefore, it is argued that it is the non-violent non-coercive power and normative voluntaristic behaviours that explain the existence and continuation of human society.[8]

The corollary of this argument can be the conclusion that merely devising mechanisms and enforcing measures to control violence will not solve the problems created by it. Raising the level of non-coercive power and developing non-violent behaviour and social relationships can probably be effective means. Because the norms of non-violence and non-violent relationships will result in displacement of and eventual elimination of violence. In other words, the place of violence will be gradually taken over by non-violence. This can be judged by the resonance effect that non-violence values and actions are generating in the world, e.g., green peace movement, pugwash movement, the Sarvodaya movement and other peace initiatives.[9]

Universal Disapproval of Violence

There is a universal disapproval of violence. Wars are fought, the war-mongers say, for establishing peace. The modern state has an elaborate apparatus to control violence. There is unlimited condemnation of violence and glorification of the values of non-violence and peace from all quarters. The major religious traditions extol the virtues of love and peace and abhor violence and hatred. Although the languages are different, their message is the same. The Jams follow the teachings of Lord Mahavira: "know other creatures' love for life, for they are alike you. Kill them not: save their life from fear and enmity." And, the Buddha has said, "here monks and disciples dwelt pervading the entire world everywhere and equally with his heart filled with love, compassion, sympathetic-joy and equanimity, abundant, grown, great measurements, free from enmity and free from distress". In the words of Prophet Muhammad, "A perfect Muslim is he from whose tongue and hands mankind is safe. If you are able, keep your heart from morning till night and from night till morning free from malice towards anyone. This is one of my laws, and he who loveth my laws verily loveth me. The greatest enemies of God are those who are entered into Islam and do acts of infidelity, and who without cause, shred the blood of men". The Hindus consider non-violence as their supreme duty – Paramo Dharma. Christianity and its norms of conduct as enunciated by Jesus Christ are based on the principles of love: "Love your enemies, do good to them that hate you, bless them that curse you. Greater love hath no man than this, that a man lay down his life for his friends." The Tamil classics extol the values of non-violence. Thiruvalluvar teaches through 'Thirukkural' that:

> Those who are devoid of love appropriate all they have to themselves; but those who posses, love consider even their bones to belong to others. (Kural 2, chapter 8)
>
> Sorrow never comes upon the kind hearted. (Kural 5, chapter 25)
>
> It is the determination of the spotless not to give sorrow to others, although they obtain wealth, which confers greatness. (Kural 1, chapter 32)
>
> It is the determination of the spotless not to do evil in return even to those who have been at enmity with and done to them. (Kural 2, chapter 3)

> The crown of all virtues is non-violence: next is freedom from falsehood. (Kural 3, chapter 33)
>
> The path of rectitude is the path of non-violence. (Kural 4, chapter 33)

Yet we the practitioners of these religions and followers and admirers of these great saints and their teachings for creating a better human society indulge in all kinds of discriminatory behaviour which is devoid of concern for the other. Human society remains compartmentalised into innumerable vertical and horizontal divisions resulting in differentiations and discriminations of all kinds leading to many types of conflicts and violence. The rich and poor, the haves and have-nots, the elites and masses, the high castes and the low castes and the many categories of social groups that have come to exist serve more as causes for discriminations, tensions and conflicts than harmonious social relations. Different sects of the same religion are fighting to destroy each other. Terrorism is sending shockwaves throughout the world. Violence is becoming a social phenomenon threatening the very fabric of human society. The family, the fundamental social institution which determines the character of any society, has not been permitted to conduct its legitimate role and the positive familial values are not reflected in contemporary society. Positive traditional values, on the whole, have been relegated to the background and the new values that have emerged do not appear to be conducive to social progress in the sense in which we consider progress as an approximation towards a qualitatively better peaceful non-violent society.

Therefore, it is imperative for us to search for ways to bridge the gap between the precept and practice and to promote values which will be directly helpful for the realisation of our ultimate goal of a world without violence.

Inculcating Non-violence

To what extent is it possible to inculcate in human beings values of non-violence to change their attitudes? Value inculcation is possible only under the assumption that individuals are not genetically predisposed to violent behaviour and that human nature is not basically violent. These assumptions have been validated by scientists, who have emphatically asserted on the basis of their findings that:

1. it is scientifically incorrect to say that we have inherited any tendency to make wars from our animal ancestors;
2. war or other violent behaviour is genetically programmed into our human nature;
3. in the course of evolution there has been a selection for aggressive behaviour;
4. humans have violent brains; and
5. war is caused by instinct.

Therefore, there is every possibility to promote non-violent behaviour and non-violent social relationships through value inculcation and development of non-violent and altruistic personalities.

The human being is essentially and basically good and non-violent. It is the brutalisation that makes him or her violent. Gandhi's view on human nature becomes very relevant in this context. On the basis of various writings of Gandhi in his autobiography, *Young India*, *Harijan* and others, what Raghavan Iyer wrote that gives a clear Gandhian view of human nature and original goodness of human beings.

> "Gandhi declared that 'the brute by nature knows no self-restraint, and man is man because he is capable of, and only in so far as he exercises, self-restraint' ... . 'Man becomes great exactly to the extent that he works for the welfare of his fellowmen. The differences between men are merely those of degree, not of kind. We were, perhaps, all originally brutes. I am prepared to believe that we have become men by a slow process of evolution from the brute ...' 'Non-violence is the law of our species, as violence is the law of the brute ...' 'I am an irrepressible optimist ...' 'My optimism rests on my belief in the infinite possibilities of the individual to develop non-violence. Man's nature is not essentially evil. Brute nature has been known to yield to the influence of love. You must never despair of human nature ...' For Gandhi as for Confucius, an evil man is one who does not change, not one who cannot be changed. The consequence of the doctrine of original goodness is that humanity cannot be divided into good and bad; there are only evil acts, no wholly evil men. I have been taught from my childhood, and I have tested the truth by experience that the primary virtues of mankind are possible of cultivation by the meanest of the human species. It is this undoubted universal possibility that distinguishes the human from the rest of God's creations ...' Clearly, the divinity of man manifests itself according to the extent to which he realises his humanity, i.e., his

oneness with his fellowmen. For Gandhi, as for Spinoza, men must unite themselves 'by bonds that make all of them as one man'. To Spinoza and Goethe, and to Gandhi, the unity between all men, though veiled from common sight, was in fact as 'real' as the idea of separateness is to man still under the spell of his senses … ."[10]

We agree with Gandhi and Confucius that human nature is naturally and essentially good. Violent behaviour is a learned behaviour and not due to any inherent or inborn factors but on account of human brutalisation. This offers scope for changing violent human behaviour patterns. Through state terrorism, police bullets and army control, terrorism cannot be stopped. More radical and fundamental measures have to be devised to elicit and increase the goodness in humans. If humans are capable of self-direction, which indeed humans are, there are infinite possibilities of the individual to eschew violence and develop non-violence, in other words in the possibility of 'debrutalisation' and 're-humanisation' of human beings. It is this possibility that gives us the clue to make efforts to solve the problems of violence.

The greater the predominance of non-violence power, the greater the progress and vice versa. By accumulating the forces of moral voluntaristic power, positive values of life are activated and the normative structure altered and societies taken to higher realms of existence which are characterised by qualitative differences in human life.

Gandhi's theory of non-violence would state that:

1. Non-violence is the law of the human race and is infinitely greater than and superior to brute force.
2. In the last resort it is of no avail to those who do not possess a living faith in the God of Love.
3. Non-violence affords the fullest protection to one's self-respect and sense of honour, but not always to possession of land or money, though its habitual practice does prove a better bulwark than the possession of armed men to defend them. Non-violence, in the very nature of things, is of no assistance in the defence of ill-gotten gains and immoral acts.
4. Individuals or nations who practise non-violence must be prepared for sacrifices. It is, therefore, inconsistent with the possession of other people's countries, i.e., modern imperialism which is frankly based on force for its defence.

5. Non-violence is a power which can be wielded equally by all children, young men and women or grown-up people, provided they have a living faith in the God of Love and have therefore equal love for all mankind. When non-violence is accepted as the law of life it must pervade the whole being and not be applied to isolated acts.
6. It is profound error to suppose that whilst the law is good enough for individuals it is not for masses of mankind.

The question is as to how to make non-violence a living principle on which day-to-day life can be organised? How to generate a non-violent power to usher in progress towards building up non-violent social orders globally? Gandhian answer to these questions is that individual transformation through Satyagraha (truth force) can develop a society with less violence and without violence.

In a Gandhian social order the individual person holds the key to social development and progress. Gandhi's ideal was a Rama Raj, a Utopia, a stateless democracy where there was no use of force in any form whereas society acquired an equilibrium by individual perfection. Whereas he advocated individual reformation, he was not for unrestricted individual freedom. In an ideal non-violent state, i.e., a Sarvodaya state, "the individual person would be a help not a hindrance to his neighbours. Society would consist of well-planned villages where life would be regulated through cooperation, bread-labour and mutual love". In his non-violent state, "life will be an oceanic circle whose centre will be the individual always ready to perish for the village, the latter ready to perish for the circle of villages till at last the whole becomes one life composed of individuals never aggressive in their arrogance but ever humble, sharing the majesty of the oceanic circle of which they are integral units. The outermost circumference will not wield power to crush the inner circle but will give strength to all within to derive its own strength from the centre". The individual will voluntarily transform himself/herself into a Satyagrahi, one who decides through vows to follow the path of truth and non-violence. The power generated by Satyagraha will produce a democratic polity, a trusteeship oriented economy, an egalitarian social system and an altruistically oriented personality system, all essential components of a non-violent society. In such a non-violent society individuals as Satyagrahis, i.e., those who follow the path of truth generate non-violent power which can overcome the power based on exploitation, injustice and violence. But Gandhi was practical enough to realise that such an ideal society was impossible to attain. He would be satisfied if we accept such a non-violent society as our ideal and make efforts to approximate it, which would constitute progress according to him.

However, as Acharya Tulsi says, "Like darkness and light, both violence and non-violence are eternal entities. The more powerful the violence becomes, the more strenuous efforts would be needed for propagating non-violence. The relevance of non-violence would ever increase with the onslaught of violence. That violence could not be eradicated from the world should not force non-violence to cease its activities. In fact, non-violence is not to be conceived in any manner less powerful than violence. The only requirement is to awaken this supine force."[11]

Towards a Non-violent Social Order

An effective solution to the problems of escalating violence lies in promoting non-violent social orders. Inculcation of positive human values, including non-violence, is only possible in a democratic polity through an enlightened education system. Under dictatorship, education is used as an instrument of suppression and 'brainwashing' not for enlightenment or positive development of character. In a democracy, we have to make our education system value-oriented and more effective in order to develop persons with strong positive character traits. For a sound value education we need committed teachers, enlightened parents and motivated students and, above all, a well-thoughtout education policy and its effective implementation. Such a system of education within an appropriate socio-political framework can surely bring into existence a large number of responsible, socially oriented, civic conscious, compassionate, citizens. It is through education that we can bring about personality development and individual transformation in a direction that foster the desired changes needed for a non-violent social order. The types of society we have at present are reflections of the types of relationships between individuals. The interrelationships and interactions of the individuals depend upon the personalities of the individuals, that is, the systems of values, beliefs and attitudes they adhere to. The individual, right from the time of its birth, internalises the values, beliefs and attitudes of others by the process of socialisation. Internalisation of the culture of the society or what we call socialisation of the child takes place in the family, school and peer-group situations. Socialisation does not stop with the children; it is a continuous process. Adult socialisation takes place through the multiplicity of interactions in which the adult is engaged. Children and adults at any age can acquire new values and discard old ones (de-learning and re-learning). Education is a continuous process from birth to death and, therefore, values can be imbibed at any stage of life.

Values constitute the core of a personality. As individuals imbibe new values, their attitudes and actions change. Inculcation of different values can bring about a radical transformation of the entire personality structure. This justifies a well-thoughtout value education programme,

It is universally recognised that the root cause of violence is the ego-centric behaviour of the individual or groups. Insecurity and over-concerns of the ego can create fear psychosis which results in violent behaviour, A 'perfect individual' can have no fear. It is the individual's desires, early childhood experiences, group identification and attachment to personal belongings that can create different kinds of fear. It is fear of death, of losing one's name and wealth and the desire to perpetuate and improve one's own status and the status of one's offsprings that create all kinds of fear, jealousies and prejudices which are responsible for the manifestations of different types of violence in human behaviour. Therefore, the fundamental prerequisite for reconstruction of human society on the foundations of peace is reduction in ego-centricism and group centricism and simultaneous development of altruism. Pitirim Sorokin very correctly maintains that there shall be no peace in the true sense of the world or survival of human kind in a dignified manner without developing greater and greater elements of altruism in human society.

Sorokin continues, "No human group can survive without a minimum of altruistic conduct among its members ... without a minimum of altruism, all the sick, incapacitated, and aged members of a group would soon die. For a thoroughgoing egoist there is no reason to engage in such an unpleasant activity as the care of the aged and infirm. Only love, sympathy and compassion can motivate it. Hence, a society consisting of only thoroughly egoistic members could not survive ... Real altruism begins only when this minimum is transcended; when an individual freely sacrifices his rightful interests in favour of the well-being of another, refraining from harming him, even though his legal right entitles him to do so, and helping him in various ways though no law demands of him such action ... Genuine altruism is pure also in its motivation; altruistic actions are performed for their own sake, quite apart from any considerations of pleasure or utility. The sublimest form of altruism is formulated in the Sermon on the Mount: Altruism preached but not practiced is a sham, or hypocritical, pseudo-altruism. Real altruism must manifest itself not merely in speech, reactions and ideology but in overt actions."[12]

As mentioned earlier, human history since the dawn of civilisation does not offer any proof that violence can be eliminated by counter-violence – state violence by any control mechanisms or legislative measures. But it has been proved beyond doubt that by love and care even hardened criminals can be brought back to a peaceful existence. Therefore, undoubtedly, the only way to solve the problems of violence is to inculcate values of non-violence and develop altruistic personalities. The Gandhian values of non-violence, i.e., values of righteous conduct, truth, peace, love, dignity of labour, self-reliance, self-control, equality, Sarvodaya, sacrifice and Satyagraha, when properly inculcated, will develop altruism and altruistic personalities who will work for the creation of greater social harmony and well-being nationally and globally. With substantial increase in attitudes of love, compassion, kindness and 'sympathetic joy' expressed through interactions and interrelationships with individuals there is bound to be a qualitative improvement in social reality. A truly non-violent person radiates peace and peace values to others. His/her very presence in a social group will be a source of positive inspiration for others. This is what Gandhi proved by his life and missionary actions. Of Gandhi's message and mission, what Professor George Catlin says is significant and worthy of our attention: "It was the mission of the Mahatma to be our educator in non-violence and to call the world's attention in this age when the wars of the international anarchy become ever more hateful and destructive of the very body of civilisation, of the need for an education in the beauties of ahimsa. He left to others to elaborate as statesman, schemes for world government. His task was fulfilled if he went to the root of the matter and pointed out the need for a new mental medicine, a new psychiatry, a new 'cure of souls'. What he had to preach was very old, for he brought men back beyond Tolstoy to the Sermon of the Mount, and the Buddha and, as he held, the Gita. He was intoxicated by the essential spirit of all true religions. But what he had to preach was also very new, for it is what the most modem educational psychologists have tested out in the training of small children, and what some of us say must be applied to political relations as well. What, then, is his message?' The old message that those who are called should observe the quadruple disciplines of chastity, poverty, spiritual courage and unflinching love of truth; that they should practise charity to all, even towards the animal creation as St. Francis also said, and non-violence in thought and deed; that they should more consider the intentions of their hearts than engage in metaphysical speculations about life after death or in probings of the inscrutable will of God; that they should prefer to suffer themselves, which give to men an imagination and a sympathy for human kind, than to cause sufferings; that they should be forbearing, meek, charitable, long suffering, for against these things there is no law."[13]

Serious and sustained threats to the survival of the environment and the well-being of humankind pose the greatest challenges to the 21st century. Our increasing reliance on personal and structural violence is the crucial cause of these destructive threats. Mahatma Gandhi's values, ideas and action strategies do offer an adequate response to these challenges. Gandhi was a crusader for truth and non-violence, non-violent values and actions. He said, "My mission is to convert every Indian every Englishman and finally, the world for regulating mutual relations". Gandhi's non-violence is a positive transcendental concept embodying the components of compassion, altruism and love. There is perhaps no other hope for this strife-torn world, not only in the 21st century but for all centuries to come, but to accept the Gandhian paradigm for establishing a qualitatively better, sustainable social order nationally and globally. "For Gandhi, a living faith in God, defined as truth, love and non-violence – encompassing all religions – is the unconquerable source of non-violent power. The spirit and reality of non-violence is the basic law of human life; violence is a violation."[14]

It is imperative and urgent that we increasingly make use of Gandhian ideas and action strategies for a 'global non-violent awakening' and consequent qualitative social transformation and dignified human survival. For this we should develop a new world view, a Weltanschauung, based on Gandhian ideas of life and "a universe woven into human hopes and visions for a better future", a better world. Such a Weltanschauung will embody the Gandhian paradigm of 'compassionate constructiveness' and encompass the rise of all (Sarvodaya), the rich and the poor, the oppressors and the oppressed. It will avoid "violence which divides humankind for the well being of some, and promotes non-violence which will unite us for the well being of all."[15]

The very survival of planet earth is contingent upon this new Weltanschauung. Let us enter the dawn of the 21 century realising the need of this new Weltanschauung and resolving to do what we can to improve the quality of human life.

Conclusions

To conclude, in the word of Swami Ranganathandaji of the Ramakrishna Mission:

> "Gandhiji stands as an archetypal man ... Gandhiji is the example of a leader who is not guided by the passing moods and passions of the populace, but who turns and guides these in the direction of the vision of human excellence that he has experienced for himself. His stress on truth and non-violence is the only beacon light in a world enveloped in the darkness of selfishness and exploitation, hatred and violence. He alone could look calmly and compassionately into the blood-shot eyes of contemporary man. Modern world conditions engendered by science and technology call for the transformation of energies of hatred and violence, competition and strife, into the moral forces of co-operation and service, love and peace. The moral education of modern man, in step with his intellectual attainments and technical achievements, is the most urgent task facing humanity today ... . The stress on love and service may sound unrealistic in the present national context of suspicion and hatred ... . But in human relations, hatred and destruction can never be a long-term measure. After short spells, it has to be transformed into, and yield place to, love and construction. By holding high this banner of love and service through thick and thin in the midst of his socio-political programmes and activities, and the banner of truth and non-violence in his personal life, Gandhiji has left an imperishable legacy which, as years pass, humanity in India and elsewhere will recognise as the only values capable of expressing the dignity and worth of man, as the only hope of civilisation and progress, and as the only guarantee of the march of human everywhere to all round growth and fulfilment."[16]

Notes

1. D.G. Tendulkar (1953) *Mahatma*, Vol. V1, Bombay: Vithalbhai K. Jhaveri and D.G. Tendulkar, pp. 157–58.
2. Justice Philip Edward Archer (1994) "Relevance of Gandhian Thought", in *Indian Horizon*, B.R. Nanda (ed.), New Delhi: Indian Council for Cultural Relations, Vol. 43, No. 4, p. 269.
3. King Coretta Scott (1994) "Legacy of Nonviolence", in *Indian Horizon*, B.R. Nanda (ed.), Vol. 43, No. 4, New Delhi: Indian Council for Cultural Relations, pp. 259–60.
4. Joan V. Bondurant (1959) *Conquest of Violence: The Gandhian Philosophy of Conflict*, Bombay, Calcutta, Madras, Karachi: Oxford University Press, pp. 23–26.
5. Severynt Bruyn and Paula Rayman (1979) *Nonviolent Action and Social Change*, New York: Irvington Publisher, Inc., p. 3.
6. Joan V. Bondurant, op. cit.
7. John Galtung (1968) "Violence Peace and Peace Research", *Journal of Peace Research*, Vol. 5, No. 3, Oslo, Norway, pp. 5–6.
8. T.K.N. Unnithan and Yogendra Singh (1969) *Sociology of Non-violence and Peace*, New Delhi: India International Centre.
9. T.K.N. Unnithan and Yogendra Singh (1969) *Mahatma Gandhi's Nonviolence and 21st Century*, Annamalai Nagar: Publication of Annamalai University, pp. 10–12.
10. Raghavan Iyer (1973) *Political and Moral Thoughts of Mahatma Gandhi*, New York: Oxford University Press.
11. Acharya Shri Tulsi (1968) *Speech on Nonviolence*, Anuvrat Vishva Bharti, Rahsamad-313326, Rajasthan (Mimeograph).
12. Pritim Sorokin (1961) *The Reconstruction of Humanity*, Bombay: Bhartiya Vidya Bhawan, pp. 61–63.
13. George Catlin (1939) "The World Mission of the Mahatma", S. Radhakrishnan (ed.), *Mahatma Gandhi: Essays and Reflection on His Life and Work*, Bombay: Jaico Publishing House, pp. 281–85.
14. Glenn D. Paige (2002) *Non-Killing Global Political Science*, Centre for Global Nonviolence, Honolulu: University of Hawaii, USA, p. 82.
15. Ibid.
16. Swami Ranganathananda, *Eternal Values for a Changing Society*, Vol. IV, Bombay: Bhartiya Vidya Bhawan, pp. 281–82. (This article was first published in *Anasakti*, Vol. I, No. 2, New Delhi: ICGSR, 2003).

6

Understanding Gandhi's Ahimsa

BALWANT BHANEJA

Was Gandhi a personification of Indian traditions to whom non-violence came natural and was inevitable? On this, one must rely on Gandhi's own candid evaluations of himself. His autobiography* provides one such authentic source. Mohandas Gandhi, popularly called as Mahatma Gandhi, believed that there was no other God than truth, and that the only means for realisation of truth was ahimsa.

Truth to Gandhi was synonymous with God. What he strove to achieve through ahimsa was ultimately to seek moksha (spiritual liberation). His autobiography entitled, *The Story of My Experiments with Truth*, is about his persistent search about whether such quest steeped in dharma, or right action, is feasible. In Hindu, Buddhist and Jain scriptures, Ahimsa refers to non-injury in thoughts, words and deed. In 1927, when the autobiography was published, Gandhi was 58 years old. There were still many non-violent struggles to be fought, e.g., Hindu-Muslim unity, abolition of caste-based untouchability, advocacy of home-spun swadeshi clothing, and above all, gaining India's independence from the British rule.

---

* *The Story of My Experiments with Truth*. London: Penguin Books, p. 464. First published in Gujarati and English by the Navjivan Publishing House in 1927 and 1929 respectively (2 vols.; reissued as 1 vol. in 1983).

His autobiography provides insights into shaping of his core beliefs on which his non-violent instrument of political action, satyagraha, the truth force, was later founded.

On his concept of ahimsa, Gandhi writes:

> Ahimsa is a comprehensive principle. We are helpless mortals caught in the flagration of himsa. The saying that life lives on life has a deep meaning in it. Man cannot for a moment live without consciously or unconsciously committing outward himsa. The very fact of his living-eating, drinking and moving about – necessarily involves some himsa, destruction of life, be it ever so minute. A votary of ahimsa therefore remains true to his faith if the spring of all his actions is compassion, if he shuns to the best of his ability the destruction of the tiniest creature, tries to save it, and thus incessantly strives to be free from the deadly coil of himsa. Such an individual will then constantly grow in self-restraint and love for others. (p. 319)

Aparigraha and Samabhava

To understand ahimsa, Gandhi relies on the teachings of the Hindu epic, the Bhagavad Gita, his "infallible guide of conduct", especially its two principles of aparigraha (non-possession) and samabhava (equability). Gandhi writes:

> Words like aparigraha (non-possession) and sambhava (equability) gripped me. How to cultivate and preserve that equability was the question. How was one to treat alike insulting, insolent and corrupt officials, co-workers of yesterday raising meaningless opposition, and men who have always been good to one? How was the one to divest oneself of all possessions? Was not the body itself possession enough? Were not wife and children possessions? Was I to destroy all the cupboards of books I had … . (pp. 244–46)

Raising such honest doubts, he asks: "Was I to give up all I had and follow Him?" Straight came the answer: "I could not follow Him unless I gave up all I had." Drawing upon his familiarity as a barrister with the maxims of equity in English jurisprudence, Gandhi's interpretation of aparigraha is that of a 'trustee' in the service of the poor and the disadvantaged:

> I understood the Gita teaching of non-possession to mean that those who desired salvation should act like the trustee who, though having control over great possessions, regards not an iota of them as his own. It became clear to me as daylight that

> non-possession and equability presupposed a change of heart, a change of attitude. (p. 245)

It is this 'change of heart' aspect of ahimsa which was central to Gandhi. How to bring in such a change within oneself?

Renouncing his material possessions, Gandhi takes a number of steps. To begin with, he lets his life insurance policy lapse. With regards to his wife and children, he is convinced that God who created them, would also take care of them. Next, he sent his life's savings to his elder brother who had brought him up as a son, informing that henceforth he should not expect anything from him, as all his future savings would be utilised for the benefit of the larger community, who he now regarded as his family. He finds it a terrible responsibility to be a parent, and subjects love for his children also to the test of these two principles.

> It is never children's fault. 'Who can say thus far, no further, to the tide of his own nature?' Who can raise the impressions with which he is born? It is idle to expect one's children and wards necessarily to follow the same course of evolution as oneself. (p. 246)

Purity of Heart

To Gandhi, purity of heart, a life-long goal, is of utmost importance. It can be achieved through subduing senses and carrying out selfless service. "To attain perfect purity, one has to become absolutely passion-free in thought, speech and deed; to rise above the opposing currents of love and hatred, attachment and repulsion" (p. 453). Without self-purification, he feels that observance of ahimsa will be an empty dream. Purification of mind can lead to the purification of one's surroundings, and eventually extend its impact to broader society. At the same time, Gandhi is realistic to concede that the path of self-purification is not an easy one. He admits: "I know that I have not in me as yet that triple purity, in spite of constant ceaseless striving for it. That is why the world's praise fails to move me, indeed it very often stings me. To conquer the subtle passions seems to me to be harder far than the physical conquest of the world by the force of arms" (p. 453).

In practising ahimsa, Gandhi provides another helpful suggestion, distinguish between the actor and his actions. Hate the sin and not the sinner. Gandhi finds that one's inability to make such distinction "leads to the poison of hatred spread in the world" (p. 254). He knows it is a precept easy to understand, but difficult to practice. In Gandhi's own words,

> Man and his deed are two distinct things. Whereas a good deed should call forth approbation and a wicked deed disapprobation, the doer of the deed, whether good or wicked, always deserves respect or pity as the case may be. (p. 254)

The last part of his statement appealing for respect and empathy for the doer of the deed, whether good, bad, or ugly underlines his compassion which is in many ways similar to the antidote of 'loving kindness' as applied for subduing personal hatred in Buddhism. He takes on the challenge of equability in reaching out to his opponents in India and South Africa. Gandhi elaborates:

> The ahimsa is the basis of the search for truth. I am realising every day that the search is in vain unless it is founded on ahimsa as the basis. It is quite proper to resist and attack a system, but to resist and attack its author tantamount to resisting and attacking one self. For we are all tarred with the same brush, and are children of the Creator, and as such the divine powers within us are infinite. To slight a single human being is to slight those divine powers, and thus to harm not only that being but with him the whole world. (p. 254)

The Truth Principle

Gandhi throughout his life remained a seeker of truth. Since his childhood, he had a strong conviction that morality is the basis of things, and that truth is the substance of all morality. For him, truth is the sovereign principle for executing morality. His definition of truth keeps on expanding, bringing in numerous other principles within its fold.

> This truth is not only truthfulness in word, but truthfulness in thought also, and not only relative truth in our conception, but the Absolute Truth, the Eternal Principle, that is God. There are innumerable definitions of God, because His manifestations are innumerable. They overwhelm me with wonder and awe and for a moment stun me. But I worship God as Truth only I have not found Him, but I am seeking after Him ... But as long as I have not realised this Absolute Truth, so long must I hold by the relative truth as I have conceived it. That relative truth must, meanwhile, be my beacon, my shield and buckler. (p. 15)

Gandhi's truth is the search for Universal Absolute. Such definition of God has in it a belief about spiritual unity that Divine permeates everything in this universe. God's names and forms may vary, but same divinity is in all. The oneness towards all creeds in all lands comes natural to Gandhi. His spiritual quest for the Universal Absolute in this sense comes close to the Vedantic notion of Brahman which points that everything in the universe originates from Brahman (Absolute), exists in Brahman and unfolds through it, and ultimately dissolves in Brahman.

Books and Mentors

In addition to the Bhagavad Gita, Gandhi mentions a long list of books and mentors in his autobiography, starting with Leo Tolstoy by his book, 'The Kingdom of God is Within You'; and John Ruskin by his 'Unto This Last', and Edwin Arnold's 'Light of Asia'. There are common strands running through these works of an alternative vision of a society, grounded in compassion and non-killing, challenging the prevalent institutions in their respective societies of slavery, serfdom, colonisation and industrialism. Gandhi's two ashrams in South Africa – Phoenix (1904) and Tolstoy Farm (1910) – were inspired from these works. Tolstoy's 'Kingdom of God' makes an abiding impression on him. He is also influenced by Tolstoy's description of the Sermon on the Mount. Mathew's gospel is all about a spiritual quest, a divine search, in which the seeker dispossesses himself of all of his worldly possessions in order to gain that one pearl of great value – God. The notion of trusteeship is seeded into Gandhi's mind from Ruskin. The latter's strong revulsion against human exploitation caused by industrialism, brings about in him, an "instantaneous and practical transformation" (p. 274).

Gandhi is so impressed with Ruskin's book that he translates it later into his mother tongue Gujarati, entitling it 'Sarvodaya' (the welfare for all). Sarvodaya later formed the basis of Gandhi's vision of his alternative non-killing society, and served as a catalyst for his decision to enter into active politics. Gandhi is captivated by Ruskin's ethics of dignity of labour and the necessity of bread labour. He summarises the teachings of 'Unto This Last' as follows:

1. That the good of the individual is contained in the good of all.
2. That a lawyer's work has the same value as the barber's; in as much as all the same right of earning their livelihood from their work.
3. That a life of labour, i.e., the life of the tiller of soil and handicraftsman, is the life worth living (pp. 274–75).

Gandhi felt that first of these conclusions he knew. The second he had dimly realised. The third had never occurred to him. The book made it clear to him that the second and the third were contained in the first – that the good of the individual is contained in the good of all.

Gandhi had many mentors. On spirituality, he thought highly of Raichand Jain whose advice on Bhagavad Gita and Vaishnavism he frequently sought. On secular matters, he had high regard for many nationalist leaders like Lokmanya Gangadhar Tilak, Sir Firoz Shah Mehta, Dadabhai Naraoji and Gopal Krishan Gokhale.

Ahimsa and Political Action

Gratitude and non-hatred for his opponents are two hallmarks of Gandhi's ahimsa. He is unable to hate anyone, even his ultimate adversary – the British Empire. He is a strong champion of its judiciary and other institutions. To show his goodwill to the colonialists, he goes as far as to involve himself in the recruitment campaigns for the British during the First World War. This brings him criticism from others. He persists with this as he had done the same in South Africa during the Boer War thereby gaining respect of ruling leadership for the social and political reforms for Indian working class émigrés. It is in the ambulance corps he finds a niche where he and his fellow workers could volunteer in the war effort.

The desire for service arises in Gandhi from a deep sense of public duty and a belief that one must be loyal to the state one lives in. Eventually, this notion of loyalty and self-discipline becomes a focal point of training volunteers for his civil disobedience movement. To be considered eligible for his call of civil disobedience, his peace volunteers must render "a willing and respectful obedience" to the state laws. Gandhi clarifies that this is not just an ordinary compliance to a law, but "the willing and spontaneous obedience" required of a true Satyagrahi.

For Satyagraha action Gandhi carefully chooses his causes, initiated often in places by him where the flagrant abuse and exploitation is obvious and known. In addition to truthful moral ground for protest, like a diligent lawyer he goes a step further in examining and analysing the situation from both the sides. And, when convinced that morally the political action is justifiable, he approaches his adversary on the imminent need for change. Only failing those approaches, he takes the recourse of Satyagraha.

Satyagraha: The Truth Force

Insisting a high moral character, Gandhi demands of his co-workers that they be civil, non-conspiring, and under no circumstance counter violence with violence. He believes if the cause being fought is just and truthful, the method of Satyagraha would bring in a change of heart in his opponents. In this, his open and non-secretive deliberations are always aimed at engaging his adversary in a dialogue.

Forgiveness is an essential component of Gandhi's truth force. Without much philosophising, Gandhi writes about a simple act of sublime forgiveness he learnt from his father. As a lad of fifteen, his innocent confession, written as a letter apologising for his pilfering money from his ailing father's wallet, brings tears to the father's eyes. Both father and son are unable to resist crying at the young Gandhi's act of repentance. Gandhi writes: "A clean confession combined with a promise never to commit the sin again, when offered before one who has the right to receive it, is the purest type of repentance. When such Ahimsa becomes self-embracing, it transforms everything it touches. There is no limit to its power" (p. 41). This father-son episode to him is more than just an expression of a father's love; for him it is pure ahimsa.

The gap between ideal and practice of ahimsa at political level came as shock to him when during the civil disobedience movement in the Kheda district in Gujarat, he noticed the lacking discipline among his volunteers. Before any massive deployment of non-violent civil disobedience workers in a political action, he feels that it would be imperative "to create a band of well tried, pure hearted volunteers who thoroughly understood the strict conditions of Satyagraha" (p. 423).

He is disappointed at his co-workers' shallow understanding of Satyagraha, and accepts that a long-term serious effort will be necessary to develop a large trained cadre of civil disobedience workers, or Shanti Sainiks, the members of his non-violent peace brigade. A Satyagrahi devoid of hatred for his opponent can compel the later in the spirit of love and personal suffering, gaining thereby a higher moral ground over the opponent psychologically. A scrupulous and conscientious observance of this rule is essential for those wanting to join the ranks of Satyagrahis.

Whether in private or in public, Gandhi holds that one should consider always the faults of others, however big, to be insignificant and negligible, while one's own, however insignificant and small, to be big and feel repentant for them. It is only when one sees one's own mistakes in this light, there are possibilities of one's genuine transformation. Once Gandhi realises that he has made a mistake, he does not rest till he has confessed to it, even though such confession may bring upon him a lot of ridicule and embarrassment. He has a full section in his autobiography on the subject of failure in Kheda campaign under the title "A Himalayan Miscalculation" (pp. 423–24).

Ahimsa and Gandhi

One of the original contributions of Gandhi is to bring together the non-violence tenets in Buddhism and Jainism with truth, the Advaitic non-dualist notion of oneness of reality as in the Upanishads. For Gandhi, God and truth are interchangeable terms. God is truth, and truth is God too. Truth is not something that can be realised by mere meditation and reading books; for Gandhi it is experiential, requiring a heart-felt practice of ahimsa in thought, words and deeds. Ultimately, end and means to him must merge into one.

While doing this, Gandhi places himself without fear amidst the weak and the poor and stands with them like one of their own as their companion in suffering. Spirit of sacrifice to him is supreme as it originates from pure heart and conscience. Hence, work done in that spirit Gandhi finds in accordance with his Atma Dharma, a call of conscience, as described in the Bhagavad Gita. It comes very close to Gandhi's truth force. Key ingredients of Gandhi's ahimsa can be summarised as: a belief in unity of life and brotherhood of mankind; non-injury in thought, word and deed; sense of sacrifice based on the values of equability and detachment; trusteeship in public service; love of one's opponent; compassion and forgiveness; voluntary respect for state laws; and penchant for openness and dialogue.

For Gandhi, ahimsa is a work in progress. It is a fundamental tool for one's continual search of truth that can bring change at individual and societal levels. Gandhi is able to use it effectively for societal reforms in South Africa and India, and later as an instrument for political change, during the independence movement in colonial India. He uses it with great conviction and thought against a democratic institutional framework prided by the British. He has a strong belief that there are unending non-killing solutions to resolve problems whether these be social or political. Beauty of Gandhi is that he practices what he preaches.

A few months before his assassination in 1947, Gandhi remarked that his life has been his message. In his autobiography, he reveals himself with all his warts in hope that his "experiments with truth" will encourage others in actualisation of their self. He lives by his example practising non-attachment and equability with compassion and humility, and encourages others to do so. He shows that the precept of ahimsa is not only for the extraordinary, but for everyone.

Ahimsa to Gandhi is not a refuge for cowardice. He has no place for cowards in his truth force. To him, ahimsa is in fact the only way to merge into the Absolute, without fear uttering God's name unto one's last breath. It's a perfect mokhsa that every Hindu aspires towards as part of his faith, but only a few are able to accomplish that. Gandhi's last words on being hit by the three bullets of his assassin were: "Hey Ram". O God! It tantamount to forgiveness of his killer.

Gandhi's life shows that practising non-violence requires an earnest desire to adhere to such other human values as truth, righteousness, justice, love and peace. His life confirms that faith-based non-violent approach can bring in genuine personal and political transformation and strengthen one's confidence in self to reach out to others as equals without proselytising and coercion. These Gandhian characteristics have been now widely tested over a century, and continue to inspire others interested in a non-violent social and political action across the globe.

Gandhi's life also raises the question of how much value the contributions of profoundly inspired persons should, either secular or spiritual, be factored into the training and development of ahimsa practitioners? Gandhi's life in particular points in that direction, that is, in order to employ non-violent methods such a person must have the highest moral order so as to embody non-violence within. He has to be morally credible to such a degree that his presence itself should become conducive to transform a climate of violence into that where his presence may generate respect and tolerance among disputing parties, which may subsequently lead to reconciliation and amity.

Though Gandhi saw himself as a devout Hindu, his concept of Hinduism varied from the orthodoxy of the prevalent times. He was not afraid to admit or challenge its shortcomings, giving these orthodoxies a vital reinterpretation. He looked within his faith the values that connected with Hindus, and peoples of other faiths. He followed the religious precepts and interpretations that united cultures and people instead of dividing them.

In an attempt to highlight Gandhi's unique contribution in discovering "non-violent political action", Gandhi's persistent spiritual quest has been played down by his greatest Western admirers, treating spirituality and character development as secondary and politically inconsequential.[1] The Bhagavad Gita that Gandhi revered is not just a story of physical warfare and justification of fighting, but it is about spiritual struggle between those engaged in dharma (right action) and adharma (not right action). It is a dialogue of learning between a seeker of the highest moral character (Arjuna) and the provider of supreme divine knowledge (Lord Krishna). The Gita is not about war, but how to achieve the peace within when the battles are waging both in and out. It is therefore also called, "The Song of Divine Love". However, to say that these elements from scriptures were conducive to Gandhi's approach, and that Gandhi drew upon these largely to win Indian masses will be an oversimplification.[2] Similarly, to describe Gandhi's Satyagraha concept a rather philosophical term close to "essence of being" will be to miss its creative origins that drove Gandhi in his search for truth as defined in ancient Vedas and the Bhagavad Gita.[3]

His constant use of religious terminology and theological language in explanation or justification of a social or political act was to enhance his own understanding of ancient scriptures as well as to share his unique socially relevant insight with the masses.

Notes

1. Political scientist Gene Sharp's classic works, *The Politics of Nonviolent Action* and *Gandhi as a Political Strategist* based on the analysis of Gandhi's life and teachings not only refute the popular assumption that power is derived from violence and can be controlled by greater violence, but these also describe the methods and dynamics of non-violent action.
2. Gene Sharp (1979) *Gandhi as a Political Strategist*, Boston: Porter Sargent, p. 7.

3. Gene Sharp, ibid., p. 14. On unique contribution of Gandhi, Sharp points out that while religious groups as the early Quakers, had practised non-violent action as a reaction to persecution, the link between the moral qualities of non-violence and the technique of action in social and political struggles was rarely made, except by individuals such as Tolstoy, and even then remained on the level of ideas. It remained of Gandhi to make the most significant political experiments to that time in the use of non-cooperation, disobedience and defiance to control rulers, alter policies, and undermine political systems. With Gandhi's experiments with the technique, its character was broadened.

7

Gandhian Vision of World Order

R.S. YADAV

The present century witnessed a number of unprecedented events in the form of rise and fall of communist revolutions, growth of means of communication, development of international organisations, and emergence of Afro-Asian states on the global scene. Simultaneously, there have also been "hot wars" and "cold wars" between nations and unparalleled growth and development of weapons of mass destruction. One perennial thrust, however, throughout the century has been the quest for global peace. At the same time, manifold efforts by nation-states through the mechanisms of balance of power armaments (deterrence), disarmament (test ban treaty and NPT), international organisations (League of Nations and the United Nations) and Marxist and structuralist models have also been made to achieve the goal of peace in the world.[1] But these efforts did not yield substantial results and hence some scholars designed and recommended in the early 1960s numerous blueprints for a "preferred world order" for the future.[2] Their recommendations, published in the form of numerous books and research articles, were based on five agreed core values (war prevention, peace, poverty eradication, ecological balance, and removal of alienation), which they consider to be of fundamental importance for the establishment of a peaceful world order in future.[3] But their proposals also met similar fate as that of the earlier policies followed by nation-states. Thus, the quest for peace has not been fulfilled despite persistent efforts by various individuals, nations, and international bodies, which have been working in this direction throughout the century. Consequently there is need to adopt a design which would be based on entirely different assumptions and methodology and which may provide an alternative to these existing approaches. The Gandhian paradigm to a great extent could be considered in this context. Raja Rao made a prophecy several years back that "he expected to see a rebirth of satyagraha by the end of this century, because it is the only form of popular resistance to oppression that has nay chance of success against the military and technological might of the modern state."[4] As we have recently seen in the non-violent satyagraha launched by Gandhian activist in his crusade against corruption, this prophecy now seems to be coming true. In the present-day competitive world, which is loaded with highly destructive weapons, only a Gandhian model provides an alternative as all other methods of persuasion, cajoling, or threats have failed to bring about a long-lasting peace to the world. Consequently, we must now understand that "peace can be brought about only by peaceful methods". Thus, the present paper is a modest attempt to analyse the Gandhian world order model in this context.

The thrust of this paper is three-fold: (i) to highlight the conceptual parameters of the Gandhian vision about the world order; (ii) to make an effort to examine as to how this model could be put into operational use; and finally, (iii) on the basis of the above-mentioned analyses, to make an evaluation of the relevance of this model in the contemporary, polarised post-Cold War world.

II

Before a conceptual analysis of a Gandhian world order is made, it must be made explicit at the outset that Gandhi never presented at one place or at one time a systematic model for the future world. Rather it was during his involvement in South Africa, during his struggle for Indian freedom, and in his concerns for the finding means to solve problems of war and peace, that one finds certain elements on the basis of which his model of a preferred world could be developed. From this, however, it should not be concluded that his interest in international affairs was peripheral.[5] In fact, he followed the developments on the international scene quite closely. His understanding and knowledge of international events was as sound as about national affairs.[6]

While visualising a future world order, Gandhi neither analysed it in terms of an isolated phenomenon such as at the individual, family, village, society, state, national and international levels, nor did he hold the view that these could be understood by studying the different level like "man, the state, and the international system" as some scholars have done.[7] He was of the opinion that the problems of war and peace are not isolated issues but interrelated concepts and hence they are not amenable to any piecemeal solutions. For a precise understanding of these issues, one has to look at the individual and his total environment, because only an integrated picture could reveal the real notion of the world. Consequently, a Gandhian world order could be discussed by analysing two core factors: (i) individual; and (ii) his socio-economic milieu.

Unlike the prevalent approaches, states or international organisations are not the basis of the Gandhian vision. The central part of this thesis is that the individual is basically good by nature. Due to the goodness of his character, he is responsive to the love and affection of his fellow-beings. This led him to another assumption, namely, that love is the law of life and hence the fundamental virtue among all human beings is love.[8] But Gandhi did not stop here. He knew that whatsoever be the inner goodness in man, it will not automatically be enough as a basis for the achievement of the goal of world peace. According to him, man is activated in the pursuit of truth, because it is only through truthful means that the goal of peace can be achieved. In this context, he gave the theory of social change by which the individual could transform himself for the preferred world order. This transformation, according to Gandhi, would be brought about through self-discipline and by using the technique of non-violence for the resolution of conflicts. For this, man needs to develop a sense of dedication, commitment and perseverance. Even, the habit of self-sacrifice and suffering is to be acquired for the cause of truth. Subsequently, a number of traits for the service of others – such as knowledge, faith, virtue, brotherly kindness, charity, humility, patience, temperance, godliness and diligence – need to be aroused by self-efforts. For de-escalation of conflict, voluntary suffering provides the basic appeal to change the heart of the adversary.

Thus, Gandhi believed in the basic transformation of man for the preservation of world peace. His man was bound by the force of truth rather than by any external conditions imposed on him either by the state or by the environment. This kind of peace would apply equally to his interpersonal relations, as well as in the field of international affairs. As the transformation of the self is based on self-discipline and voluntary self-sacrifice, this ideology is not for the weak, non-committed, idle, or fearful. Rather it is for those who have commitment to the values of truth and non-violence and want to pursue these values as goals without any fear or pressure.

The second conceptual level of a Gandhian world order is the socio-economic milieu of the individuals in the form of state, society and the international system. Gandhi believed that there is need to transform the socio-economic structure as well. Politically, Gandhi considered the state as a soulless entity which perpetuates violence. Through his experiences, he visualised the existence of the coercive and tyrannical power of the state. Consequently, he was in favour of a state which serves the cause of humankind and in this context society could play a very vital role. The latter could always hold the state responsible for the welfare of the individuals. Hence, Gandhi pleaded for decentralisation of powers of the state up to the grassroots level so that violence is replaced with a responsible welfare system which in turn will ultimately establish a society based on cooperation, mutual adjustment and self-sacrifice. Later, he thought, similar qualities will be extended to the global community of nations. Gandhi felt that centralised, industrial, unresponsive, coercive and impersonalised states are not conducive to the development of a cooperative and amicable world order. Hence, the need of the hour is to transform these states accordingly.

Like the political aspect, transformation of economic structures is equally essential. The Gandhian economic order was also based on decentralisation of resources and capital through small-scale industries and self-sufficiency of village economy. He was against the industrialisation and use of big machines. Simultaneously, he advanced the concept of trusteeship where individuals manage and hold properties as trustees of the community and not for their own benefit. Besides, Gandhi wanted that individuals should also limit their demands and wants. This voluntary cut in one's wants will promote real happiness on the one hand and will enhance his/her capacity for the service of humanity, on the other.

Thus, Gandhi was in favour of transformation of socio-economic structures in a manner which would lead, in the long run, to the promotion of equality, cooperation, independence and capacity for service among the individuals. Simultaneously, forces generating tensions and violence will be done away with. These developments will automatically strengthen the forces and scope for global peace and security among the states. This process, along with the transformed individuals, will facilitate the growth of a world order based on justice, equality and peace, and devoid of conflict and violence.

All this, in Gandhi's view, will facilitate the growth of a world federation in which individuals, states and the international system will work in harmony with each other. They will be like oceanic currents supplementing and complementing each other rather than creating obstacles for each other. The main attributes of a Gandhian world order could thus be summed up as follows:[9]

- This world federation envisaged by Gandhi would be formed by fully independent states and there would be no place for imperialism, exploitation, injustice and disparity among those nations.
- All the members of the international system would be given equal status in the international organisation. The smallest state should feel equal to the tallest one.
- The membership of this organisation would be on a voluntary basis and members would be ready to serve the cause of humanity at large.
- Non-violence should be the creed of such an organisation. Al the individuals and states joining it must have deep convictions about a peaceful world order.
- The Gandhian model does not consider a mere reform in the existing international bodies. Rather it demands a fundamental departure on the basis of its own value system, because Gandhi was critical of both the League of Nations and the United Nations system on various counts.
- Moral precepts of *dharma* will be the guiding force to settle disputes between states. Even amicable means like negotiations, mediation and arbitration may be used.
- To mitigate the challenge of a new world transformation, states should adhere to the means of satyagraha and not to any violent or coercive techniques.
- Though there is no place for large-scale and mighty force in this organisation, a small international police force could be kept to meet the need for the maintenance of law and order.
- This body should have faith in complete disarmament. Till such consensus emerges, even one state should take an

initiative for voluntary disarmament as this will be an eye-opener to other who will soon follow suit.

Gandhi also suggested that until such time this long-term objective is achieved, we should adopt short-term measures to deal with any contingency arising before the emergence of a new world order, or an armed attack by the aggressor, or the occupation of territories by external powers. In all the three situations, Gandhi recommended the use of self-sacrifice and non-cooperation through the use of non-violent means against the adversary without any ill-will against any one.

III

To implement the above conceptual paradigm, Gandhi also suggested some operational techniques to achieve the goal of a world order of his conception. These methods, like his model, are a departure from existing techniques and are unique and important in their own way. Gandhi wanted this goal to be achieved by the pursuit of satyagraha through the means of non-violence. This technique, Gandhi believed, could be used both by the individuals as well as by the communities. Similarly, it could be applied to achieve the goals at the domestic as well as at the international level.

A Gandhian approach is based on the goodness of man. Hence, it is believed that an aggressor is also a human being who is not without heart. So he could also be converted into a good human being by the examples of sacrifice. Besides, unlike Spinoza, Morgenthau, Niebuhr and others, Gandhi did not think that violence is innate to human nature and that man cannot be expected to renounce violence in his dealings with others.[10] That is why, Gandhi remarked: "Not to believe in the possibility of permanent peace is to disbelieve in the godliness of human nature."[11] Creed of sacrifice is important not only in the case of individuals but also in the case of nations. In the context of the latter, it must be ready to sacrifice everything, except honour. Though doubts have been raised as to whether dictators like Hitler or Mussolini could be transformed in this way or whether this method is relevant in the nuclear age where the machines and not men are involved in the warfare, Gandhi was fully convinced that this philosophy is tenable in both situations. In the first case, a non-violent satyagrahi should not wait for the pity on the part of anybody. Besides, this type of resistance will be unique for a dictator as he also possesses the same soul as possessed by a non-violent resister.[12] In the case of nuclear warfare, Stephen King-Hall believed that in an age when deterrent effects of the use of available weapons would be suicidal and destroy civilisation, violence has outlived its usefulness.[13] In this context, Gandhi believed that the sacrifice of the large humanity will change the perceptions of those who push the buttons of these weapons.[14] That is why, he was emphatic in his remark that "in this age of atom bomb, unadulterated non-violence is the only force that can confound all the tricks put together of violence."[15]

Gandhian satyagraha, however, seeks to liquidate antagonism, but not the antagonist. It is neither coercive nor redemptive. It is rather a middle course of ethical compulsion which can be substituted for war because it satisfies many qualities of war, such as mass appeal, aggressiveness, suffering and romance. But it is always pursued by way of love and not hatred towards anybody. Nor does it contain any sort of vengeance towards anybody. Rather, a satyagrahi is always open for "any honourable opportunity for peace."[16]

Gandhi also perceived that at the international level, non-violence should be supported by national freedom. He was opposed to any kind of imperialism and exploitation in the community of nations. Though Gandhi was an ardent supporter of nationalism, his vision was not narrow. It transcended the boundaries of nations and acquired an international status and recognised humanity at large as his family. Similarly, he felt that till the great powers of the world renounce their imperialistic aims, peace is an impossibility. It will be possible only it great nations stop believing in mutual competition and in adding to their worldly possessions which kill the soul. Consequently, a true international body is constituted when all the nations, big or small, comprising it are fully independent. The nature of that independence will correspond to the extent of non-violence assimilated by the nations concerned. Moreover, in a peaceful world society, "based on non-violence, the smallest nation will feel as tall as the tallest and the idea of superiority and inferiority will be wholly obliterated."[17]

Simultaneous to the policy of non-violence, there is need among the states to renounce war as an instrument of national policy and resort to disarmament voluntarily. If disarmament is resorted to by one nation, there will be no fear of destruction and it will be an eye-opener for others. This will lead to the emergence of a true international body where each nation could participate on equal terms without fear.[18] Gandhi conceived of an international body whose strength comes from the character of individuals composing it, rather than from armaments possessed by states. Thus, "a bold and unconditional acceptance of the non-violent method with all its glorious implications" will lead to the emergence of a peaceful and just world order.[19]

IV

After analysing the conceptual and operational aspects of the Gandhian model, it becomes essential to evaluate it in terms of its utility in the contemporary international situation. Some scholars have rightly pointed out some limitations of the Gandhian technique. First, it is pointed out that the pursuit of non-violence involves the use of coercion (may be physical or moral) against whom it is used.[20] As C.M. Case has remarked: "The non-violent coercion is, and ought to be, a two-edged sword ... it causes ... . Inconvenience and suffering to those who wield it, as well as to those against whom it is invoked."[21] Secondly, it requires courage of the highest order for sacrifice, even to the extent of accepting death. This is too rigorous a discipline for a common man to follow. Despite these limitations, one must note that Gandhian coercion is not with ill-will or hatred. It is, in fact, for the pursuit of truth. Similarly, the achievement of global peace is a very ardent task and the last hope to save the humanity. Hence, any sacrifice is meagre for the attainment of the ultimate goal of world peace.

Another suggestion has come in the form of "convergence of peace models" of the East and the West.[22] It is pointed out that it will transcend the limitations of both the models and will lead to the emergence of a real model for world peace. But it is very difficult to assimilate the two models based on contradictory assumption, such as centralised/decentralised, Hobbesian/anarchist, violent/non-violent, and state-oriented/ individual-oriented.[23] Besides, all existing models are based on the reformation of existing institutions, whereas Gandhi was in favour of reform in human beings. Thus, the latter will be more suited to durable and long-lasting peace.

It is also believed by some people that the Gandhian approach to world order could not be operationalised as a matter of state policy. It is observed that "peace is not and never can be the direct object of policy."[24] Though it is certain that a foreign policy serves different objectives of states, the long-term goal of all policies, however, is peace. In this respect, the Gandhian principles of unilateral disarmament and equity among nations do away with imperialism and exploitation among states and could be channelised to attain the long-term objective of global peace. Moreover, development of countries is always feasible only when peace prevails at the global level. In this context, at least for the developing nations, quest for peace is a paramount necessity. Hence, the Gandhian vision of peace could be conceived as a long-term goal for nations to attain a just and equalitarian world order.

Gandhian ideas could not be called "utopian" as various scholars call them. One will agree with the viewpoint that his utopianism is "resilient and challenging" because it deals with man-made inequities and injustices which could be done away with. Secondly, Gandhian ideas give an individual a responsibility to do something for peace rather than to pass this burden on to somebody else (as, for example, state or the international system.)[25]

Here it is pertinent to point out that the Gandhian vision is considered very difficult to be practicable both at the national and international levels. But if looked differently, one finds that through no other existing model can one compel the mighty powers to surrender to the demand for a just and equalitarian world order. Even in the past, whether it was the case of Indian independence or the goal of the end of apartheid in South Africa, it was only the moral precepts of Gandhi, and not any so-called realistic ideologies, which actually worked. At present, the international scenario is such where one cannot get any concession through the use of force from the major powers of the day. So, the Gandhian approach is the only available choice. Thus, despite numerous difficulties in pursuing the Gandhian values, the latter will have to be applied as a last resort to achieve peace.

Thus, the Gandhian world order model is more relevant in the present-day world where uncertainties loom large and every other alternative for the establishment of peace has failed. Hence, the Gandhian perspective needs a fair trial. This vision is more important also because it cures the root cause of conflict without aiming at a mere reform at a superfluous level. It is based on the fundamental principles of the reform of individuals which is so vital for a long-term peace. Gandhi's ideas may seem a little bit difficult to be implemented, but they still constitute the easiest alternative available to the present generation.

For a successful implementation of this model, there is a need to have the firm conviction about the desirability of peace. This is possible only through reading and practising Gandhism and communicating it to humanity at large. Though the process to reach the goal will be very slow, a non-violent world order based on justice, equality and freedom for all the nations could be built eventually.

Notes

1. For details see, Biraja Shankar Rath, "Gandhi and International Conflict Resolution", in Anima Bose (ed.), *Peace and Conflict Resolution in the World Community* (New Delhi: Vikas Publishing House, 1991), pp. 121–23.
2. In this direction numerous volumes were published under the World Order Models Project (WOMP) and by various scholars independently. Prominent works among them are: Rajni Kothari, *Footsteps into the Future* (New Delhi: Orient Longman, 1974); Ali A. Mazrui, *A World Federation of Cultures* (New York: Free Press, 1971); Richard Falk, *A Study of Future World* (New York: Free Press, 1971); *Exploration at the Edge of Time* (Philadelphia: Temple University Press, 1972); Johan Galtung, *The True Worlds: A Transnational Perspective* (New York: Free Press, 1972); Saul H. Mendlovitz (ed.), *On the Creation of a Just World Order* (New Delhi: Free Press, 1975); Jagdish Bhagwati (ed.), *Economics and World Order: From the 1970s to the 1990s* (New York: Macmillan Co., 1972); Ali A. Mazrui and Hasu Patel (eds.), *Africa and World Affairs* (New York: The Third Press, 1973); Grenville Clark and Louis B. Sohn, *World Peace Through World Law* (New York: Knopf, 1966); Harnam Singh (ed.), *Studies in World Order* (New Delhi: Kitab Mahal, 1974); and Hedley Bull, "Models of Future World Order", *India Quarterly*, 31 (1), January-March, 1975.
3. Saul Mendlovitz (ed.), *On the Creation of a Just World Order*, New York: Free Press, 1975, p. xii.
4. Cited in Harold A. Gould, "Rabin and the Rebirth of Satyagraha", *Times of India*, 10 November 1995.
5. For instance, see Homer A. Jack, *The Gandhi Reader* (Bloomington: Indiana University Press, 1956); and R. Payne, *The Life and Death of Mahatma Gandhi* (New York: E.P. Dutton, 1969).

6. Rashmi-Sudha Puri, "Gandhi and the Second World War", *Indian Journal of Political Science*, 38 (1), January-March 1977, p. 30.
7. Kenneth N. Waltz, *Man, the State, and War: A Theoretical Analysis* (New York: Columbia University Press, 1954).
8. For details regarding Gandhian application of law of love in international relations, see James Warren Gould, "Gandhi's Contribution to the Practice of the Law of Love in International Relation", *Gandhi Marg*, October 1979, pp. 436–51.
9. For detailed discussions on these aspects see P.S. Muhar, "Gandhian Approach to World Order", in Harnam Singh (ed.), *Studies in World Order*, Delhi: Kitab Mahal, pp. 374–408; and S.C. Gangal, "Gandhi's Views on World Affairs", in Verinder Grover (ed.), *Political Thinkers of Modern India*, Vol. 7 (New Delhi: Deep & Deep Publications, 1981), pp. 755–64. Also see, Minoru Kasai, *Gandhi and the Contemporary World*, Pune: Centre for Communication Studies, 1980, pp. 765–74; J.D. Sethi, "Twelve Point Gandhian Agenda for Peace Movements", pp. 775–803; J.B. Kripalani, "The Gandhian Approach to World Peace", pp. 820–27 and "Gandhi and Future of World Peace", pp. 831–40 in Grover's Volume; Anima Bose (ed.), *Peace and Conflict Resolution in the World Community* (New Delhi: Vikas Publishing House, 1981) and *Dimensions of Peace and Non-violence: The Gandhian Perspective* (New Delhi: Gian Publishing House, 1986), K.P. Misra and S.C. Gangal (eds.), *Gandhi and the Contemporary World: Studies in Peace and War* (New Delhi: Chanakya Publications, 1981); and D.N. Pathak, "Gandhi's Word-View: Intimation of a Peaceful World Society", *Gandhi Marg*, February 1983.
10. Biraja Shankar Rath, op. cit., p. 125.
11. *Harijan*, 16 May 1936.
12. V.P. Gaur, "Modern Search for Peace: The Gandhian Way", *Gandhi Marg*, 14 (2), July-September 1992, p. 385. Also see Durganand Sinha, "Ahimsa as Conflict Resolution Technique and Instrument of Peace: A Psychological Appraisal", in Anima Bose (ed.), *Peace and Conflict Resolution in the World Community*, New Delhi: Vikas Publishing House, 1981, pp. 57–58.
13. See Stephen King-Hall, *Defense in the Nuclear Age* (London: Gollancz, 1959) cited in K.S. Murthy and A.C. Bouquet, *Studies in the Problems of Peace and War* (Bombay: Asia Publishing House, 1960), p. 202.
14. For the justification of nonviolence in contemporary times see, Kathleen Lonsdale, *Is Peace Possible*? (London: Penguin, 1958); Stephen King-Hall, *Defense in the Nuclear Age* (London: Gollancz,

1959); K.S. Murthy and A.C. Bouquet, *Studies in the Problems of Peace and War* (Bombay: Asia Publishing House, 1960), pp. 201–04; and Durganand Sinha, op. cit., pp. 60–61.

15. *Harijan*, 16 November 1947.
16. *Young India*, 19 March 1931.
17. M.K. Gandhi, *For Pacifists* (Ahmedabad: Navajivan Publishing House, 1949), p. 88. Also see *Harijan*, 11 February 1939.
18. Ibid.
19. *Harijan*, 16 May 1936.
20. See D.C. Grover, "Dimensions of Gandhian Satyagraha in Contemporary World", *The Indian Journal of Political Science*, October 1968, pp. 232–34.
21. C.M. Case, *Nonviolent Coercion: A Study of Methods of Social Pressure* (London: Allen & Unwin, 1923), pp. 404–05.
22. Hanna Newcombe, "Convergence of Peace Models", *Gandhi Marg*, July-September 1992, pp. 379–81.
23. Ibid., p. 380.
24. E.H. Carr, *Conditions of Peace* (New York: Macmillan, 1942), pp. xxiii-xxiv.
25. Richard Smith Beal, "Faint Light on an Uncertain Prospect: Gandhian Insights on World Order", *Gandhi Marg*, July 1979, p. 214.

8

Gandhi's Approach to Resolution of Conflicts through Non-cooperation

MANISH SHARMA

Mahatma Gandhi is remembered as one of the most popular and prominent leaders who made extraordinary contributions towards attaining India's independence. And, it has never happened in the history of the world that a leader of a new political and spiritual idealism has had during his lifetime such a mass following as has Mahatma Gandhi. His doctrine has spread to different parts of the world like Egypt, Palestine, Ceylon, South China, Haiti, Santo Domingo and even Philippines. He became actively involved in Indian politics at a time when the country needed proper guidance and the national movement was on the brink of losing its ground and direction. Displaying a remarkable leadership quality during the independence movement, Gandhi successfully guided the nation to achieve its long desired goal. He was the one who transformed the freedom movement from an elite movement into a movement of the masses and persuaded the common people to oppose the colonial rule. Besides, he enthused the common man to correlate himself to the national ethos and made him a part of the freedom struggle. Appropriately, he is called "Father of the Nation" because he acted as the guardian of the nation at its hours of crisis. He rightly deserves that status and he will be remembered as the great man who shaped India's destiny to independence.

For Gandhi, the non-cooperation means refusal to assist a government which does not listen to the people's just grievances and has in their view become corrupt.[1] If the government persistently refuses to cooperate with the people, the people in turn should refuse to cooperate with the government.[2]

However, the complete significance of the Mahatma's leadership can be examined and appreciated if an attempt is made to understand the circumstances in which he took the leadership of the crusade to free India and the strategy he adopted during the independence movement to confront the British rulers in India.

By the time Gandhi returned from South Africa in 1915, several methods of national emancipation had been tried in the country and the Indian freedom fighters were clearly divided into two camps, led by the moderates and the extremists, respectively. The moderates were losing their grip over the situation and were gradually becoming ineffective to retain their control over the youths in India. Their failure to get political advantages as a result of the repeated rejections received from the government weakened their stature before the youths in the country. Their hold over the young mass was also threatened by the extremists who provided an alluring alternative means to gain quick results. The extremists, on the other hand, were not able to sustain the initial gain achieved by them through violence against the formidable opposition of the mighty British Empire. The British Government employed its superior punitive capacity to suppress the spread of violence in different parts of the country and restrict the activities of the extremists. As a consequence, in the absence of an able leadership, there was no effective supervision over the freedom fighters. In other words, the independence movement was on the verge of becoming rudderless. There was no unity between the Hindus and the Muslims. Before Gandhi many of the political leaders of high status had already applied several methods of national emancipation which include both the method of passive resistance and the terrorists-like activities. As Gandhi found all these methods unsuitable, he placed before the country his own method of resisting evil or injustice, which he had practised and perfected in South Africa and which has been regarded as his "most original contribution to political thought".[3] This method is known as 'Satyagraha'.

Further, the Jallianwalabagh massacre in 1919 had created a widespread resentment against the British and there was crave for revenge against the perpetrators of cruelty in India. The people were demanding quick retribution for the tragedy and expected the freedom fighters to punish the wrong doers. They were claiming for the blood of the persons responsible for the bloodbath and the situation was favourable for the occurrence of violence. Against all this backdrop Gandhi shouldered the responsibility of the freedom struggle by taking over the leadership of the Indian National Congress.

Means and Ends Relationship: Gandhi's Philosophy of the Purity of Means

While Gandhi assumed the leadership of the Indian National Congress, the main task before him was to bring unity among the leaders of the two factions – Hindu and Muslim – and achieve the target of gaining freedom for India. Moreover, along with attempting to assuage hurt feeling of the common people at the hands of the British, he had to show an exemplary performance as a leader of the masses because the people had known him as a successful campaigner for the cause of the suffering people; they had high expectations from him.

To meet all these challenges Gandhi had to choose the right method. However, as a champion of peace and non-violence, he could not approve the violent methods of the hardliners and as a man of action, he could not follow the method of appeal as preferred by the moderates and wait for things to happen. In other words, he neither wanted to make India free through bloodshed nor wished to be a mute spectator to the misrule of the British. In his wish to bring independence to India, Gandhi did not favour a method which was unacceptable to his conscience. He was not unscrupulous while he attempted to achieve his objective.

According to Gandhi, both the means and the ends were of equal importance or they were the two sides of the same coin. According to him, "The means may be likened to a seed, and the end to a tree; and there is just the same inviolable connection between the means and the end as there is between the seed and the tree."[4] Therefore, he did not follow the principle of "the end justified the means"; rather for him, if the means were good, automatically the end would be good. Therefore, the selection of the just and pure method was as important as the attainment of the end. Besides, if the end was important, then the means were most important. In practice, he desired to free India from the British rulers with the help of a non-violent and pure method which was honourable and moral in its character. He believed that an unethical means never brought a good result and to him violence was always bad and unethical. Hence, he did not prefer violent means for challenging the bad governance of the rulers. He felt that instead of adopting the principle of 'blood for blood' it was easier to win over the enemy with the help of non-violent means. According to him, violence resulted in more violence and there was the possibility of inviting the severe oppressive power of the government if a violent means was opted for opposing the government. He was certain that it would be impossible for him to face the British rulers with any unethical and immoral method. Therefore, he chose to confront them by attracting the attention of their conscience and reason to their own misdeeds. He wanted to challenge the rulers on moral grounds. He preferred to awaken their conscience by his rational approach. Gandhi decided on this method to attain his objective as he was convinced that violence would be a failure in the long run and only peaceful means would bring an everlasting result and independence to India and the result of this approach could be seen in the form of independence in 1947.

For Gandhi, non-cooperation is a process of evolving strength and self-reliance. It is a universal doctrine because it is as applicable to family relations as to any other. It means nothing less than training in self-sacrifice. It cannot be carried on except in an atmosphere of non-violence. The other nomenclature of non-cooperation is non-violence. Rejection is as much of an ideal as the acceptance of a thing. It is as necessary to reject untruth as it is to accept truth. We are all familiar with this fact that all religions teach us that two opposite forces act upon us, and that the human endeavour consists in a series of eternal rejections and acceptances. Non-cooperation with evil is as much a duty as cooperation with good.

Non-violent Peaceful Resistance: The Gandhian Method

Gandhi provided a new answer to the complicated questions of resolving all kinds of conflicts. As mentioned above, he had already experimented his ideals of truth and non-violence in South Africa in very ably opposing the practice of exploitation and discrimination against the blacks and propagated for racial equality and after coming to India, he applied those methods to win freedom for his countrymen. Further, he supported the cause of peaceful resolution of conflicts and preferred a method sans violence in an age when the principle of humanism had been savagely attacked by the might of the weapons of mass destruction. Therefore, he got the recognition of being the apostle of peace who vindicated the cause of spiritual and moral approach to social and political problems. Though like Gokhale, Gandhi wanted to spiritualise politics and mix moral values into politics, but he went a step further in his efforts to cleanse politics by bringing religion into it. To him, politics without moral principles did not serve the cause of soul. For him, the road to salvation was in the service of one's country and of humanity. He loved both his friends and foes. He also believed that bad means could not be justified because they would bring bad end. Against all odds Gandhi selected the peaceful means to fight the powerful British and achieve freedom for the masses. This accorded him the position of the most popular leader of the Indian independence movement.

Moreover, Gandhi was a very pragmatic leader. He had a clear understanding of his position. He was quite aware of his own strength and also the power and limitations of his adversary and accordingly selected his means to achieve his target. The success story of South Africa had convinced him that if an appeal was made to the head and heart of the adversary and the reason of the opponent was awakened, it would not be difficult to achieve the goal. Through these experiments, he had realised that even a very powerful opponent would succumb to the pressure of his own reason. That is why, Joan Bondurant called him a 'True Karmayogi – a practical man'. Besides, his faith in the Eastern culture also gave him the moral strength to pursue the path of non-violence. He was a committed follower of Eastern ideas which strongly supported the notions of peace and non-violence. In accordance with the struggle, he remarked that, "two paths are open before India today, either to introduce the Western principle of 'might is right' or to uphold the Eastern principle that truth knows no mishap, that strong and weak have alike a right to secure justice."[5] He believed, "To use violence for securing rights may seem an easy path, but it proves to be thorny in the long run, those who live by sword also die by sword."[6] He felt that violence bred violence and a violent means would not result in a good end. He had pointed out that violence would destroy many and would divide the survivors fighting endlessly.

Similarly, Gandhi was against any form of exploitation and injustice. He did not support tyranny on anybody. He propagated that evil must be opposed but the methods against the same should be non-violent and moral ones. The opponent must be dealt with mutual respect, love and affection. He believed that only through love an enemy could be permanently won. The resolution of conflict lies in non-violence and not in violence as he had a deep feeling with regard to the futility of violence as a method to solve a problem and because of this attitude he did not want to be a follower of violence. He had a strong conviction that through the uncivilised means of violence, nothing could be achieved. Thus, he said, "The barbarous method is warfare, open or secret. This must be ruled out if only because it is impracticable. If I could but persuade everyone that it is always bad, we shall gain all lawful ends much quicker. The power that an individual or a nation forswearing violence generates is the power that is irresistible. But my argument against violence is based upon pure expedience, i.e., its utter utility."[7] Likewise, he was so much against violence that he desired no emancipation, no Swaraj through the use of sword.[8] To him, non-violence was the weapon of the strongest and unless a person had sufficient moral strength he would use non-violence as a means to achieve something.

The Philosophy of Non-cooperation

On account of the above mentioned facts, Gandhi, after a long battle and maturity, opted non-cooperation as the novel means to challenge the might of the British government. According to him, non-violence with non-cooperation would serve double purpose: it would counter the vindictiveness of the government and also unite the common masses in their struggle for independence. His experiment with truth and non-violence as methods of resistance as applied in South Africa helped him to consider peaceful non-cooperation as the most suitable technique to be employed in the freedom movement in India. He understood that it would be impossible for the innocent peace-loving people to oppose the powerful rulers through violent means; rather; if the conscience of the British was awakened and if the British were to see reason it would be easier for the Indians to gain freedom. He emphasised, "Non-co-operation is therefore the only remedy left open to us. It is the cleanest remedy as it is the most effective, when it is absolutely free from all violence."[9] He further added that, "Non-co-operation is the only method which will either bring freedom or purge the regime of its evils."[10]

Therefore, he believed that people's mind could be changed by the force of love and reason. If the heart of the opponent could be touched by the power of love and reason, it would not be difficult for somebody to win over his opponent and achieve his objective. Gandhi thought that Swaraj could also be achieved through the power of love and reason. He asserted that, "We want to win Swaraj by changing people's ideas through the force of love and reason and this has obliged the Government also to rely on reason."[11] He was fully convinced that love and compassion could be used to resolve all kinds of conflicts.

In fact, Gandhi was an avowed supporter of peace. He had always put emphasis on the peaceful method of resistance. Even in non-cooperation movement he did not want anybody to be a party to any violent activity. He was so much attached to non-violence that he considered non-violence as the essential part of the non-cooperation movement. That is why, he declared, "Non-violence is the most vital and integral part of non-cooperation."[12] While fighting for Khilafat, Gandhi expounded the uselessness of the power of the sword. He believed that the power of the sword was less effective than that of love. According to him, "The sword makes men cruel. After fighting with one another like so many bulls, till they all get exhausted, the opponents salute each other and become friends. Anyone who shows weakness will humiliate himself. The other method is, instead of using physical force against the opponent to employ soul force and win ascendancy over him. This ascendancy is accepted no tout of fear but out of love, and so both become equals. One does not consider it humiliating to admit another's moral superiority. The other takes no pride in being morally superior. Hence, both behave respectfully towards each other. We must give up the very thought of overcoming the English by sword."[13]

In this respect, Gandhi had pointed out that the practitioners of non-cooperation needed to purify themselves. Unless one was purified one was not capable of becoming a true soldier of the non-cooperation movement. Taking his argument a bit further he had stated that the practice of untouchability prevalent in the Hindu society was against the principle of purification and it could hamper the non-cooperation movement as it needed the active involvement of all sections of the society and the involvement and participation could be possible only if there was unity among all sections. Therefore, he declared, "Non-co-operation is a science of purification. Unless we have purified ourselves, we cannot employ it. So long as we regard one of limbs as untouchable, we ourselves, the Hindus, and our neighbours, the Muslims and others, will remain the untouchable that we have become."[14] Gandhi's argument, thus, is quite convincing in this context.

Similarly, Gandhi always advocated that an opponent could be reached through non-cooperation. The heart of an adversary could be changed only by putting moral pressure on him through non-cooperation. However, at the same time, he also warned against the misuse of the power of non-cooperation and directed that a person practising non-cooperation must observe strict discipline in his conduct. He must maintain restraint in his behaviour towards his so-called adversary. In his opinion, "Non-co-operation is a process of purification and we must continually try to touch the heart of those who differ from us, touch their minds and their emotions but never their bodies. Discipline and restraint are the cardinal principles of our conduct and I warn you against any sort of tyrannical social ostracism."[15] Thus, Gandhi was not only aware of the effectiveness of non-cooperation to confront an enemy, but he was also conscious of its susceptibility to be misused.

Accordingly, Gandhi contended that while a person remained engaged in non-cooperation it was imperative for him to avoid violence as violence had no place in non-cooperation. Adoption of violence even in an indirect form was prohibited by Gandhi. Therefore, he said, "So long as we are associated with the movement of non-co-operation, we shall not directly or indirectly advocate violence at present or in the future nor create an atmosphere of preparedness for violence. Indeed we hold it contrary to the spirit of non-violent non-co-operation to which we have pledged our word."[16]

Moreover, Gandhi was more concerned with the cause of the evil than its symptoms. He gave more importance to wipe out the cause of the evil than to do away with the evil doer. To him, non-cooperation was a process which could cure the system from all evils, so he advised that the aim should be to go to the root cause of the problem and think of the remedy to purge the system of its defects. He regarded non-cooperation as an effective method to tackle the cause of a problem. In his own words, "Non-co-operation is essentially a cleansing process. It deals with causes rather than symptoms."[17] As a matter of fact, Gandhi was a true fighter in the war of Indian independence. He was always prepared to suffer for the sake of the nation. He honestly believed that through sacrifice India could be made independent. Thus, there was nothing to boast or bluff about non-cooperation. By becoming a participant in non-cooperation one has to work for the nation. To Gandhi, "Non-co-operation is not a movement of brag, bluster, or bluff. It is a test of our sincerity. It requires a social and silent self sacrifice. It challenges our honesty and our capacity for national work. It is a movement that aims at translating ideas into action. And the more we do, the more we find that much more be done that we had expected. And this thought of our imperfection must make us humble."[18]

Role of Non-cooperation, Passive Resistance and Civil Disobedience

Gandhi had differentiated non-cooperation from passive resistance and civil disobedience. He thought that a weak person adopted the method of passive resistance to challenge his opponent where violence could be allowed. For a moment the weak did not employ violence in passive resistance because he could not use it due to his weakness, but use of violence was not excluded from passive resistance. Passive resistance, according to Gandhi, "covers the suffragette movement as well as the resistance of the nonconformists. Passive resistance has been conceived and is regarded as the weapon of the weak. Whilst it avoids violence, being not open to the weak, it does not exclude its use if in the opinion of the resister, the occasion demands it."[19] Accordingly, it is dependent on expediency or an opportunity to humiliate and harm the opponent.

On the other hand, by civil disobedience, Gandhi meant refusal to render obedience to law made by the state. According to Gandhi, if the law of the state was discriminatory and immoral, the citizens had the right to disobey the law. Thus, he said, "Civil disobedience is civil breach of immoral statutory enactments."[20] By civil disobedience the evil intentions of the state or the other agencies could be exposed.

Though Gandhi did not object to the use of the word "passive resistance" for his method for want of a more suitable expression in English, yet he always maintained that Satyagraha should not be confused with passive resistance. According to Gandhi, the one was as different from the other as the North Pole from the South. Passive resistance was conceived of as a weapon of the weak and avoided violence on the ground of expediency, but did not exclude its use, if in the opinion of the resister the occasion demanded it, whereas Satyagraha was a weapon of the strong and exclude the use of violence in any shape or form.

Method of Non-cooperation

While describing the process in which the non-cooperation movement could be waged, Gandhi explained that "Non-cooperation predominantly implies withdrawing of cooperation from the state that in the non-co-operator's view has become corrupt and excludes civil disobedience of fierce type described above. By its very nature it is even open to children of understanding and can be safely practised by the masses. Civil disobedience presupposes the habit of willing obedience to law, without fear of their sanctions. It can therefore be practised only as a last resort and by a select few in the first instance at any rate."[21] Thus, according to Gandhi, it was possible for all the people who were of sound mind to be the participants in the non-cooperation movement whereas civil disobedience was for the few selected people who had the deep conviction of the faulty nature of the law made by the state. A meek and mild person could also start non-cooperation against his powerful opponents and show his resentment against them as well.

Gandhi did describe in detail the various techniques to be used by the practitioners of non-cooperation. He explained that in non-cooperation movement, the people could adopt different means for not cooperating with their adversaries. Besides boycotting the wrong doers, those who practised non-cooperation might observe strike or could cease work or begin hartal (strike). Gandhi believed that opposition to the immoral conduct of an authority or a person could be expressed through these means peacefully. At the same time, he also warned against the misuse of these means. He stated, "Strike, cessation of work and hartal are wonderful things no doubt, but it is not difficult to abuse them."[22] This could, according to Gandhi, be quite effective in the process of conflict resolution.

Satyagraha as a Method and a Way of Life

Gandhi contended that the most effective means for a fighter in non-cooperation was the weapon of Satyagraha. According to him, Satyagraha had a far more superiority than any other means because it had a moral base or foundation. Satyagraha was based on truth and non-violence and these were more desirable than anything else. In Gandhi's view, there was no substitute for truth and non-violence and ultimately only these could prevail.

To Gandhi, Satyagraha "is literally holding on to Truth and it means therefore, Truth force. Truth is soul or spirit. It is, therefore, known as Soul-force. It excludes the use of violence because man is not capable of knowing the absolute truth and therefore not competent to punish."[23] Further, redefining Satyagraha, he said, "Its root meaning is 'holding on to truth'; hence, truth force. I have also called it love force or soul force. In the application of Satyagraha I discovered in the earliest stages that pursuit of Truth did not admit of violence being inflicted on one's opponent,"[24] but that he must be weaned from error by humility, patience and sympathy. It is because of the fact that what appears to be truth to one may appear to be untruth to the other. And patience means self-suffering. So, the doctrine came to mean vindication of truth, not by infliction of suffering on the opponent, but one's own self.[25]

In fact, Gandhi's concept of Satyagraha is a natural outcome of his faith in the supremacy of truth. It was the result of his realisation of truth as he regarded truth as the ultimate reality. He believed that it was the moral duty of all to protect the foundation of truth. To him, a supporter of truth should put all his might to safeguard the cause of truth. A votary of truth must work with determination to establish the supremacy of moral and spiritual principles. Propagation of truth was the final goal of a lover of truth and Satyagraha was the practical application of truth. The term "Satyagraha" was coined in South Africa to distinguish it from passive resistance.

Gandhi emphasised that a Satyagrahi should acknowledge the omnipotence of truth in his heart. Within his heart a Satyagrahi knows that truth must be established, if necessary even at the cost of one's life. "It (Satyagraha) is also called Soul-force because a definite recognition of the Soul within is a necessity if a satyagrahi is to believe that death does not mean cessation of the struggle but a culmination."[26] A Satyagrahi should be prepared to make any sacrifice for the protection of truth.

According to Gandhi truth does not need any artificial support. It is self-reliant. He contended, "Satyagraha is self-dependent. It does not require the assent of the opponent before it can be brought into play."[27] Gandhi was of the opinion that a Satyagrahi would definitely try to change the heart of his opponent by making an appeal to the reason of his adversary. By gentle convincing arguments a Satyagrahi would attempt to make his opponent see logic and be aware of his misconduct. Through his self-sacrifice a Satyagrahi would make effort to bring changes in the thinking of his so-called enemy. "And a Satyagrahi never injuries his opponent and always appeals, either to his reason by gentle argument, or his heart by the sacrifice of self, Satyagraha is twice blessed; it blesses him who practices it, and him against whom it is practiced."[28] Gandhi thought that everybody had a soul and in his heart everybody knew what was right and what was wrong; if an attempt was made, everybody would see reason. In his view, even the hardest opponent's heart could be changed by humility and self-suffering.

Regarding Satyagraha and passive resistance, Gandhi said that passive resistance was a weapon of the weak. If a person was unable to openly resist his opponent, he would adopt the method of passive resistance. In contrast, Satyagraha was the weapon of the brave. It could be practised by only such persons who had total conviction to truth as a Satyagrahi was convinced of the supremacy of truth and he did not require any violent means. As stated earlier, Satyagraha differs from passive resistance greatly. The latter has been conceived as a weapon of the weak and does not exclude the use of physical force or violence for the purpose of gaining one's end, whereas the former has been conceived as a weapon of the strongest, and excludes the use of violence in any shape or form.[29] Rather, it was the sacred duty of a satyagrahi to make endless endeavours for the vindication of truth.[30]

While narrating the concept of Satyagraha Gandhi drew an analogy between the relationship within a family and the outside world. He believed that law of love regulated the domestic life within a family and because there was no use of violence in the family, the family life had been continuing since time immemorial. Within a family there was mutual respect among the members in spite of the many differences among them. However, now exceptions can be seen. But one of the basic foundations of the family structure was the sacrifice of its members. Thus, Gandhi asserted, "This doctrine of Satyagraha is not new; it is merely extension of the domestic life to the political. Family disputes and differences are generally settled according to the law of love. The injured member has so much regard for the others that he suffers injury for the sake of his principles without retaliating without being angry with those who differ from him... his actions, whether he resists or resigns, is always calculated to promote, the common welfare of the family. It is this law of love, which silently but surely, governs the family for the most part throughout the civilized world."[31]

However, Gandhi's Satyagraha does not presuppose disobedience to the law of the state. By nature, Gandhi was a law-abiding person and he respected the laws of the society; however, he objected to the laws which were immoral and against the principle of justice. He commented that the laws which were against the interest of the citizens must be resisted. At the same time, he clarified that he was not deliberately trying to create problems for the government. He remarked that it was contrary to his creed to embarrass governments or anybody else, but he should not hold himself responsible for having caused embarrassment when he resists the wrong of a wrong doer by refusing assistance in his wrong doing.[32]

Role and Duties of Non-cooperator

The idea of non-cooperation as conceived by Gandhi does not presume social and political disintegration. It does not believe in the subjugation of one by the other. It teaches to respect even the rights of an opponent. Non-cooperation, Gandhi opined, "will not succeed unless we create an atmosphere of perfect freedom, unless we prize our opponent's liberty as much as our own. The liberty of faith, conscience, thought and action which we claim for ourselves must be conceded equally to others."[33]

Gandhi was so deeply attached to the principle of non-violence that he always emphasised on the use of this method to achieve one's objectives. Non-violence and love should be the only weapons in the fight for a just cause. According to him, violence should never be used as a means by a practitioner of non-cooperation movement. This means violence should never be used even as a last resort. He felt that when people became restless, impatient and vindictive they used to adopt violent methods to achieve their goals. Hence, he had warned against the use of violence in the non-cooperation movement: "The real danger of violence lies in the people resorting to non-co-operation becoming impatient and revengeful."[34] And that is why Gandhi had to withdraw his non-cooperation movement in 1922.

Similarly, Gandhi believed in self-discipline. To him, those who were participants of non-cooperation should observe certain restraints. A non-cooperator should always consciously avoid violence; even the very thought of violence should be abominable to him. Prescribing what to do while practicing non-cooperation, he advised, "it is infinitely more necessary that we non-co-operators control our speech, control our movements and free them even from any danger or any smell of violence. Let our speech and our pen be free from any violent thing."[35] To him, non-violence was not merely abstention from physical violence, it included violence in any form.

Gandhi had emphasised that a participant in non-cooperation movement had certain duties towards others as basically non-cooperation movement did not mean disregarding the sentiments and feelings of others. Rather, a non-cooperator should be respectful towards his opponent. He must be humble towards all. Gandhi said, "A non-co-operator must remain respectful, peaceful and humble towards all."[36] Thus, Gandhi's idea of non-cooperation was to make one more aware of his duties. Accordingly, involvement in the non-cooperation movement was not a licence to do whatever one wished. On the other hand, it put many limitations on the conduct of a participant. In Gandhi's view, non-cooperation movement was a voluntary movement and the participants were those who were convinced of its necessity and utility and they were prepared for making sacrifices for the success of the movement. In Gandhi's view, a person who had a genuine commitment only would be willing to suffer for the cause for which the movement had been launched. He said, "Non-co-operation as a voluntary movement can only succeed if the feeling is genuine and strong enough to make people suffer to the utmost."[37]

In this respect, Gandhi told that non-cooperation movement aimed at establishing the superiority of truth and non-violence as these did not need the support of others for its vindication and it was the ultimate reality and there was no need for any violence for establishing its supremacy. As a result, the movement was for the vindication of truth. He clarified, "Non co-operation too like civil disobedience is branch of Satyagraha which includes all non-violent resistance for the vindication of Truth."[38]

Non-cooperation as a Process for Resolving Conflicts

Besides describing the meaning of non-cooperation and the duties of a non-cooperator, Gandhi also narrated how the movement could be started and how an opponent could be faced during the movement. According to him, when the government became tyrannical and began tormenting the people it was the right and duty of the people to oppose the policies and laws of that government. The people should not be associated with such a government which did not serve the interests of the people; they should rather not be a party to the tyranny of the government. He emphasised that non-cooperation meant refusing to associate oneself with or be a party to the tyranny of the government and to render any support, direct or indirect, to such tyranny.[39]

Accordingly, he contended that it was the prime duty of the government to protect the interest of the people and if the government failed in its duties it had no right to rule the people. He asserted that without the willing acceptance of the people that government had no legal right to control over them, no government had the capacity to regulate the people, however powerful it might be. It was also the duty of the people to protest such a government which did not safeguard their welfare and interest. They should not be the willing abettors of the tyranny of the rulers. Therefore, he said, "As there can be no cooperation between virtue and sin, between darkness and light, so there can be none between the people and a Government opposed to their interests; by means of non-co-operation, we are proving that even the most wicked policy cannot survive if the people do not tolerate it, refuse to be a party to it."[40]

Therefore, Gandhi's advice was that all the people were to be involved in the movement of non-cooperation to make the movement a success. However, while launching the non-cooperation movement, Gandhi first targeted the classes which were trapped by the government to implement its policy of oppression. Gandhi felt and commented that the youths were lured by the faulty policies of the government and they were the first who were to be warned of the evil designs of the government; if the students could be convinced of the utility of the non-cooperation movement then it would be easier for the movement to succeed. Thus, he told at the very beginning of the movement, "Non-co-operation deals first with those sensitive classes upon whom the Government has acted so successfully and who have been lured into the trap consciously or unconsciously as the school going youths have been."[41]

In this context, while delivering a speech at the students' meeting at Benaras on November 27, 1920, Gandhi said, "Now I want to tell you why in the scheme of non-co-operation I have included the sacrifice from students. It is my firm conviction that the main reason why the present regime goes on and continues to perpetrate the atrocities that it does, is that we have come under the spell of its education. Before its instruction we were self-reliant and not dependent as we are today. The present system of education has rendered us more dependent."[42]

Therefore, Gandhi was convinced that the system of education that the British had introduced in India, aimed at creating dependency in the country. The people who were educated by the British were blindly following the British dictates because of their imposed educational background. They were the people who were acting as supporters of the tyranny of the government. So, unless those people changed their attitude it would be difficult to counter the evil designs of the British government.

In fact, Gandhi had evolved his own method of peaceful resistance and applied it in South Africa and later on in the freedom movement in India. He launched non-cooperation movement in 1920–21 and continued to use this method till the attainment of freedom and even up to his death. Though initially the movement was regarded as a failure by some, it provided an example to others about the relevance of peaceful means in a violent world. He could prove to the world that even a powerful opponent could be successfully challenged by non-violent means and he could be changed through the power of love. He taught the world how to manage a crisis without invoking the power of sword and how love could prevail over hatred.

If we go through the whole concept of non-cooperation and its application as expounded by Gandhi, it can be regarded that Gandhi gave a new approach to the resolution of conflicts. He expounded a new theory with regard to solving a problem. He prescribed how to meet one's enemy in a world torn by violence. He experimented the highest virtues of truth and non-violence during the Indian freedom struggle and came to the conclusion that if a person had moral force he could face any challenge against any powerful enemy. The basic philosophy behind it was that Gandhi was a firm believer in the inherent goodness of man. To him, everybody had a conscience and if he was made aware of his misconduct and his wrongs, he would see reason and behave differently. So it was not necessary to threaten him with physical violence and incur his wrath; it would be better to convince him with rational and gentle persuasion and settle the matter peacefully.

Furthermore, Gandhi was a man of moral conviction. He always believed in the supremacy of moral and ethical values. He had a strong belief that freedom could be brought to India only by such methods which were supported by the principles of morality because moral superiority could enable the Indians either to bring freedom in the country or eliminate the evils from the regime. Ultimately, he succeeded and proved to be right.

The credit of Gandhi's success lies in the fact that instead of an aggressive and militant struggle, he built up a movement of peaceful resistance in the form of non-cooperation in which the Indian masses were converted into active participants in the fight against oppression, injustice and violence. Only a person of the Mahatma's stature could transform the people into vigorous soldiers in the war of Indian independence who could face the mighty British Empire with conviction, confidence and courage. Because of his moral strength he could lead the people of India to their freedom and he could do so with the support of only of truth and non-violence. And, the whole world is a witness to it.

The real contribution of Gandhi can be realised if the background in which he took the reign of the national freedom movement is understood properly and the means he adopted to achieve are analysed in a proper way as he accomplished his goal by following a simple peaceful method at a difficult time. Moreover, he prepared the mankind for facing the crisis of a world full of violence, strife and hatred. He showed a path on which people could peacefully live in a violent world and work together on the basis of mutual cooperation and harmony. His method of Satyagraha, in fact, is a substitute for war and the concept of non-cooperation is a unique method of conflict resolution. For all his contributions he certainly deserves appreciation and rightly becomes the champion of peace and non-violence and one of the greatest personalities in the world. The vital need of this article arises not alone because of the considered, as well as the unintentional misrepresentations that a movement of this sort must inevitably call forth, but because there is contained in the truth concerning it, an active principle that is greatly needed today. Gandhi has said that his message is for humanity and his life is his message for the masses. He is looking beyond India to the world, and he is saying "return not evil for evil, but return the good for evil". The message that was Christ's two thousand years ago is the Mahatma's today. Shall we not – must we not give heed to it?

Notes

1. M.K. Gandhi (1965) *Collected Works*, New Delhi: The Publications Division, Ministry of Information and Broadcasting, Government of India, Vol. XIX, 466 (hereinafter to be cited as CWMG).
2. C.F. Andrews (1923) *The Meaning of Non-Co-operation*, Madras: Tagore and Co., p. 24.
3. P. Sitaramayya (1948) Gandhi, the Man and the Philosopher, *Amrit Bazar Patrika*, Puja Number, p. 7.
4. M.K. Gandhi (1998) *Hind Swaraj*, Ahmedabad: Navajivan Publishing House, February, p. 64.
5. M.K. Gandhi, *CWMG*, Vol. XVII, p. 17.
6. Ibid., pp. 17–18.
7. Ibid., p. 75.
8. Ibid., Vol. XIX, 1966, p. 27.
9. Ibid., Vol. XVII, p. 75.
10. Ibid., Vol. XIX, p. 36.
11. Ibid., p. 10.
12. Ibid., Vol. XX, p. 439.
13. Ibid., Vol. XVII, pp. 105–06.
14. Ibid., Vol. XIX, p. 8.
15. Ibid., pp. 104–05.
16. Ibid., Vol. XX, pp. 93–94.
17. Ibid., Vol. XIX, p. 145.
18. Ibid., p. 220.
19. Ibid., p. 466.
20. Ibid.
21. Ibid.
22. Ibid., Vol. XVII, p. 17.
23. Ibid., Vol. XIX, p. 466.
24. Ibid., Vol. XVII, p. 152.
25. Ibid.
26. Ibid., pp. 153–54.
27. Ibid., p. 153.

28. Ibid., p. 154.
29. Ibid., p. 152.
30. Ibid.
31. Ibid., p. 153.
32. Ibid., p. 350.
33. Ibid., Vol. XIX, p. 104.
34. Ibid., Vol. XVII, p. 352.
35. Ibid., Vol. XIX, p. 545.
36. Ibid., Vol. XX, p. 513.
37 Ibid., Vol. XVII, p. 390.
38. M.K. Gandhi (1981) *Young India*, Ahmedabad: Navajivan Publishing House, Vol. III, No. 12, p. 90.
39. M.K. Gandhi, *CWMG*, Vol. XIX, p. 250.
40. Ibid., p. 284.
41. Ibid., p. 234.
42. Ibid., p. 37.

Section II

Reinterpreting Non-violence: Asia-Pacific Context

9

Practical Non-violent Responses to New Forms of Violence

A.T. ARIYARATNE

The international human rights, enumerated in the international covenants of civil and political rights and of economic, social and cultural rights, cover a very broad sweep of human life. In certain respects, they highlight the advances in human thinking about the conditions necessary for human beings to live a more truly human life. One has only to compare, for instance, the content of the present-day human rights covenants with the Code of Hammurabi in Babylonia or accounts of the amphitheatre of the ancient Romans where the general public came to witness the most cruel killings of other human beings as a source of legitimate pleasure to see the immense progress that has been made in what humanity has now generally come to consider to be the ideal rights of all human beings.

Almost every government in the world has given its assent to the concept of human rights giving it a universality that is unprecedented in recorded human history. However, this leaves us with no room for complacency as the degree of suffering in the world is perhaps at a higher level now than at any time in the past. With the enormous increase in human population and the multiplication of the demands placed upon the environment by that population, or sections of that population, the level of violence in the world has registered a massive increase.

The gravity of this fact lies in the hidden dimension of the violence to be found in the world today. It is true that no human society will openly condone the imposition of suffering on other forms of life and openly derive pleasure from it as in the past. Of course, even this statement is debatable as we saw during the war prosecuted by the United Nations against Iraq. The truth is that as the world becomes ever more polarised between a global affluent and privileged minority and a poverty-stricken and powerless majority, new and hidden forms of violence are considered necessary by the former to keep the latter in check. As Mahatma Gandhi said some half a century ago, "if true freedom were to come to India, the hovels of the poor and the palaces of the rich will not be able to coexist for even a moment". There is an appearance of freedom and democracy but the substance of it is drained away in unseen and hidden ways. Both subtle and crude forms of violence are the greatest violators of human rights. Finding a non-violent response to violence is our greatest challenge.

All-encompassing Violence

What are these new forms of violence that impose unjust structures and unjust outcomes on others? We need to go back to the very definition of violence in order to understand what is sometimes not immediately visible to the eye. Any external factor interfering with the normal growth, functioning and survival of a living organism can be broadly defined as violence. When human society was less sophisticated, we could have confined the meaning of violence to the inflicting of harm by human beings on other human beings in thought, word or deed. To this type of personal violence, which imposes pain on mind and body, we could have added structural forms of violence through social, economic and political instruments of control. The most important characteristic of both these forms of personal and structural violence for our purposes was the ability to identify the person or group on whom the violence was imposed.

In the present day, however, the victim need not necessarily be an individual human being or a group. The victim of the new violence can be as small as a living cell or micro-organism that has its integrity, which is the result of millions and billions of years of evolution, violated by the sophisticated instruments of modern science that probe it without having any comprehensive understanding of the probable outcome. On the other hand, the victim can be as big as the planet itself, including the entire biosphere, atmosphere and stratosphere, which humanity is abusing in a manner unprecedented in history. To add to the complexity of the problem, the imposer of the violence and the victim are difficult to identify, and quite often they happen to be both the subject and object of violence.

Those of us who believe in 'Sarvodaya' (welfare of all) also believe in a concept which is of Gandhian origin, meaning the well-being or awakening of all. Ours is a universal thought for the well-being of all life where personal and structural violence as well as identifiable and unidentifiable violence are neither condoned nor permitted. Our ideal is to create a human society where the human mind and the social, economic and political institutions created by human beings and their relationship with nature in its microscopic and macroscopic dimensions sustain themselves with the least opportunity for self-destruction. This demands a reappraisal of the Sarvodaya and Gandhian approaches to counter violence and to disseminate new thinking, techniques and technologies.

Now I would briefly look at the situation in Sri Lanka as analysed by the Sarvodaya Shramadana Movement (hereafter, SSM) to which I belong and give a few examples of the processes we are trying to release to ensure peace within human personalities and human communities as also between human beings and nature itself.

SSM has worked in the villages of Sri Lanka for over thirty-four years. At present, it is working in over 8,000 villages which constitute more than a third of the village communities in the country. Sarvodaya is involved in all aspects of community development under ten broad basic human needs. They are: environment, water, clothing, food, housing, health, energy, communication, education, and cultural and spiritual needs.

'Sarvodaya' means the awakening of all in every aspect of human life. SSM believes in six aspects of integrated development: at the levels of the human being, the family, the village and urban community, the national and the world community. These are the spiritual, moral, cultural, social, economic and political aspects of life. For a world where peace, non-violence and justice will prevail, human beings and society should awaken simultaneously at all these levels.

However, the political and economic mismanagement of our country since independence has resulted in an appalling degeneration of commonly accepted social norms and values which prevailed for at least the two millennia for which we have recorded history. The inevitable result is that in every profession, from teaching to farming and from religion to judiciary, there is a moral and spiritual decay in the quality of the personalities involved in those activities.

The ensuing frustration and desperation conspire to bring about a fear psychosis in which even homicidal tendencies become a means to survive. It is not necessary that everybody would take it that far. But certainly a substantial minority in Sri Lanka has already demonstrated a frightening capacity to resort to such actions in order to survive. The young people in the southern parts of the country who attempted twice to overthrow the prevailing system by violence and the militant youth and even children in the north who are still on the battlefield clearly demonstrate this fact. The equally harsh and more repressive instruments of official violence are just as much subjected to this fear psychosis and homicidal mania as their opponents. In the meanwhile, the vast majority of people, whatever their political or racial group, are enveloped in fear and even marginally become subscribers to these evil tendencies. The custodians of values, including the religious personalities, are no less victims of this total social malaise.

In our societies the most powerful establishments for changing the course of society for better or worse in the short term are the governments. Even though we call ourselves democratic countries, those who run governments are the political leaders and small coteries of their supporters. To varying degrees and perhaps at a much more intense level than those of others, the survival instinct and fear psychosis get control over them.

The SSM is not functioning in a vacuum. It works in the reality of this environment. Thousands of its workers, spread across the length and breadth of the country, are a witness to the air bombings, cannon fire, landmine explosions, foot mines, disappearances, burnings on tyres, and unauthorised arrests – all of which constitute nothing but violence and human suffering. They also do witness the apparently carefree and happy-go-lucky affluent lifestyles of a minority who are insensitive to the realities of what is happening in the rest of the country. They zoom about in their airconditioned cars and enjoy sumptuous meals at five-star hotels as if these are normalities in everyone's life.

In this world of contrasts, of poverty and affluence, of fear and sensuality, any practical response with the intention of having an impact has to be manifold and all-embracing. The portfolio of activities should include the awakening of the personalities of unborn children to the creation of a popular mass of consciousness of the people in the country of critical proportions to enable them to realise the grave situation and the way out of it.

While the physical energies and resources of people and the remnants of sanity still prevailing in social structures are utilised to the maximum, the priority for SSM is creating a critical mass of spiritual consciousness. With extreme caution, the spiritual energies have to be differentiated and harnessed from religious resources, but taking care not to hurt the religious susceptibilities of people. A kind of socially engaged Buddhism, Hinduism, Islam and Christianity have to be brought to the fore to get individuals, groups and communities to practise meditation, cultivate respect for life, and radiate loving kindness far and wide.

Material resources have also to be harnessed and directed to bring about a realisation of the utter futility of violence and the alternative sustainable social system that can be put into place by non-violence. Satisfaction of basic, secondary and tertiary human needs can be initiated by releasing processes through constructive non-violent action, and participatory and sustainable village-level socio-economic structures can be created so that democracy evolves from below rather than imposed from the top.

Backlash

SSM has initiated these processes in its three decades of work so that its presence as a non-violent integrated movement for total change is being felt nationally. The surest indication is that in subtle and devious ways the government itself has launched an all-out attack on the movement and its leaders. Throughout its existence it has on occasions been at the receiving end of governmental displeasure. But, in the last three years, this has reached an unprecedented level. It will not be exaggerating to say that no other organisation except one that has embedded itself in the people could have survived the government sponsored campaign of distortion and obstruction.

The first portent of things to come was when, within a week of the swearing in of the new President, I was interrogated by the chief of the National Intelligence Bureau. The weekly educational radio programme that the SSM had conducted for several years was suddenly stopped and TV and radio coverage of its activities was completely blacked out. Then using the excuse of the Presidential

Commission to investigate NGOs, the police began to question its workers. Foreign funds pledged to it by donor agencies that also assist the government were blocked by the finance ministry.

This was followed by a calumnious campaign against the SSM and myself personally in the largest circulation government-controlled newspapers in which, among other things, we were falsely accused of selling babies abroad for profit. In the middle of these attacks, my family and I began to receive anonymous death threats and we were followed by unidentified men in vehicles. A very large printing machine we had ordered to print low-cost books for the poor was confiscated by the customs authorities. The Central Bank stepped in to restrict our children's savings programme and rural savings and credit programme and ordered us to return our savings deposits. These are just some of the highlights. There are a large number of other obstacles that have been put in our path.

Initial Measures

How are we going to face these new forms of violence which are intended to break our spirit and force us to acquiesce in the injustice that is rampant in our country? From our past experience we have learnt that when there is violence and injustice imposed on us, patiently continuing to do whatever work that can be done helps to diffuse the adversities and the work that was previously being obstructed can be continued. Of course, there is a waste of time and resources on account of the damage that would already have been done.

The injustice and violence have been imposed on us on account of the ignorance regarding the value of the work that we are doing. On the basis of that realisation, we regard awareness creation and conscientisation through educational programmes as having a very useful role to play. Once the ignorance is dispelled, the erstwhile opponent becomes friendly, subscribes to our ideals, and supports our work. But there are some who cannot be changed this way because they are quite aware of the valuable work that the SSM is doing but still persist in wilfully obstructing our work. If they happen to be administrators working on the instigation of the political authorities and who know very well that they are working against the spirit of the law and justice, then another course of action has to be resorted to, that is, to take resort to courts of law to get justice.

During the present period, the SSM has had to resort to this course of action owing to the continued injustices imposed on us by the abuse of power and vitiation of the law. The difficulty is that there are now an increasing number of laws that are no longer based on the principles of justice, but are drafted and legislated merely to suit the temporary convenience of the government. Likewise, it is possible that judicial appointments will be made not on the basis of merit and justice but on the basis of the consideration to further the unjust purposes of the appointing authority. As a result, the general public is losing faith not only in the law but also in the administration of justice. Still, one has to try it out. Only if we fail to get justice by resorting to legal institutions will the next course of action have to be considered. For a non-violent revolutionary movement like the SSM, this is non-violent direct action.

However, unlike during the times of Mahatma Gandhi when he launched his non-violent satyagraha campaign against the British rule in India, at the present time the non-violent direct action has to be directed against rulers who are a part of the general population of the country. They have used and misused the democratic processes in both a subtle and crude manner and claim democratic legitimacy for their tyrannical attitude towards their opponents. They believe that their election victories give them the right to define their own rules in their own interests. For instance, they have created and used illegal goon squads to intimidate, kidnap, torture and kill dissenters even if they were unarmed and non-violent. Therefore, to resort to non-violent direct action is more difficult today than it was during Gandhi's time.

Final Option

Under today's circumstances, the votaries of non-violence and social justice have to depend almost exclusively on the spiritual consciousness they can awaken within themselves. They have to aggregate these energies into a critical mass capable of affecting the mass psyche of the general population. The external manifestations of such a course of spiritual action that is directed to bringing about a change will manifest itself in the form of fearlessness and sacrifice.

The final possibility that is open to the SSM is direct political action. Although the SSM does not believe in power and party politics and has stayed away from it ever since its inception, this very system has caused and is causing untold damage to its work. Now, the present regime has launched an all-out attack to make the movement ineffective and destroy it completely. But people in thousands of villages want it to exist and succeed. The people's strength of the organisation has in recent years expanded as a result of the oppression the movement has been subjected to. Therefore, it has become both necessary and possible to confront the unjust and violent power and party political system by people's power and replace it by a participatory alternative system of politics. The SSM has decided to take to this kind of political action if all other efforts to bring about sanity and justice do not succeed.

Among the objectives of such a political campaign will be:

1. to introduce non-violence and justice as the fundamental value systems into the political life of the country;
2. to disband the highly concentrated political and economic centres at the top of the hierarchy and re-establish village-level political authorities ensuring protection of people's lives, their properties, life support systems, and the environment;
3. to ensure the justice of laws affecting the general population as against the discriminatory legislation that protects the privileges of a few;
4. to ensure the freedom and integrity of the judiciary and noninterference with the administration of justice;
5. to re-establish the dignity and worth of civil servants to function under the law without duress or interference from the political authorities;
6. to ensure the freedom of the press and media so that they can play an independent and investigative role befitting a Participatory democracy;
7. to promote a true open economy in which the private sector, the public corporation sector, and the non-governmental and cooperative sector are given equal opportunities and incentives for production, marketing, and financial and resource management; and
8. to promote the evolution of a democratic political system from below where the ultimate objective of an enlightened Sri Lankan community with diverse cultures but equality before law is achieved.

Under the existing constitutional and political realities in Sri Lanka, these objectives cannot be achieved without confronting politicians and their institutions. However, the objective of the confrontation is not to grab power. It is to ensure the achievement of the objectives sketched out above. Therefore, the SSM has decided to form a political organisation and get it registered with the Commissioner of Elections so that if the present regime continues, it can be challenged electorally.

In this article, we have concentrated on the tragic issues directly affecting human life in Sri Lanka and the immediate socio-political issues relating to the need for a non-violent alternative. This does not mean that we should give less importance to the violence inflicted upon our life support systems by inappropriate applications of science and technology. Violence done to living cells, to human beings, and to the planet as a living organism should also be our constant concern.

10

Revalidating Gandhi

Non-violent Action in the Globalising India

VIDYA JAIN

The article addresses the most critical issue of social justice in the globalising India and offers study of Gandhian techniques of non-violent action. The hegemonistic paradigm of globalisation has sought to undermine not only the normative-centric social values and economic justice but also tends to dehumanise the world web. In this context, non-violent action is the imperative of time in order to realise social justice for marginalised section of society.

The article also tries to assess and re-evaluate the relevance and efficacy of the Gandhian techniques of non-violent action in the context of India. Since marginalised and deprived people are left behind in the development syndrome and so Gandhian vision of harmonious society has to be revalidated in the present context.

In this article, the author argues that there is enduring relevance of Mahatma Gandhi's philosophy for social transformation through non-violent actions. A non-violent revolution, Gandhi said, is not a "programme of seizure of power" but a "programme of transformation of relationships" among communities, classes and people. His non-violent non-cooperation movement was also intended for social justice. That is why, he had given a clarion call to the people not to cooperate with those who were the "enemies of social justice". Gandhi clearly wrote: "I have always held that social justice, even to the least and the lowliest, is impossible of attainment by force. I have further believed that it is possible by further training of the lowliest by non-violent means to secure redress of the wring suffered by them. That means is non-violent non-cooperation." Gandhi, therefore, favoured a society in which all are equal and there are no exploiters to exploit the weak and poor. Today, his concept of social justice has become more relevant in the light of a mushroom growth of exploiters in the new form of MNCs and corporate tycoons.

The relevance of Gandhian thought will continue to grow as the contradictions which the modern civilisation creates but cannot deal with will continue to grow and hence the civilisation crisis which we are undergoing deepens. These contradictions are the production of weapons of mass destruction, the violent nature of social orders, violence and destruction of nature and of various life forms on this earth, the structural violence of absolute and relative poverty violence in everyday life, an erosion of inner life of humans, etc. Gandhi has a special place in today's world which is the highest stage of the violent social orders.

Gandhi's concern for the poor prodded him to launch non-violent movement for the empowerment of grassroots people through basic education, liberation of women and fighting against injustices perpetrated upon by the dominant over the dominated. At the same time, he was in favour of involving the rich in his nation-wide programme for alleviation of poverty. That was a unique experiment that encouraged Gandhian followers like Vinoba Bhave for Bhoodan movement.

Gandhian Satyagraha and Swadeshi movements were aimed at assertion of human dignity for all Indians, especially the poor, downtrodden and marginalised sections of society. Gandhi essentially believed that non-violent movements are indispensable for resolution of conflicts, which emanate from poverty, economic exploitation and unemployment.

Gandhi had developed Swadeshi movement during our struggle for freedom as a weapon to cut the roots of colonial economic interests and exploitation as well as to utilise our local resources and talents. Swadeshi is the only way to solve the problems of exploitation and inequality caused by globalisation.

Challenges of Globalisation

The twentieth century was a strange and contradictory century. It was the bloodiest century in history with two world wars and a number of bitter and endless conflicts. The last decades have put the world on the path of globalisation where phenomena of intolerance, terrorism and war are inherent.

If we look at the balance sheet of development and human well-being, achievements and deficits, profit and people, power and poverty, global over-class and local under-class, universalism and particularism, totalitarianism and democracy, homogenisation and pluralism, hegemony and equilibrium, masculinity and feminity and above all global village and fractured civilisation, a disastrous picture of new world (dis)order emerge. The basic nature of world cosmos (truth, beauty and goodness) is shattered.

Though formal colonial rule has been handed down, Western domination and control continues to have an impact on the vast majority of the non-Western world in ways which are more subtle and sophisticated but no less destructive and devastating. The newly independent nations, after freeing themselves from their colonial masters, asked for development aids from the same colonisers. The donor comes with a new agenda of neo-colonialism. As a result, even though formally independent, the dominant West controls global politics and economics in one way or the other.

In politics it controls through UNO, while in economics it dominates the globe in IMF, World Bank, WTO and so on. Dominating the information and technologies it is capturing the global cultural scene through films, music, foods and fashions. Global culture is brought by a variety of social and cultural developments such as the existence of a world satellite information system, emergence of consumption and consumerism, the cultivation of cosmopolitan lifestyles, emergence of global sports (e.g., cricket in the place of local village sports), spread of world tourism, the decline of sovereignty of nation-states, global health problems like AIDS, etc. It maintains the global militancy through its virtual monopoly over high-grade weapons and asking everybody to sign treaties like NPT and CTBT.

Globalisation is not a simple but a complex set of processes, which operate at political, economic, social, cultural and ideological levels. By catching hold of economy the West wishes to have a cognitive and ideological superiority over the rest of the world. The charming concepts, such as the of global village, are fake and illusionary and it is nothing else than concentration of wealth, power and knowledge in the hands of West.

Globalisation has generated widespread social, economic and cultural insecurity. It is not the cross-cultural interaction of diverse societies but an imposition of a particular culture on all others. It is the predation of one class, one race, one nation and often one gender. In 'global' the dominant 'local' seeks global control. The global is not universal human interest; it represents a particular interest and culture which has been globalised through its reach and control.[1] It is not merely economic colonisation but imposition of cultural autocracy. The capitalist is riding over the science, technology and media for the expansion of their exploitation network.

The liberalisation of trade has led to the enslavement of people. The industrial technological development, military supremacy, cultural hegemony, arrogance of English language, dehumanising competition, commodification and commercialisation have all endangered the very existence of human souls and mother nature. The world "composed of autonomous individuals and big market, is not the world that anyone lives in – not even the free enterprises of welfare liberal ideologies. This world is a world without families. It is also a world without neighbourhoods, ethic communities, churches, cities and towns, even nations (as opposed to states)."[2]

The world is currently witnessing the worst phase of human history in which more wars have taken place, new forms of conflicts have emerged, civil wars are rampant, human rights are violated and human poverty is on the increase.

In this era of global crisis, which is in fact a civilisation crisis, many contradictions emerge like (a) the production of weapons of mass destruction, (b) the violent nature of social order, (c) destruction of nature, (d) the structural violence of absolute and relative poverty, and (e) increasing violence in everyday life.

Impact of Gandhi on Non-violent Movements

Gandhi has a special place in today's world which is the "highest stage of the violent social order". On the other hand, innumerable non-violent movements are going on in different parts of the world. These are essentially for acquiring justice for all and for ending exploitation of all kinds which is essence of violence. These non-violent movements create the peace paradigm and are three-fold:

1. These provide more sustainable, appropriate model of development as against Marxism and capitalism, viz., peace paradigm (Gandhian model).
2. These aim at spiritual transformation – a more popular and secular phrase in recent decades has been "cultural revolution" creating "culture of peace".[3]
3. Modern era is said to be an era of social movements as from regional to global, there is a sense of connection with history (the continuity with previous social struggles).

Gandhi stands out as an apostle of peace and non-violent change. We can make following observations on the impact of Gandhi on peace and non-violent social movements:

1. The disarmament movement against weapons of mass destruction cannot be violent. The philosophy of non-violent social action is the very heart of thought and the political practice of Gandhi.
2. The highest level of non-violent political action was India's national movement led by Gandhi.
3. Every social movement aspires to be a mass movement. The universal suffrage, women's rights, trade unions, peasant struggles, dalit (backward caste and class) movement, and above all national movement were mass movements.
4. There is a greater degree of voluntarism in these movements. The hierarchy does not pertain to centralist organisation. There is a widespread acceptance of the rule that the decisions be taken by consensus and not be split vote.
5. One important aspect of a movement is the symbols that it uses. The symbols used in these social movements are not of aggression but are symbols of non-violence, harmony, togetherness, human love and oneness.
6. The most important impact that Gandhi makes is with respect to the method of politics. Gandhian method was the method of non-violent civil disobedience. In this method, the individual, his initiative, transformation and self-discipline are central. In this process of political action, the idea is not to hurt, defeat or overpower the enemy but to transform, reform and uplift him by moral transformation.

Gandhian Activism in India

There were many non-violent, Gandhian-style movements in India including:

(i) *Sarvodaya Movement:* The vehicle for the development of the theory and practice of India's nonviolent revolution has been the Sarvodaya (welfare of all) movement. The experience of the Sarvodaya movement's first 21 years under the guidance of Vinoba Bhave, the initiator of the campaigns for voluntary land gifts in the form of *Bhoodan* and *Gramdan* (village gifting), has been very revolutionary. Vinoba's influence in shaping the movement's strategy remained paramount. Vinoba's "gentle, gentler, gentlest" approach helped to revise the concept of *Gramdan*. Under this, the participants agreed to surrender to the village community the ownership of 5 per cent their land holdings in the village for distribution to the landless but were allowed to retain possession of 95 percent of them.

(ii) *The J.P. Movement:* This was inaugurated by Jai Prakash Narayan, a leading Gandhian socialist leader, in 1973 against the Indira Gandhi's government. Students were mobilised to campaign against corrupt politicians, black-marketeering, profiteering and hoarding by capitalists that led to price rise, the evasion of land reform laws and unemployment. The people organised *satyagrahas* at nearly three thousand places and on five hundred occasions. The police beat up and arrested large number of people, including political leaders. Despite great provocation, *satyagrahis* remained non-violent.

(iii) *The Total Revolution:* Jai Prakash's protest against the government of Indira Gandhi was what he called his campaign for "total revolution" in India. This followed the old Gandhian path of deploying political discontent to drive forward a wider movement for all-round social, economic and cultural change. Gram Sabhas (Village Assemblies) were established and people were mobilised.[4]

(iv) *The Chhatra Yuva Sangharsh Vahini (Students and Youth Wing):* JP started an organisation called the Chhatra Vahini – a non-violent army to work for his total revolution. This is a great example of non-violent student and youth movement.

Recent Non-violent Movements

(i) *Anti-liquor Movement by Women:* In recognition of the strong movement against liquor which has been inspired by Gandhi and which brought about mobilisation of many women within the struggle and prohibition was implemented in many parts of India. Mrs Vimla and Sunderlal Bahuguna started a far more powerful movement in Uttarakhand, an Indian state. They launched a *satyagraha* (plea for truth) against the awarding of a contract to sell liquor in the village near their Ashram. Afterwards, this became a nation-wide movement supported by many political parties.

(ii) *Chipko Andolan (Hugging to Trees):* The Chipko Andolan was started by Gandhian activists. This was a protest against the forest policy of the government in the Uttaranchal division of Uttar Pradesh. With the extensive constructions of roads in the region in the 1960s trucks were able to enter the hills and remove timber on an unprecedented scale. Politicians took bribes to ensure that timber felling contracts were awarded to industrialists and timber dealers at concessional levels. This caused lack of fuelwood for daily cooking as well as fast run-off causing floods and landslides. Then, the villagers decided to protest against cutting of trees under the banner of this movement, which was women-centric in its earlier phase.

(iii) *Narmada Bachao Andolan (Save the Narmada Movement):* One of the most powerful campaigns of civil disobedience since 1980 has been against the construction of a huge dam on the Narmada river. The organisation which was formed to fight against this project was Narmada Bachao Andolan is described as environmentalist. The chief stated goal of the movement is creating an alternative political culture based on Gandhian principles. It has been driven by a very Gandhian belief that modern developmental projects supported by the state-run roughshod over the economic needs and civil rights of the mass of the rural poor, and that the only way to counter such tyranny is through non-violent mass resistance. The two main leaders, Medha Patkar and Baba Amte, have used fasting as a weapon. Narmada Bachao Andolan is best seen, therefore, as a campaign for economic and civil rights that employs the Gandhian style of *satyagraha*.

Gandhi has considerable influence on Chipko Andolan and Narmada Bachao Movement, especially in adoption of his technique of non-violent protest and policies against heavy industrialisation by environmental activists.[5]

(iv) *The Swadeshi Movement (Self-Reliance):* The ultimate goal of Gandhism is to establish Panchayati Raj (local self-government) at village level, the economically self-sufficient, politically self-governing and culturally non-violent village republic, which is the guarantee of democracy, true humanism, non-violence and lasting peace to realise this true village democracy.

Urbanisation and industrialisation have stolen the works of potter, weaver, blacksmith, carpenter and other self-employed workers in the village. The millions of poor people in rural areas have lost their works and dying of hunger and sickness. Thus, the Swadeshi movement is the humble reply to excessive mechanisation. It means use of local raw materials, exchange in the local markets and control of local territory as well as society. "The Swadeshi movement is not just a technical alternative. It involves a belief that truth and non-violence shall be ultimate victors."[6] It is a belief of incorporation of human values within the body of science and technical practice.

The movement run on non-violent lines. Swadeshi is an anti-colonial concept. It refers to the structures of power which colonise both externally and internally. It is search for our own identities.[7] Like individuals, communities and nations too have their own identity. Global economy has no concern for the local identities, the contexuality, the ecology, style of life, experience and indigenous skills.

Swadeshi is the key concept in Gandhi's philosophy. It is not merely an economic doctrine but also has ideological implications. In Swadeshi Gandhi not only envisaged economic salvation of India but also found an answer to psychological and political problems.

The Gandhian approach to development stressed on "equity" (i.e., "justice" in distribution and exchange). Gandhi's concept of "development" (Swaraj) is based on a notion of "community" and an ethic of "justice for all". Thus, Gandhi's Swaraj (development) goes hand in hand with the concept of "local self-reliance" (Swadeshi). In *Hind Swaraj* Gandhi developed a conceptualisation of independence (i.e., Swaraj) which was not mearly restricted to political independence. He had an ideal of Swaraj. Swaraj, for Gandhi, was economic, cultural and social development as well as political independence. For Gandhi, the concept of Swaraj meant India should undergo a major structural transformation. Such economic, political and cultural change should be gradual and evolutionary. The key to successful "home rule" would be self-reliance. He believed that each step along the way should be completely integrated so that basic harmony of the nature and humans would not be harmed. Such development will not create unemployment and poverty. Rather, it will minimise the costs of disruptive aspects of change to individuals, and maximise local self-reliance and indigenous technologies.

Swadeshi is the search for our nation's identity. Gandhi says, "My nationalism is as broad as my Swadeshi. I want India's rise so that the whole world may benefit. I do not want India to rise on the ruin of other nations."[8] He further says, "No nation on earth has risen without adopting Swadeshi as the principle of life."[9] For Gandhi, Swadeshi was a positive concept based on what a community has in terms of resources, institutions and structures. Imposed resources, institutions and structures leave people unfree and non-sustainable. Swadeshi for Gandhi was central to the creation of peace, freedom and sustainable development. Swadeshi or self-organisation in economic affairs is the basis of economic freedom, without which there can be no political freedom or self-rule. Swadeshi is Swaraj (self-rule).

For Gandhi, Swaraj and Swadeshi are complementary. For true Swaraj, Swadeshi is an important imperative to be foilowed. "Swaraj is my birthright. Swaraj is the birthright of all people", Gandhi says, Gandhi's Swaraj does not imply governance by a centralised state but decentralised self-governance by local communities. During the period of external domination, when people are denied economic and political freedom, it requires peaceful non-cooperation with unjust laws and regimes which Gandhi realised and stated in *Hind Swaraj*: "As long as the superstition that people should obey unjust laws exists, so long will slavery exist."[10] And, a non-violent resistance can remove such a superstition. The word 'Swadeshi', however, was not coined by Gandhi himself. It was in vogue in the national movement even before his emergence on the political scene. In fact, Dadabhai Naoroji, Sri Aurobindo, Tilak, Gokhale, Ranade and others propounded the doctrine of Swadeshi.

Swadeshi extends to all aspects of institutionalised life: economic, political, religious and cultural. Ramashray Roy discusses Gandhi's concept of Swadeshi in terms of his General Sociological Theory of Self and Society.[11] Basically, Gandhi was opposed to excessively rapid capitalist development and disruption of local communities. He anticipated the modern notion of appropriate technology. He emphasised the importance of local people's knowledge to solve local problems.

The idea of Swadeshi is as old as national consciousness. Arising spontaneously and mostly in an unorganised and isolated manner, the Swadeshi movement in the early phase gathered widespread support from the vernacular press and the local efforts of innumerable faceless men. It created a patriotic sentiment which served as moral force to boycott foreign goods.

Gandhi's deep interest, support and propaganda for Swadeshi had deep linkages with the economic problems of unemployment amongst people. He encouraged both men and women to ply *charkha* (small machine on which threads are made by hands), spin *khadi* and boycott foreign goods. It promoted a deep sense of love for goods manufactured within the country and their use generated the spirit of selfless sacrifice amongst the masses.

Swadeshi is not obsolete in today's context. It is the creative alternative to the rule of centralised nation-state as well as the rule of global corporations and institutions such as WTO. Economic freedom requires reduced control by the World Bank, IMF, WTO, the G-7 and global corporations. It is freedom for the people to have secure livelihoods, to have control over the policies and resources that make their livelihoods.

Swadeshi, as conceived by Gandhi, was not against either internationalism or universal brotherhood. He wanted India to be a self-dependent state as only such a nation can support the world. He was of firm belief that a weak state could neither sustain itself nor help others. According to him, the main aim of Swadeshi was the protection of the home industry. Gandhi did not favour isolation of India from the world. He categorically asserted that his Swadeshi provided for foreign import if it was useful for the country or the people. In his opinion, Swadeshi which excluded the use of every foreign things, no matter how beneficial it may be, was its narrow interpretation.

A couple of years back, the idea of Swadeshi was considered outdated. To the economist it was anti-economic, to the intellectual it was anti-modern, to the industrialist it was anti-technology, to the media it was an amusement, and to the policy maker it was an embarrassment. The combined column of all these powerful groups created a deep prejudice against the idea of Swadeshi in India and outside.[12]

But now the Swadeshi view has overcome the entire unfair attempt to label it as irrelevant and obsolete. Today, many intellectuals admit that Swadeshi is not a reactionary idea. Many industrialists agree on Swadeshi as the idea of strengthening Indian industry and projecting India as multinationalist. Swadeshi means trusting our own geniuses to handle our own problems unique to ourselves.

The Swadeshi ideology is not redundant or outmoded. It has scientific value. In fact, no country has risen to heights without paying proper attention to its indigenous institutions and resources. China has shown it to the world. It does not mean that we isolate ourselves from the world or the process of liberalisation should be reversed. What we need today is a well-conceived, multi-pronged strategy by which we can realise the economic growth on a sustainable basis. We should put more emphasis on social policies, education, poverty and raising standards of living of people. This can be achieved only by reformulating India's development policy. We have to place greater emphasis on labour-intensive sector than on the capital and technology. This type of economic policy would be real Swadeshi.

Gandhi's policies are revolutionary. These follow from his personal experience. After all he gave up all types of privileges by choosing simplicity in his life. His philosophy involves strengthening the individual, family, community and society which in turn by its very nature weakens, fundamentally, the hold of the existing market and state framework. Even though Gandhian economics appeal to economic elites but they are threatened by it, because its objective is to eliminate elitism and thereby the elite. Just as addicts do not want to give up addictions, elites do not want to give up their elitism. The major appeal of the Gandhian economic is to the masses to which he belonged. No government has promulgated Gandhian policies.[13] The need today is to resuscitate a positive, an inclusive, a generous Swadeshi, to build and renew confidence in our abilities and skills in our people and knowledge system.

Notes

1. See, Vandana Shiva, "Arthic Swaraj or Economic Slavery?" *The Observer,* February 3, 1998.
2. Robert N. Bellah, "Community Properly Understood: A Defence of 'Democratic Communitarianism", in Amitai Etzioni (ed.), *The Essential Communitarian Reader,* p. 17.
3. M.L Handa, 'Global Peace Movements: The Highest Stage of Social Movements and the Impact of Gandhi', in Mahendra Kumar (ed.), *Non-Violence: Contemporary Issues and Challenge,* Gandhi Peace Foundation, New Delhi, 1994.
4. David Hardiman, *Gandhi in His Times and Ours,* Permanent Black, New Delhi, 2003.
5. Ramchandra Guha, 'Mahatma Gandhi and the Environmental Movements', in A. Raghuramaraju (ed.), *Debating Gandhi: A Reader,* Oxford University Press, New Delhi, 2006.
6. Sunil Saharabudhey, 'The Machine', in A. Raghuramaraju (ed.), *Debating Gandhi: A Reader,* Oxford University Press, New Delhi, 2006, p. 192.
7. Erik Erikson, *Gandhi's Truth: On the Origin of Militant Non-Violence,* W.E. Morton, New York, 1993.
8. M.K. Gandhi, *An Autobiography: The Story of My Experiments with Truth,* Navjivan Publishing House, Ahmedabad, 1940.
9. *Collected Works of Mahatma Gandhi,* Publication Division, Government of India, New Delhi 1958, Vol. XV, p. 379.
10. M.K. Gandhi, *Hind Swaraj,* Navjivan Publishing House, Ahmedabad, 1938, p. 29.
11. Ramashray Roy, *Self and Society: A Study in Gandhian Thought,* Sage Publications, New Delhi, in collaboration with the United Nations University, 1985.
12. S. Gurumurthy, "Swadeshi and Nationalism", *Seminar,* No. 469, New Delhi, September 1998.
13. Ramesh Diwan, *"Mahatma Gandhi, Amartya Sen and Poverty",* *Gandhi Marg,* Vol. 20, No.4, January–March, 1999.

11

Global Constitutionalism and Japan's Constitutional Pacifism[1]

AKIHIKO KIMIJIMA

It is noteworthy that discussions of global constitutionalism have become very common in recent years. The Japanese academia is no exception (Urata, 2005; Mogami, 2007; Kimijima, 2009). Caution is required, however, because various authors use the term and concept differently. There are several different kinds of global constitutionalism. My own understanding will be discussed further later in this article, but perhaps it is helpful to mention some of its elements here.

I use the terms "constitution" and "constitutionalism" in a broader sense. Constitution is a set of fundamental principles for regulating power in a given political community, and constitutionalism is a project to regulate the exercise of power by rules, laws and institutions. With an emergence of global political community, we can talk about global constitutionalism. I understand that global constitutionalism is a project in which counter-hegemonic global civil society regulates the exercise of hegemonic power relying on rules, laws, institutions and other non-violent means. Global constitutionalism also refers to global civil society's efforts to replace military options with civilian options in coping with the issues of human rights violations, conflicts and humanitarian crises. In this sense we have witnessed the increasingly common practice of global constitutionalism in recent years.

The *heiwa shugi* or "pacifism"[2] of Japan's post-war constitution has been, and continues to be, an issue of intense debate and political contention. Article 9 is radical in its language of total rejection of war and militarism. It is a mixture of power politics and idealism. On one hand, it was a provision of complete disarmament of the axis state by the allied powers, but immediately it came to be seen as an obstacle to the US-Japan military alliance that fought the Cold War. In spite of Article 9, Japan's rearmament has steadily continued. On the other hand, the Japanese people embraced Article 9, and anti-militarism became a culture of post-war Japan. The Japanese people have resisted revising Article 9, and because of this the process of Japan's comeback as a major military power has not yet been completed.

In this article, I elaborate global constitutionalism and the "pacifism" of the Japanese Constitution and connect them. Both in Japan and the United States there is an argument that Japan should revise Article 9 and send the 'Self-Defence Forces' overseas more frequently, and, in doing so, Japan would contribute more to international peace and security. I disagree with this as I think that Japan's contribution to international peace is not in the Japanese government's dispatch of its forces as a US ally but the Japanese people's participation in global civil society's efforts to create peace by non-violent means with Article 9 preserved. I will explain this by linking the "pacifism" of Japan's Constitution with global civil society's efforts in global constitutionalism.

Global Constitutional Thinking

Constitution is "the system or body of fundamental principles according to which a nation, state, or body politic is constituted and governed," according to the *Oxford English Dictionary*. Although the written constitutions framed and adopted by the peoples after the American and French Revolutions are the paradigms of modern constitutions, we can talk about constitutions in a broader sense. It is often said that wherever there is a political community there is a constitution. Now that we have overlapping political communities such as local, national and international, we find three levels of constitutions, viz., city ordinances, the sovereign states' constitutions, and the United Nations Charter. It is not difficult to see the rudiments of a constitution of international society in the Charter of the United Nations (Fassbender, 2009).

At stated earlier, constitutionalism is a project to regulate the exercise of political power by rules, laws and institutions. In the modern sovereign state system, the major exercise of political power is the exercise of state's power – police power and military power. As a result, a project to regulate the exercise of these powers through a state's constitution and its laws is the typical form of modern constitutionalism. In the post-modern world, although constitutionalism of individual states continues to be most important, probably it is insufficient for regulating the exercise of power.

We have been witnessing a phenomenon of globalisation of the exercise of political, military, corporate and monetary powers beyond national borders. The worldwide deployment of the US military forces using overseas bases and the worldwide activities of multinational corporations and investors are obvious examples. If the political, military and corporate powers are exercised globally, our project of constitutionalism will need to create the means and mechanisms to regulate globally exercised power. We need a project of global constitutionalism.

At this moment, I think it is useful to trace the history of global constitutional thinking. We at once notice that there have been numerous world order proposals since the early 19th century. When examining the world order, people have often worked from an analogy of the domestic order. People thought of international society as an imperfect domestic society and perfecting international society by domestic analogy became their task. Hidemi Suganami has explored in detail how the world order proposals in the 19th and 20th centuries were based on thinking of domestic analogy (Suganami, 1989). According to Suganami, many of the 19th century world order proposals used their own states' constitutions as models.

Post-Hiroshima-Nagasaki Moment

When we trace the history of global constitutional thinking, we also notice the research on global constitutionalism and the world government movement in the post-World War II United States. Two research publications are important. One was the *Preliminary Draft of a World Constitution*, usually known as the Chicago Draft of a World Constitution, which was written in 1948 by the Committee to Frame a World Constitution – a group organised chiefly around scholars at the University of Chicago (Committee to Frame a World

Constitution, 1948). Another was Grenville Clark and Louis Sohn's magnum opus, *World Peace Through World Law* (Clark and Sohn, 1966). This book, first published in 1958 as an outcome of two lawyers' collaborative research since October 1945, is a provision-by-provision proposal for revision of the United Nations Charter aiming to strengthen its functions for world peace.

It was the atomic bombings of Hiroshima and Nagasaki that propelled these scholars and lawyers toward global constitutional thinking. Robert M. Hutchins, Chancellor of the University of Chicago, who organised the Committee to Frame a World Constitution, told his radio audience as early as August 12, 1945 that the shock of Hiroshima made him realise the necessity of a world state (Boyer, 1994: 38). In addition to serving as President of the Committee to Frame a World Constitution, Hutchins was very active in promoting the cause of world government. The world government movement had momentum for a couple of years in post-war America. For Clark and Sohn, the United Nations Charter was inadequate and a strengthened United Nations was a prerequisite for world peace. It is important to be reminded that the United Nations Charter, signed in San Francisco on June 26, 1945, predated the advent of nuclear weapons. Unlike the Chicago Draft, the Clark-Sohn proposal was not an argument for a world government but for a combination of universal and complete disarmament of sovereign states, strengthening the UN's conflict resolving functions, and establishing the standing UN Peace Force. In any case the Clark-Sohn proposal was conceived as their expression of drastic, new thinking in the nuclear age, or, I would like to say, in the post-Hiroshima-Nagasaki age.

Kai Bird and Martin J. Sherwin wrote in the biography of J. Robert Oppenheimer that "(t)he scientists knew that the gadget was going to force a redefinition of the whole notion of national sovereignty" (Bird and Sherwin, 2005: 289). In 1946, Oppenheimer believed that without world government there would be no perpetual peace but that world government could not be realised soon. He argued that all states should agree to renounce their sovereignty in terms of nuclear energy (ibid.: 341–42). Both the Chicago Draft and the Clark-Sohn proposal were examples of a redefinition of the notion of national sovereignty. They represented a tendency to limit state sovereignty and delegate some aspects of it to world institutions. These are forms of global constitutionalism. And, as Suganami says, their global constitutional thinking was based on thinking of domestic analogy. It is true that they were too legalistic and static, lacking strategies of transition. However, their intention was to stimulate discussions on future world order, and both of them were aware of the impact of the Cold War. As the Cold War intensified, these ideas became marginalised. And, after the end of the Cold War, discussions on global constitutionalism have been revitalised.

Theory and Practice of Global Constitutionalism

World Order Models Project's Conception

Among the theories of global constitutionalism after the Cold War, the most useful one for our purpose is that of the World Order Models Project (WOMP) (Falk, Johansen and Kim, 1993). Led by Saul Mendlovitz and Richard Falk, the WOMP began in the 1960s as a kind of successor to the Clark-Sohn proposal, and it became an international joint research project with participation by scholars of Europe, Japan, and the Global South.

According to Falk and others, global constitutionalism refers to a set of international norms, rules, procedures and institutions for realising peace, economic welfare, social justice, and ecological balance for global society. They think, the world now comprises three systems. The first is the states system, which is made up of territorial states and the corporations, banks, military forces, and media that support them. The second is international governmental institutions including the United Nations system. And, the third system is composed of the non-state actors and individuals who act through NGOs, various kinds of citizen groups, social movements, and other vehicles. Presently, the world can be conceived as a three-layered structure comprising the states system, the UN system and global civil society. A set of transnational norms, rules, procedures and institutions for realising peace and other values should permeate all three layers. While we must work to achieve democracy within the states system and the UN system, collaborations and partnerships among civil society organisations, states and the UN are also important (ibid.: 9).

One possible direction of global constitutionalism is an integration of sovereign states and the creation of world government. This could take the form of strengthening the United Nations' powers and functions, which was the direction that the Chicago Draft and the Clark-Sohn proposal pursued. Besides the practical political difficulties of this course, there is the paradox of creating a greater power of world government in order to regulate the powers of sovereign states. A world government would sit far away from the global citizenry and it would be an enormous challenge for them to control it. The problem of "deficits of democracy" would be serious, and it may be that demerits would outweigh merits. In contrast, WOMP's global constitutionalism does not seek a centralisation of state power, but it emphasises the global citizenry's effort to control state power from below.

In my (this author's) view, when we observe a form of power and its exercise in present global society, we notice the following phenomenon: although there is no world government nor a single power centre in the present world, various actors such as G8 governments, multinational corporations, the WTO, finance capitals, dominant mass media, and think tanks, interacting with one another, constitute a giant power complex, or informal global power (Gill, 2008: 183–205). This informal global power makes decisions that influence tens of millions of people in the world. A project to regulate the informal global power complex is what I call a project of global constitutionalism.

Among the exercises of informal global power, it is particularly important to regulate two of them ... the military power of the US and its allies; and the power of actors of global capitalism.[3] They are the pillars of the informal global power complex. The exercises of these powers have brought direct and structural violence and threatened human lives and the global natural environment. Thus, to design and practice global constitutionalism that regulates these powers is an urgent task.

When we seek to regulate informal global power, constitutionalism of individual states ... parliamentary democracy and judicial review ... plays a certain important role, but in global society as a whole "deficits of constitutionalism" occur, so to speak. In addition to regulations based on individual states, transnational and global regulation of power is required. Here, multilateralism and international organisations are extremely important (Mogami, 2007). So far, discussions on global constitutionalism have centred on these aspects. However, "deficits of constitutionalism" have also clearly been seen in the United Nations. On one hand, all member-states are bound by the Security Council resolutions. On the other hand, when permanent members of the Security Council decide to go to war, the United Nations has no power to stop them. This is an example of "deficits of constitutionalism". And "deficits of democracy" have been a problem of the United Nations and, accordingly, democratising the UN is also our task (Patomaki and Teivainen, 2004). I believe that, finally, the actors who regulate informal global power will be global citizens and their associations or, in other words, global civil society. By regulating informal global power, they protect their human lives, their human dignities, and their human rights. By doing so they will be empowered.

When we design and practise global constitutionalism, in order to regulate the exercise of informal global power, strategy is necessary, but it must not be a static, legalistic blueprint like the Chicago Draft. I understand that global constitutionalism is a process in which counter-hegemonic global civil society intervenes in the dynamic power relations of global society.[4]

Accomplishments of the 1990s and Beyond

We witnessed global constitutionalism operating in the 1990s. On several occasions in the 1990s, global civil society succeeded in regulating military power. These instances included the World Court Project, which elicited from the International Court of Justice an advisory opinion on the illegality of the threat or use of nuclear weapons (Dewes, 1998), and the International Campaign to Ban Landmines (ICBL), which worked with the Canadian government (the Ottawa Process) and achieved the Convention on the Prohibition of Landmines (Cameron, Lawson and Tomlin, 1998). Both are cases in which NGOs took the initiative, created NGO networks, and worked in league with like-minded governments to regulate military power. It is characteristic that many governments that worked with NGOs were middle powers or small powers.

Recently, ICBL has again succeeded in achieving a treaty to regulate military power. This time ICBL and other NGOs formed the Cluster Munition Coalition, an NGO network for achieving a cluster munition ban treaty, worked with the Norwegian government (this time the Oslo Process), and accomplished the cluster munition ban treaty. In addition, the International Coalition to Ban Uranium Weapons (ICBUW), an NGO network seeking a uranium weapons ban treaty, has been very active and its impact remains to be seen. All of these cases represent examples of the practice of global constitutionalism.

How to Regulate US Military Power?

Arguably, regulating the exercise of the US military power may be the most important task of global constitutionalism because the US military power is the primary pillar of the informal global power complex. The "mission" to regulate it is probably the most difficult.

The US President with the involvement of the US Congress exercises the US military power. Regulating the war-making powers of the President and Congress is, firstly, an issue of constitutionalism in the United States. Second, international law experts scrutinise the legality and legitimacy of a specific exercise of the US military power. These are important elements of global constitutionalism, but we need more than that.

The impact of the US military power ... its presence and its exercise ... is global (Calder, 2007; Johnson, 2000, 2004, 2006, 2010). Tens of millions of people all over the world have been influenced by the US military. As affected parties, these stakeholders think that they should have a chance to express their opinions. In theory, citizens of other countries can convey their opinions to the US government by way of their own governments, but, in reality, there are alliances of government elites between the US and its allies and its client states, and government elites in, for example, Tokyo, Seoul and Manila usually ignore their citizens' opinions. For both domestic and global constitutionalism, US citizens play pivotal roles. First, they elect the US President and the US Congress, and their votes may influence the exercise of the US military power. Second, citizens of other countries approach US citizens by way of international NGOs, and US citizens may help influence the US public opinion and lobby the US Congress, providing an avenue of domestic expression for these international NGOs.

The United States has 716 military bases in foreign countries.[5] These bases support the exercise of the US military power and, thereby, cause direct and structural violence to the people living in the vicinity. There are movements against the US military bases all over the world. These movements, on the occasion of the World Social Forum in Mumbai in 2004, formed the International Network for the Abolition of Foreign Military Bases, and they consolidated their network when they held their international conference in Ecuador in March 2007 (Yeo, 2009). The Network includes US NGOs among its members, and it has a potential to develop a strategy for influencing the US public opinion.

Replacing Military Options with Civilian Options

For our task of regulating military power, it is important to notice that there have been worldwide efforts to replace military options with civilian options when dealing with conflicts and humanitarian crises. They, are seen in the spheres of government, international organisations and global civil society. People have increasingly realised that civilians can better perform many functions currently carried out by soldiers, such as peacekeeping. We can observe the trend that military options have been replaced by civilian options in many areas.

A practical manifestation of this trend on the governmental level is the development of the civil peace service in European countries (Wallis and Junge, 2002). This is a project that trains civilian peace workers to use non-violent means to manage conflicts, sends them to conflict areas in other countries at government expense, and has helped them with post-conflict peace building. This project was proposed in Germany in the early 1990s and became a reality at the end of the 1990s. It is a government-NGO partnership for which Germany's Federal Ministry for Economic Cooperation and Development provides funding, and which is implemented by German NGOs. Currently, in Germany, each year about 100 people undergo four months of training in non-violent conflict resolution and other skills, and then are sent to Balkan countries, Latin America, Africa, and other places for two years. The project is an important part of Germany's development assistance policy. While Germany's civil peace service is the most advanced, Austria, France, the Netherlands, Switzerland, Sweden and Italy have their versions of civil peace service projects. In some countries, conscientious objectors can join a civil peace service project as an alternative to military service.

An important instance of practice by an international organisation is the Kosovo Verification Mission, which the Organisation for Security and Cooperation in Europe (OSCE) sent to Kosovo during the conflict there. When the Kosovo conflict erupted, the OSCE sent over 1,000 civilian observers to the area in an attempt to deter the conflict from becoming violent. Researchers and the NGO activists often claim that sending thousands of foreign civilians into conflict areas can prevent conflicts from becoming violent, and the Kosovo Verification Mission can be seen as exactly that kind of attempt. Because the mission was forced to withdraw before its activities were fully implemented, it is difficult to assess its result, but Paul Rogers, professor of peace studies at the University of Bradford, thought highly of the mission and its activities in Kosovo and suggested the need for developing this kind of large-scale civilian observer forces (Rogers, 2002: 125).

It is global civil society that has made the most efforts to replace military options with civilian options in dealing with conflicts and humanitarian crises. There are many NGOs engaging in unarmed civilian peacekeeping (Weber, 1996; Moser-Puangsuwan and Weber, 2000). These NGOs send peace teams comprised of multinational, trained, unarmed citizens into conflict areas, where they accompany local human rights activists and lawyers who might be targets of attack from military groups. The international civilian presence is an attempt to prevent killings and keep conflicts from turning violent. Having foreigners accompany local activists sends a message that international society is watching and, thereby, deters violence using the eyes of international society. Among the NGOs of this kind, probably Peace Brigades International (PBI) has been most visible, and PBI's activities in Guatemala in the 1980s established a paradigm (Mahony and Eguren, 1997). Based on the accomplishments of these NGOs, Non-violent Peaceforce, a new NGO that aims to send out more global and large-scale peace teams, was proposed at the Hague Appeal for Peace in 1999 amid the NATO's bombing of Yugoslavia. With the support and participation of numerous NGOs worldwide, Nonviolent Peaceforce was founded in 2002 and it began sending civilian peace workers to Sri Lanka in 2003 (Kimijima, 2008).

The above-mentioned examples are cases where conflicts and humanitarian crises have been dealt with internationally. In defending one's own community against invasion, I think that Gene Sharp's theory of civilian-based defense (Sharp, 1990, 2005) is relatively well known. It constitutes another area in which military options can be replaced with civilian options. I think, these trends of the military being replaced by the civilian are also one aspect of global constitutionalism.

The Genealogy of the Japanese Constitution

Now, we turn to the Japanese Constitution. Before we begin the discussion on the "pacifism" of the Japanese Constitution, I think it is useful to trace the legislative history.[6] The making of the Constitution of Japan of 1946 was an important component and probably a climax of the allied occupation. In October 1945 the Supreme Command for the Allied Powers (SCAP) suggested to the Japanese government the necessity of constitutional revision for demilitarisation and democratisation. In response, the Japanese government established the Constitutional Problem Investigation Committee.

With members of distinguished constitutional scholars of the time, the Committee worked on the issue of whether or not constitutional revision was necessary and, if so, how to revise the 1889 Constitution. After preliminary deliberations, the Committee decided to prepare its draft revision of the 1889 Constitution and principal members of the Committee worked on a draft. Meanwhile, suddenly on February 1, 1946, the *Mainichi* newspaper published the Committee's draft as an exclusive story. The Japanese public opinion denounced it as too reactionary. SCAP realised that they could not rely on the Japanese government for the task of constitutional revision, and they decided to prepare a draft constitution by themselves. On February 8, the Japanese government submitted its draft revision to SCAP. SCAP, for their part, were preparing their draft constitution from February 3 to 12. On February 13, at the meeting of representatives of the Japanese government and SCAP, SCAP officials flatly rejected the Japanese government's draft as totally inadequate for demilitarisation and democratisation and presented, instead, the draft constitution they had written (the so-called MacArthur Draft). The Japanese government resisted, but they had no choice but to accept the MacArthur Draft. The Japanese government's draft revision based on the MacArthur Draft was submitted to the Imperial Diet in June 1946. After several months of substantial debate, and with small changes to the Japanese government's draft, the Imperial Diet passed the Constitution of Japan and it was promulgated on November 3, 1946.

While SCAP officials played a decisive role in making Japan's new constitution, as this legislative history shows, I must emphasise two things. First, many SCAP officials who wrote the MacArthur Draft were New Dealers, or American liberals. In a way they pursued their ideals in a project of constitution-making in Japan. Second, when these Americans wrote the draft constitution for Japan, they referred to the Constitutional Research Association's "Outline for Draft Constitution". The Constitutional Research Association was a non-governmental body of independent and critical Japanese intellectuals who were concerned about post-war constitutional reform. The SCAP officials thought highly of their "Outline for Draft Constitution" and they used it as one of the sources of their draft constitution. One could perhaps say that liberals of both the US and Japan worked together on this project.

Furthermore, when the Constitutional Research Association prepared the "Outline for Draft Constitution," they referred to the draft constitutions written by Japanese intellectuals and citizens in the Freedom and People's Rights Movement in the 1880s (Koseki, 1998: 32; Dower, 1999: 358). The Freedom and People's Rights Movement was a popular movement seeking constitutional democracy against the conservative, oppressive regime. Unlike the conservative 1889 Constitution the government enacted, draft constitutions written during the process of the movement showed liberal democratic nature with much emphasis on human rights protection. As a result, the genealogy of the 1946 Constitution is as follows: the draft constitutions in the Freedom and People's Rights Movement (1880s) ... the Constitutional Research Association's Outline for Draft Constitution (December 1945) ... the MacArthur Draft (February 1946) ... the Constitution of Japan (November, 1946). It is important to note that the constitutional thought of human rights and democracy in the 1880s in Japan has flowed into the 1946 Constitution.

The "Pacifism" of the Japanese Constitution: Origin and Trajectory

> We, the Japanese people, desire peace for all time and are deeply conscious of the high ideals controlling human relationship, and we have determined to preserve our security and existence, trusting in the justice and faith of the peace-loving peoples of the world. We desire to occupy an honored place in an international society striving for the preservation of peace, and the banishment of tyranny and slavery, oppression and intolerance for all time from the earth. We recognise that all peoples of the world have the right to live in peace, free from fear and want.
>
> (second paragraph of the Preamble to the Constitution of Japan)

> Aspiring sincerely to an international peace based on justice and order, the Japanese people forever renounce war as a sovereign right of the nation and the threat or use of force as means of settling international disputes.
>
> In order to accomplish the aim of the preceding paragraph, land, sea, and air forces, as well as other war potential, will never be maintained. The right of belligerency of the state will not be recognised.
>
> (Article 9 of the Constitution of Japan)

Textually based in the Preamble and Article 9, the *heiwa shugi* or "pacifism" is one of three fundamental principles of the Japanese Constitution, in addition to popular sovereignty and protection of fundamental human rights. For the post-war Japanese people "pacifism" has been a national identity and the 1946 Constitution has often been called the "Peace Constitution".

Article 9 came from General Douglas MacArthur and his staff. While it was a provision of complete disarmament of the axis state by the allied powers, it contained an idealist nature as well. It has been argued that the "outlawry of war" movement and the 1928 Kellogg-Briand Pact influenced the idea and language of Article 9 (Fukase, 1987: 121–24; Dower, 1999: 369–70).[7] The "outlawry of war" movement was a very active peace movement during the 1920s in the United States, and it was one of the driving forces behind the Kellogg-Briand Pact (Cortright, 2008: 62–66). One could perhaps say that the US peace movement was behind Article 9. It is an irony of history that Japan, which had violated the Kellogg-Briand Pact and had begun the Asia-Pacific War, came to have Article 9, which can be seen as a reinforced Kellogg-Briand Pact. At the same time, the Kellogg-Briand Pact has been reinforced as Article 2 Clause 4 of the United Nations Charter.[8] Article 9 of the Japanese Constitution and Article 2 Clause 4 of the UN Charter share the spirit of the age.

Article 9 was conceived as providing *security against Japanese militarism*. Those who were offered security were the allied states, the people of East Asia, Japan's age-old emperor system, and the Japanese people themselves who suffered under the prior military regime. The *security of Japan* was not a major concern of Article 9. The Preamble suggested that Japan rely on the United Nations for its security. Theoretically speaking, Article 9's self-restraint on military sovereignty and the UN's collective security are compatible, but the UN's collective security remained unrealised as a result of the Cold War. Historical records suggest that Douglas MacArthur envisaged that the US military presence in Okinawa would provide Japan with security (Koseki, 1998: 201). And, the Japanese government chose to seek security through a military alliance with the US.

The atomic bombings of Hiroshima and Nagasaki and the adoption of Article 9 gave birth to Japan's world government movement. Some people in Japan thought that, in addition to the necessity of international control over atomic bombs, Japan, disarmed by Article 9, required world government.

From the final years of occupation, when the Cold War intensified, the US government wanted Japan to rearm and to revise Article 9, and Japan began to rearm during the Korean war. In the 1950s conservative politicians made efforts to revise Article 9, but they failed due to opposition from the Japanese people. Nevertheless, Japan's re-armament continued and expanded steadily through numerous pieces of legislation based on the US-Japan Security Treaty and through subtle interpretations of Article 9. This phenomenon is sometimes called "interpretative constitutional revision". As a result, "Two Legal Systems" have existed in post-war Japan, one based on Article 9 and the other based on the US-Japan Security Treaty; needless to say, there have been tensions between the two.[9]

The Japanese people have embraced the 1946 Constitution and Article 9. Whenever the Japanese government has taken military action, Japanese citizens have opposed it and brought the issue to court. Consequently, there have been numerous lawsuits challenging the constitutionality of governmental action under the US-Japan military alliance. As a result, large parts of the peace movement in post-war Japan have taken the form of constitutional lawsuits (Yamauchi, 2001). This situation has had both positive and negative impacts. It has been positive because citizens have taken the initiative in challenging governmental military actions by relying on the constitution. At the same time, it has been negative because the issue of peace and security has been narrowed to a legalistic debate on constitutional interpretation, and, as a result, efforts to form pacifist, alternative policies to military commitment have been insufficient. It is ironic that, although an idea like civilian-based defense is most suitable for post-war Japan under Article 9, it has not interested the Japanese people.[10] In any case, the issues addressed by constitutional lawsuits have included the US troops stationed in Japan (Sunagawa case in 1959), Japan's Self-Defense Forces (Eniwa and Naganuma cases in the 1960s and 1970s), Japan's financial contribution to the Gulf War in 1991, and the Self-Defense Forces' actions in Iraq since 2003, among other things. In most of these cases the courts have avoided making any judgment on the constitutionality of these governmental actions, and Japan's Supreme Court has avoided making a decision on the constitutionality of the Self-Defense Forces. However, there have been some lower court decisions that have found the US troops stationed in Japan and the Self-Defense Forces as being in violation of Article 9. Constitutional scholars have played important roles as well. They have placed Article 9 in a comparative and historical perspective, brought out its potential, and provided plaintiffs in lawsuits with strong constitutional interpretations. Since the 1960s, in constitutional lawsuits, the plaintiffs and constitutional scholars have used "the right to live in peace" clause in the Preamble as one of their arguments. This was far earlier than the United Nations General Assembly resolutions confirming people's right to peace (1978, 1984) (Roche, 2003; Urata, 2005: 143–67, 203–23).

When we look back at the 60-year history of Article 9, it looks as if Japan's peace movement had little success in resisting the expansion and reinforcement of the US-Japan military alliance. But had it not been for Japan's peace movement, the posture of the US-Japan military alliance would have been very different from the present one. I think that Japanese citizens and constitutional scholars, by dint of 60 years of practice, have elevated pacifism from a marginal, obscure idea to a respectable, alternative principle of political order.[11] Global civil society has noticed these efforts, and it has referred to Article 9 in its documents in the past ten years.

One of the features of the Japanese Constitution is its perception about the actors who create peace. Judging from the Preamble and Article 9, we can say that it assumes that the actors who create peace are not the government, but rather the people. And, although it does not explicitly mention NGOs or civil society organisations, I understand that it assumes NGOs and civil society organisations to be the actors creating peace. Here, the Japanese Constitution's emphasis on the people as principal actors for peace resonates with the practice of global constitutionalism. Tadakazu Fukase sums it up most exactly:

> The problems of war and arms, and of peace and disarmament, are no longer problems of the government's exclusive power or final say; they are under the direct and indirect direction and control of the sovereign people. Not only in domestic society, but also in international (world) society, the people, as individuals and as voluntary groups (NGOs and other groups which lobby the UN), and by means of their partial and total public opinion, are guaranteed the status and rights to exercise their initiative in solving problems relating to war and peace and to arms and disarmament, or to influence or apply pressure regarding them. (Fukase, 1987: 194–195)

"Pacifism of Inaction" and "Pacifism of Action"

So far, people have tended to understand Japan's "pacifism" solely as a "pacifism of inaction," that is, pacifism as a prohibition against governmental military action. That is one of the reasons for Japan's peace movement's inability to effectively rebut the realist argument in the 1990s. The realists argued that in order to contribute to international peace and security Japan should revise Article 9 and send the Self-Defense Forces overseas. Restraining Japanese military power is an important responsibility of the Japanese people, but it is only half of the "pacifism" of the Japanese Constitution. An integrated reading of Article 9 and the Preamble suggests the other half of Japan's "pacifism," that is, a "pacifism of action".

It should be noted that Article 9 and the Preamble are complementary and need to be read concurrently. While Article 9 rejects war and militarism (direct violence), that is, it aims at negative peace, the Preamble states that the Japanese people are determined to make every effort to overcome "tyranny and slavery, oppression and intolerance" and "fear and want" (structural violence) throughout the world and create a just world order, that is, they are engaged in a search for positive peace. Read this way, the Japanese Constitution requires a "pacifism of action". In other words, the Japanese people's engagement with peace activities in the world is a necessary component of the "pacifism" of the Japanese Constitution. Given this, there are many possibilities for the Japanese people to make contributions to international peace and security.

As I have discussed above, global civil society's efforts to regulate military power and replace military options with civilian options are noteworthy. Ideas and practices of civilian-based defense or unarmed civilian peacekeeping are just a few examples of the vast possibilities. There are numerous NGO activities for peace in which the Japanese people can participate. Supporting and participating in these activities are a practice of a "pacifism of action" that flows from the Japanese Constitution (Kimijima, 2010).

Japan's Contribution to Global Constitutionalism

The Japanese People's Engagement with Global Peace Efforts

Indeed the Japanese people have engaged with global peace efforts in the past 60 years. Naturally, the experiences of the atomic bombings of Hiroshima and Nagasaki have had an enormous impact on the Japanese people. *Hibakusha*, or "survivors of atomic bombings," have constituted a core of the Japanese people's movement for nuclear weapons abolition. In the 1990s this movement participated in the World Court Project and played a very important role.

Under the US-Japan Security Treaty, there are numerous US military bases in Japan, particularly in the island of Okinawa. Okinawans have been victims of militarism during the Asia-Pacific War (1931–1945) and the US military occupation (1945–1972), and even after Okinawa returned to Japan as well. Their suffering due to military forces ... both Japanese and American ... have made them strong anti-militarists.[12] Because the US military bases in Okinawa have been playing significant roles in the global projection of US military power, Okinawa's peace movement is important as an actor to watch global operations of US military power and as a member of the International Network for the Abolition of Foreign Military Bases.

Among the recent trends of replacing military options with civilian options, Nonviolent Peaceforce (NP), an international NGO that practises unarmed civilian peacekeeping, has drawn support from the Japanese people. Nonviolent Peaceforce Japan was established as an affiliate in Japan, and it has been instrumental in NP's project in Sri Lanka. The important point is that Nonviolent Peaceforce Japan consciously links the "pacifism" of the Japanese Constitution and global civil society's efforts to replace military options with civilian options (Kimijima, 2008).

Global Civil Society and Article 9

In the 1990s, following the end of the Cold War, when activities of various social movements, NGOs and civil society organisations became very active and influential, people realised that global civil society had developed into an important actor in world politics. The World Court Project and the International Campaign to Ban Landmines are only a few examples of this phenomenon.

In May 1999, nearly 10,000 peace activists from all over the world, including about 400 Japanese people, participated in the Hague Appeal for Peace Civil Society Conference. It was one of the largest citizen peace conferences in history. Global civil society has clearly emerged out of this conference as a principal actor to regulate power and create peace. "The Hague Agenda for Peace and

Justice for the 21st Century," global civil society's strategic plan for creating peace, is still one of the best available conceptual maps for peace studies. On the last day of the conference, the secretariat of the Hague Appeal for Peace released "Ten Fundamental Principles for a Just World Order" which summed up the conference discussions (Kimijima, 2001). The first principle is the following:

> Every Parliament should adopt a resolution prohibiting their government from going to war, like the Japanese article number nine.

Since the Hague Appeal for Peace in 1999, the Japanese people's engagement with global civil society's peace efforts has become strengthened and deepened. As a result, NGO conferences often make reference to Article 9 of the Japanese Constitution. Article 9 is quoted because it resonates with global civil society's efforts to regulate military power and replace military options with civilian ones.

One of the recent examples is the Global Action Agenda (2005) of the Global Partnership for the Prevention of Armed Conflict (GPPAC). It contains the following reference:

> In some regions of the world, normative-legal commitments play an important role in promoting regional stability and increasing confidence. For example, Article 9 of the Japanese Constitution renounces war as a means of settling disputes and of maintaining forces for those purposes. It has been a foundation for collective security throughout the Asia-Pacific region.

The Global Partnership for the Prevention of Armed Conflict (GPPAC) is a global civil society project to emphasise the primary importance of prevention of armed conflict rather than military intervention. GPPAC began as a response to UN Secretary-General Kofi Annan's 2001 report on preventing armed conflict (S/2001/574), and one of its aims has been to make the voice of global civil society heard in the UN Security Council. It partially succeeded when representatives of GPPAC spoke at the debate of the UN Security Council in September 2005. The Global Action Agenda is a product of global civil society's intense discussions on strategies and priorities for preventing armed conflicts. It was presented to Kofi Annan at the GPPAC Global Conference held at the UN in New York in July 2005 (Global Partnership for the Prevention of Armed Conflict, 2005). Article 9 is quoted in this document as well. GPPAC is another example of the practice of global constitutionalism.

Lastly, it is important to emphasise that global civil society is not a flat, harmonious space but a field where various actors interact and fight each other for hegemony or counter-hegemony (Cox, 1999). Probably we can distinguish two types of global civil society (Santos, 2005). One is the liberal global civil society that does not challenge the prevailing ideologies such as liberal democracy and neo-liberal capitalism. The other is the counter-hegemonic global civil society that seeks more participatory democracy and alternative economies. For our purpose, as a principal actor to regulate the exercise of informal global power, we will rely more on the counter-hegemonic global civil society than on the liberal global civil society.[13]

Conclusion

In closing the article, I think it is fitting to refer to the outcome of the GPPAC process in Northeast Asia. At GPPAC, in preparation for the Global Conference and the Global Action Agenda, civil society organisations met region-by-region and adopted regional action agendas. Civil society organisations in Northeast Asia – China, Taiwan, South Korea, Mongolia, Far Eastern Russia and Japan – met twice in Tokyo and adopted the Northeast Asia Regional Action Agenda (Tokyo Agenda) in February 2005. The discussions at the meetings and the contents of the Tokyo Agenda are most relevant to this article.

In post-war Northeast Asia, the US-Japan military alliance succeeded the Japanese Empire. As a result, regulating US-Japan military power is a large task for this region, and for that purpose preserving Article 9 is extremely important. In addition, creating a multilateral, common security mechanism in the region is the direction we should pursue. At the same time, it is necessary for civil society organisations in Northeast Asia to engage non-violently in conflicts and humanitarian crises in, and out of, the region. Ultimately, it is civil society, not state armed forces, that should take the initiative to create peace. All of these issues are what civil society organisations discussed, and these are the contents of the Tokyo Agenda. They resonate with my argument.

I believe it is the Japanese people's efforts to preserve Article 9 and engage in global civil society's peace activities that constitute Japan's contribution to global constitutionalism. And, as the references to Article 9 in NGO documents show, I think global civil society is ready to share Article 9 and draw on its potential.[14]

Notes

1. This article, based on a paper I submitted to the International Peace Research Association Conference held at the University of Sydney on July 6–10, 2010, was prepared with the benefit of feedback from Stephen Gill, James H. Mittelman and Heikki Patomaki, for which I am grateful. I would also like to thank the students and administration at the School of International Service at American University who gave me the opportunity to teach a graduate course on global constitutionalism in Spring 2008. Of course, it is I alone who is responsible for any and all errors. A slightly different version of this article appeared in Vol. 23, No. 3 of the *Ritsumeikan Journal of International Studies* (2011).
2. It is extremely difficult to translate the Japanese term *heiwa shugi* into English, but I use the English term "pacifism" because in the context of this article I think "pacifism" is closest to *heiwa shugi*. See also Cortright (2008: 11).
3. It is appropriate to refer to Gill's new constitutionalism here. I understand that new constitutionalism is global capitalism's project to restrain popular power or democratic control in order to secure private property rights and accumulation of capital (Gill, 1998, 2002, 2008). My conception of global constitutionalism is the opposite. However, I regret that I have not elaborated the aspect of global constitutionalism that regulates the power of actors of global capitalism in this article. I wait for another chance.
4. The author's conception of global constitutionalism resonates with what Mittelman calls civil society and organic intellectuals' project for alter globalisation (Mittelman, 2004: 94–95). This project pursues autonomy from below against globalising forces. And I would like to mention here that Teubner's conception of "societal constitutionalism" and WOMP's and the author's conceptions of global constitutionalism have similarities in that all of them emphasise the principal roles of civil society (Teubner, 2004).
5. The number of US military bases in foreign countries, 716, is based on the US Department of Defense's 2009 *Base Structure Report*.
6. On the legislative history of the 1946 Constitution, I rely on Koseki (1998) and Dower (1999).
7. Article 1 of the Kellogg-Briand Pact provides as follows: "The High Contracting Parties solemnly declare in the names of their respective peoples that they condemn recourse to war for the

solution of international controversies, and renounce it, as an instrument of national policy in their relations with one another."

8. Article 2 Clause 4 of the United Nations Charter provides as follows: "All members shall refrain in their international relations from the threat or use of force against the territorial integrity or political independence of any state, or in any other manner inconsistent with the purposes of the United Nations."
9. On Japan's rearmament and the tensions between Article 9 and the US-Japan Security Treaty, see Dower (1993). On political contention over the 1946 Constitution, see Hook and McCormack (2001).
10. Notable exceptions are Miyata (1971) and Terajima (2004).
11. On some aspects of Japan's pacifism, see Yamamoto (2004) and Kimijima (2006).
12. On Okinawa, see Johnson (2000: 34–64; 2006: 171–207); Urata (2005: 71–142).
13. As a space for counter-hegemonic global civil society, the World Social Forum is important. See Blau and Karides (2008).
14. Peace NGOs in Japan launched the Global Article 9 Campaign and they successfully organised and held the Global Article 9 Conference to Abolish War in May 2008 in Japan.

References

Bird, Kai and Martin J. Sherwin (2005) *American Prometheus: The Triumph and Tragedy of J. Robert Oppenheimer*, New York: Alfred A. Knopf.

Blau, Judith and Marina Karides (eds.) (2008) *The World and US Social Forums: A Better World is Possible and Necessary*, Leiden: Brill.

Boyer, Paul (1994) *By the Bomb's Early Light: American Thought and Culture at the Dawn of the Atomic Age*, Chapel Hill: The University of North Carolina Press.

Calder, Kent E. (2007) *Embattled Garrisons: Comparative Base Politics and American Globalism*, Princeton: Princeton University Press.

Cameron, Maxwell A., Robert J. Lawson and Brian W. Tomlin (eds.) (1998) *To Walk without Fear: The Global Movement to Ban Landmines*, Toronto: Oxford University Press.

Clark, Grenville and Louis B. Sohn (1966) *World Peace Through World Law: Two Alternative Plans*, Third Edition Enlarged, Cambridge, MA: Harvard University Press.

Committee to Frame a World Constitution (1948) *Preliminary Draft of a World Constitution*, Chicago: The University of Chicago Press.

Cortright, David (2008) *Peace: A History of Movements and Ideas*, Cambridge, UK: Cambridge University Press.

Cox, Robert W. (1999) "Civil Society at the Turn of the Millennium: Prospects for an Alternative World Order", *Review of International Studies*, 25, 3–28.

Dewes, Kate (1998) The World Court Project: The Evolution and Impact of an Effective Citizens' Movement, A Thesis Submitted for the Degree of Doctor of Philosophy of the University of New England, Christchurch, Aotearoa/New Zealand.

Dower, John W. (1993) "Peace and Democracy in Two Systems: External Policy and Internal Conflict", in Andrew Gordon (ed.), *Postwar Japan as History*, Berkeley: University of California Press, 3–33.

—— (1999) *Embracing Defeat: Japan in the Wake of World War II*, New York and London: W.W. Norton & Company.

Falk, Richard A., Robert C. Johansen and Samuel S. Kim (eds.) (1993) *The Constitutional Foundations of World Peace*, Albany: State University of New York Press.

Fassbender, Bardo (2009) *The United Nations Charter as the Constitution of the International Community*, Leiden, The Netherlands: Martinus Nijhoff Publishers.

Fukase, Tadakazu (1987) *Senso hoki to heiwateki seizonken (Renunciation of War and Right to Live in Peace)*, Tokyo: Iwanami Shoten.

Gill, Stephen (1998) "New Constitutionalism, Democratisation and Global Political Economy", *Pacifica Review*, 10, 1: 23–38.

—— (2002) "Constitutionalizing Inequality and the Clash of Globalizations", *International Studies Review*, 4, 2: 47–65.

—— (2008) *Power and Resistance in the New World Order*, Second Edition, New York: Palgrave Macmillan.

Global Partnership for the Prevention of Armed Conflict (2005) *Conference Report: Global Conference: From Reaction to Prevention: Civil Society Forging Partnership to Prevent Violent Conflict and Build Peace*, Utrecht: European Centre for Conflict Prevention.

Hook, Glenn D. and Gavan McCormack (2001) *Japan's Contested Constitution: Documents and Analysis*, London and New York: Routledge.

Johnson, Chalmers (2000) *Blowback: The Costs and Consequences of American Empire*, New York: Henry Holt and Company.

—— (2004) *The Sorrows of Empire: Militarism, Secrecy and the End of the Republic*, New York: Henry Holt and Company.

—— (2006) *Nemesis: The Last Days of the American Republic*, New York: Henry Holt and Company.

—— (2010) *Dismantling the Empire: America's Last Best Hope*, New York: Henry Holt and Company.

Kimijima, Akihiko (2001) "Nihonkoku kenpo daikyujo to hagu heiwa apiru" (Article 9 of the Japanese Constitution and the Hague Appeal for Peace), *Sekai*, 694: 90–95.

—— (2006) "Revisiting the Pacifism of the Japanese Constitution", *Ritsumeikan kokusai kenkyu (Ritsumeikan Journal of International Studies)*, 18, 3: 191–205.

—— (ed.) (2008) *Hibuso no PKO: NGO hibouryoku heiwa tai no rinen to katsudo (Unarmed PKO: Ideas and Activities of NGO Nonviolent Peaceforce)*, Tokyo: Akashi Shoten.

—— (2009) "Japan's Contribution to Global Constitutionalism", *Societies without Borders*, 4, 2: 105–116.

—— (2010) "Article 9", in Nigel J. Young (ed.), *The Oxford International Encyclopedia of Peace*, Vol. 1, New York: Oxford University Press, 151–152.

Koseki, Shoichi (1998) *The Birth of Japan's Postwar Constitution*, Boulder and Oxford: Westview Press.

Mahony, Liam and Luis Enrique Eguren (1997) *Unarmed Bodyguards: International Accompaniment for the Protection of Human Rights*, West Hartford, CT: Kumarian Press.

Mittelman, James H. (2004) *Wither Globalization? The Vortex of Knowledge and Ideology*, London: Routledge.

Miyata, Mitsuo (1971) *Hibuso kokumin teikou no shiso (An Idea of Nonviolent National Resistance)*, Tokyo: Iwanami Shoten.

Mogami, Toshiki (2007) *Kokusai rikken shugi no jidai (The Age of International Constitutionalism)*, Tokyo: Iwanami Shoten.

Moser-Puangsuwan, Yeshua and Thomas Weber (eds.) (2000) *Nonviolent Intervention across Borders: A Recurrent Vision*, Honolulu: Spark M. Matsunaga Institute for Peace, University of Hawaii.

Patomaki, Heikki and Teivo Teivainen (2004) *A Possible World: Democratic Transformation of Global Institutions*, London: Zed Books.

Roche, Douglas (2003) *The Human Right to Peace*, Toronto: Novalis.

Rogers, Paul (2002) *Losing Control: Global Security in the Twenty-first Century*, Second Edition, London: Pluto Press.

Santos, Boaventura de Sousa (2005) "Beyond Neoliberal Governance: The World Social Forum as Subaltern Cosmopolitan Politics and Legality", in Boaventura de Sousa Santos and Cesar A. Rodriguez-Garavito (eds.), *Law and Globalization from Below: Towards a Cosmopolitan Legality*, Cambridge, UK: Cambridge University Press, 29–63.

Sharp, Gene (1990) *Civilian-based Defense: A Post-Military Weapons System*, Princeton: Princeton University Press.

—— (2005) *Waging Nonviolent Struggle: 20th Century Practice and 21st Century Potential*, Boston: Extending Horizons Books.

Suganami, Hidemi (1989) *The Domestic Analogy and World Order Proposals*, Cambridge, UK: Cambridge University Press.

Terajima, Toshio (2004) *Shiminteki fufukuju (Civil Disobedience)*, Tokyo: Fukosha.

Teubner, Gunther (2004) "Societal Constitutionalism: Alternatives to State-centred Constitutional Theory?", in Christian Joergens, Inger-Johanne Sand and Gunther Teubner (eds.), *Transnational Governance and Constitutionalism*, Oxford: Hart Publishing, 3–28.

United Nations Secretary-General (2001) *Report of the Secretary-General on Prevention of Armed Conflict*, S/2001/574.

Urata, Kenji (2005) *Reflections on Global Constitutionalism: Perspectives based on the Constitution of Japan*, Tokyo: The Institute of Comparative Law, Waseda University.

Wallis, Tim and Mareike Junge (2002) *Enhancing UK Capacity for Handling Conflict: The Rationale for a UK Civilian Peace Service*, London: Peaceworkers UK.

Weber, Thomas (1996) *Gandhi's Peace Army: The Shanti Sena and Unarmed Peacekeeping*, Syracuse: Syracuse University Press.

Yamamoto, Mari (2004) *Grassroots Pacifism in Post-war Japan: The Rebirth of a Nation*, Abingdon, Oxon: Routledge-Curzon.

Yamauchi, Toshihiro (2001) "Constitutional Pacifism: Principle, Reality and Perspective", in Yoichi Higuchi (ed.), *Five Decades of Constitutionalism in Japanese Society*, Tokyo: University of Tokyo Press, 27–41.

Yeo, Andrew (2009) "Not in Anyone's Backyard: The Emergence and Identity of a Transnational Anti-base Network", *International Studies Quarterly*, 53, 3: 571–594.

12

New Media

The Power of Transnational Non-violent Politics

SELVARAJAH SENTHAN

The Question of Non-violence

After the military defeat of the Liberation Tigers of Tamil Eelam (LTTE) in May 2009 the immediate responsibility of taking forward the Eelam struggle through the non-violent means fell in the hands of Tamil diaspora in Sri Lanka as there is no democratic space in Sri Lanka for the Tamil people to struggle for their rights.

This non-violent struggle of the diaspora Tamils through the transnational politics can actually contribute a lot to regain the rights of the Tamil people in Sri Lanka. One might ridicule this argument because of the bitter experience during the 1960s and 70s in Sri Lanka. The Tamil people trusted on non-violence for three decades, but their non-violent resistance was challenged by violence. To understand the reasons behind this, it is pertinent to briefly look at the history of non-violent movement of the Tamils in Sri Lanka.

Non-violent Struggle of Tamils

As Satchi Ponnamblam (1983) records, "On 5th June 1956, the date the 'Sinhala Only' Bill was introduced by (Prime Minister) Bandaranaike in the House (of Parliament), as an act of protest, Chelvanayakam, the leader of the Federal Party, led a party of 300 Tamil volunteers and staged a sit down Satyagraha (peaceful protest) of the kind popularized by Mahatma Gandhi in the days of the Indian freedom struggle.

It was a peaceful sit down protest outside the House, on the Galle Face Green... On that day, the police were all around but allowed the Satyagrahis to be beaten up... Some Tamil Satyagrahis were thrown into Beira Lake near the Parliament House." (ibid.).

Pretesting against the 'Sinhala Only' Act, the Federal Party organized a long march called "Thirumalai Yatra" (March to Trincomalle) in April 1957, which followed a 3-day convention.[1]

After the implementation of 'Sinhala Only' Act, the government was quick to respond with an important decision that all the vehicle registration plates marked in English should be changed into Sinhala only. Accordingly, all vehicle registration numbers should start from 'Sri' in Sinhala. The Federal Party fervently protested this instruction and organised a campaign in 1958 named "Anti-Sri Campaign". Subsequently, this campaign sparked off Anti-Tamil violence in 1958.[2]

Another satyagraha opposing the 'Sinhala Only' Act was organised by the Federal Party on 20 February 1961 opposite the Jaffna Kachcheri (secretariat). The government responded to this campaign by airlifting a naval unit to Jaffna to cordon off the secretariat. However, the Federal Party expanded the campaign to Vavuniya, Mannar, Trincomalle and Batticoloa district secretariats.[3]

To show the disobedience to the law, the Federal Party launched a Federal Party Postal Service (Thamil Arasu Postal Service) in Jaffna on April 14, 1961. Party leader S.J.V. Selvanayagam issued stamps on behalf of Thamil Arasu Postal Service, as its Post Master General (Sri Kantha, 2011).

The Federal Party went on expanding the satyagraha into a civil disobedience movement. The 1961 satyagraha for Tamil rights lasted for nearly three months. The satyagrahis outside the main government offices in the major cities of the Tamil areas continued to protest against the implementation of 'Sinhala Only' Act. The government reacted by declaring a state of emergency and made use of the army to crush the satyagraha movement. The leaders and the youth leaders involved in arranging the campaign were arrested (Philips, 2007).

In May 1972, the Tamil United Front organised a massive protest against the new constitution. The protest spread even to the villages, with several youths involved in arranging demonstrations and meetings. They burnt the national flag and the copies of the new constitution. The government used the police force and arrested over 70 youth leaders (Ponnamblam, 1983).

In almost all cases, the non-violence campaigns were met with some form of violent opposition. Consequently, none of these campaigns produced any good results. The party members started questioning the use of Gandhian methods. They argued that Mahatma Gandhi succeeded in India with his concepts of non-violence and non-cooperation because he was leading a majority against a minority, however powerful, whereas in Sri Lanka, the Tamils were a minority demanding rights from a majority. And, the majority was not agreeable to give concessions.[4]

One of his earliest interviews to Anita Pratap in 1984, the LTTE leader Pirabhakaran argued the following for justifying his armed struggle against the Sri Lankan government:

> "The democratic parliamentary system, or the conventional political system in Sri Lanka, has always tried to impose the will of the majority on the minority. This system not only failed to solve the basic problems of our people but, in fact, aggravated our plight. For decades, the repression by the State has made the life of our people miserable. The non-violent democratic struggles of our people were met with military repression. Our just demands were totally ignored, and the oppression continued on such a scale as to threaten the very survival of the Tamils in Sri Lanka. It was these circumstances which led me to form our liberation movement. I felt that an armed struggle was the only alternative left to our people, not only to ensure our survival but ultimately to free ourselves from the Sinhala oppression" (cited in Sri Kantha, 2011).

When looking at the meaning of non-violence, as Jonathan Power says, it is " connected in most people's minds with passivity and non-resistance. Yet if properly deployed and organised, it can be a very powerful weapon of defence and a very effective tool for rapid social change" (Power, 2011). Its success depends on the support of the people. The logic of the non-violence is that the power of rulers depends on the consent of the people, and therefore the power depends on the cooperation of others. Non-violence undermines the power of the rulers through the deliberate withdrawal of this cooperation.[5]

But, this philosophy relates to the theory of 'power game' and supports the argument that a minority cannot undertake non-violence when faced with a formidable majority, because the power is always with the majority people and the rulers of the majority depend on the consent of the majority people, and not on the consent of the minority people. Therefore, the non-violence strategies of a minority community are unlikely to undermine the power of the majority's rulers through the deliberate withdrawal of disobedience associated with non-violence.

This was the scenario before the globalisation process began in early 1990s, and it was true in the case of Sri Lanka too. The minority Tamil people could not undertake non-violent struggle against the majority Sinhala people, because the power had always remained with the governments decided by the majority Sinhala people. The Tamil people did not have the political clout to jolt the governments by non-violence means. However, the situation has now changed due to the politico-economic transformation brought by the globalisation process.

It must be understood that this paper does not argue that the non-violence methods have never worked or cannot work for majority-minority conflicts. Ethnic conflicts differ from one case to another in nature, form and historical roots. Accordingly, the dynamics of the non-violence methods, its functions and the behaviours may vary, and produce win-win solution. Therefore, this issue needs to be further discussed and researched based on the theories of non-violence and conflict resolution in the context of historical examples – which is beyond the scope of this paper. Instead, this paper argues that the changes brought by the globalisation provide an avenue to the minority (Tamils) people to equally challenge the majority hegemony through transnational politics of non-violent strategies, and the new media can be the power tool for this transnational politics of non-violent struggle.

Changes of Globalisation

Scholars have given a variety of explanations to the process of globalisation. For David Harvey, globalisation means the shrinking of space and time, while Anthony Giddens stresses its impact of distant events on local experience. Roland Robertson highlights the increased awareness in a dwindling world, while Manuel Castells emphasises the informational effect in a globalising world. In general, all these explanations demonstrate that the latest communication technologies have contributed to the development of a 'new form of globalisation' (cited in Chabot and Duyvendak, 2002: 697).

After referring to the explanations of all these scholars, Chabot and Duyvendak conclude that "globalisation represents unintentional and deterritorialised process, while transnational diffusion (or transnationalism) involves the relatively deliberate and 'grounded' construction of cross border networks between individuals, groups, organisations and countries" (ibid).

Transnationalism is one of many changes induced by the globalisation. Hence, the transnational politics has now come under the direct influence of the dynamics of the globalisation process (Adebayo and Adesina, 2009: 6).

It is in this premise that transnational politics can be defined as the political practice of diaspora communities, the relationship that they maintain and establish with their homelands and host countries and their activities that influence the national conflict. Diaspora is a transnational community because of its organisation of life in various parts of the world crossing territories and boundaries (Senthan and Nirmanusan, 2011: 4).

As Goldring (cited in ibid.) notes a diaspora group views itself as a particular ethnic group based on its shared identity and collective memory. The ethnicity-based affection and the cultural ties in the homeland of an ethnic diaspora group can play an influential role in the conflict in the homeland. Various diaspora groups scattered throughout the world have showed such a political function and become successful in creating ethnic pro-self-nationalistic movements for the support of the struggle in their countries.

There is always an ideological importance in conditioning the formation of such ethnic nationalist diaspora movements and constructing the political identity in order to facilitate the diasporic society. Discourse is considered to be the favoured vehicle of ideology in which language is the key element (Van Dijk, 2001: 11–13). In the stream of politics, nationalism can be considered an ideology. Hence, the creation of a 'discourse of nationalism' is a result of interface between the ideology/nationalism and discourse practices. Studies have illustrated the influence of nationalist discourse in the political practices of a society and vice versa.

In Sri Lanka, the identity of Tamils has been formed as a distinctive group. Nationalism has played a crucial role in the process of identity formation of Tamils. A state and an ethnic identification are the two main conditions for the involvement of nationalism. Smith defines nationalism as an ideological movement for attaining and maintaining identity, unity and autonomy of a social group some of whose members deem it to constitute an actual or potential nation (cited in Senthan and Nirmanusan, 2011: 4). This description of nationalism well accommodates the generally referred definition of Sri Lankan Tamil nationalism that it is the conviction of the Sri Lankan Tamil people that they have the right to constitute an independent or autonomous political community. Perhaps, such a political entity can be called as 'Tamil Eelam' (ibid.).

Thus, it could be said that the non-violent struggle for freedom and justice of the moderate Tamil political parties was the core substance of the creation of Tamil nationalist discourse towards the construction of Tamil nationalism. The Vaddukoddai Resolution, adopted at the first National Convention of the Tamil United Liberation Front (TULF) on 14 May 1976, has created a deep effect on Tamil nationalism. This convention resolves that restoration and reconstitution of the free, sovereign, secular, socialist state of Tamil Eelam, based on the right of self-determination inherent to every nation, has become inevitable in order to safeguard the very existence of the Tamil nation in this country (Ponnamblam, 1991).

Recently, a referendum was held among the Tamil diaspora people in a number of western countries, including Canada and Australia, based on this Vaddokoddai Resolution. The aim of this referendum was to unite the Tamil-speaking people and endorse the Vaddokoddai Resolution of 1976. Almost more than 99 per cent of the diaspora Tamils had endorsed the resolution (*Tamil Guardian*, 2010). This example clearly shows the fundamental similarities of the development of the transnationalism of diaspora Tamils in parallel to the nationalism of the Sri Lankan Tamils. The recent transnational non-violent political practices of the Tamil diaspora people have further strengthen the conviction of the Tamil nationalism among the Tamil people.

Transnational Politics of Tamils

Presently, the process of the political identity of Tamil diaspora in the UK is evolving through the dynamics of transnational political practices and political discourse from a uni-polar identity formation process to a multi-polar formation process (Senthan and Nirmanusan, 2011: 3).

The paradigm shift has led the Tamil nation towards a transnational politics. Greater part of Tamils living in foreign countries is strongly attached to their homeland concept and their struggle for peace, freedom and justice through democratic means.

The Tamil diaspora network has started functioning independently through constructive engagement with the socio-political networks in the UK. The decisions concerning the political future of the Tamil people are taken in a democratic manner (ibid.: 9).

Through various non-violence strategies such as advocacy, non-violent resistance, diplomacy, boycotts, moral purchasing, supporting anti-war political candidates, demonstrations and national political lobbying groups, the Tamil diaspora organisations are mobilising the Tamil diaspora in the UK and elsewhere, and increasing the citizen participation in the political process. Their strategies include integration of societies and empowerment of the Tamil diaspora in terms of social, political and economic conditions in the host countries (ibid.: 10).

The Tamil diaspora is also successfully starting to integrate with global actors through its various strategies of transnational politics. It is now steadily moving into the process. In the process, they are engaging with host country governments, cross-party politicians, civil society movements, solidarity movements, media, human rights and humanitarian organisations, business communities and fellow citizens of the countries and beginning to associate with international government organisations, supranational and regional unions.

Lobbying and advocacy are done in two different ways, such as awareness raising, organising marches and demonstrations, and promoting public education and relations. Usually, diaspora people do lobbying activities in their host countries, but in some cases, this lobbying is articulated through international actors and agencies.

The engagement process has at least four phases: strengthening or empowering Tamil diaspora structure and institution, entering into geo-political arena, bringing global actors into their transnational activities, especially into political and economical activities, and working together in a common platform. Therefore, a collaborative work of the diaspora with other states and international agencies is vital for its constructive engagement. There is a great potentiality for creating sufficient resources for diaspora by collaborating with states, international agencies, regional organisations and NGOs in the current age of globalisation.

Balancing the Imbalance of the Power of Non-violence

According to the programme description of the global integration of the Bremen International Graduate School of Social Sciences, "studies of global integration explain the relationships between political, social and economic integration beyond the nation state. Globalisation brings the world to a 'single place' towards 'global integration'. The global integration means the end of the nation-state".

As the nation-states adopt these changes of integration in the 20th century, the globalisation has begun to transform the 'national constellation' into a 'post-national' one. Subsequently, the nation-states saw a sudden increase in the cross-border exchange in the economic, security, environmental and cultural spheres which in turn resulted in the emergence of 'global society' (ibid.).

This conducive global environment greatly facilitates the transnational politics of the Tamil diaspora that in turn contributes to balance the imbalance of the power of non-violence struggle in the globalising world. The changes brought by the globalisation provide an avenue to the Tamil minority people to equally challenge the majority hegemony through transnational non-violent strategies. These changes have further altered the model of the non-violence idea. In general, the power of non-violence used to be in the hands of majority people because in general the dynamics of the non-violence depends on the cooperation and consent of the majority people. But, minority community scattered throughout the world can also now equally use the power of non-violence in the globalising world. The emergence of the 'new media' has become a facilitating tool of this change of power of non-violence.

Power of New Media

When looking at the development of the new communication technologies, we see how the rise of new media has been providing a strength and support to the transnational politics.

Nowadays, non-violence activists much rely on the internet, cell phones, wireless tools, Skype, Facebook and other forms of web-based software tools for their coordination and communication of the non-violent activities across both geographical and media boundaries. As Lance Bennett (2003) observes, organisations and institutions such as unions, political parties, governments, and election campaigns will be adopting these new communication technologies to their existing missions and agendas in future.

Bennett further writes, "Due to these patterns of association, these global activists have developed models for empowering uses of digital communication media. Some activists are pursuing more empowering applications of new communication technology. The digital personal media enable the fine linkages that connect people across time, space and issues" (ibid.).

Richard Hunter has coined the term "network army" which he describes as "... a collection of communities and individuals who are united on the basis of ideology, not geography. They are held together by public communications, the Internet being a prime example".

As we can see the Tamil diaspora organisations and activists are also not an exception to the use of new media. The activities of the Tamil diaspora heavily rely on the new media to promote and organise the transnational activities.

As observed earlier, the recent period has been marked by impressive levels of global activism of the Tamil diaspora, including mass demonstrations and sustained campaigns against the Sri Lankan government. The coordination and communication of these activities are based on the various ways of the new media technologies. In many instances, the simple exchanges of information through mobile text messages and the use of internet have proved to be very useful to overcome the limit of time and space in organising such activities.

This shows the potential of the new communication technologies for altering the power relationship of political organisation and political power. As Bennett observes, "the New Media is not inherently transformative of either human communication or social and political relations. Rather, it is the interaction between the Internet and its users — and their interactions. The power of the new media enables for the creation of new spaces for discourse and coordinated action" (ibid.).

To conclude, is clear throughout this discussion that the changes brought out by the globalisation provide an avenue to the

Tamil minority people to equally challenge the majority hegemony through transnational non-violent strategies. On the other hand, the asymmetric power balance of non-violent struggle of the diaspora community of the minority Tamil ethnic group of Sri Lanka is becoming a 'symmetric' due to the changes brought by the globalisation process. The new media can be the power tool for the changing process of the power balance of the transnational non-violent struggle.

Notes

1. T. Sabaratnam, Pirabaharan, Introduction, http://www.sangam.org/Sabaratnam/PirapaharanIntro2.htm
2. Ibid.
3. Ibid.
4. South Asian Free Media Association (SAFMA), "Brief History of Ethnic Conflict", http://www.lankalibrary.com/pol/militancy_history.htm
5. Non-violence definition, http://www.wordiq.com/definition/Nonviolence

References

Adebayo, Akanmu G. and Olutayo C. Adesina (2009) *Globalization and Transnational Migrations: Africa and Africans in the Contemporary Global System*, Cambridge: Cambridge Scholars Publishing, http://www.c-s-p.org/flyers/978–1–4438–0535–3-sample.pdf

Bennett, W.L. (2003) "New Media Power: The Internet and Global Activism", in Nick Couldry and James Curran (eds.), *Contesting Media Power*, Lanham, Maryland: Rowman and Littlefield, http://depts.washington.edu/gcp/pdf/bennettnmpower.pdf

Chabot, Sean and J.W. Duyvendak (December 2002) "Globalization and Transnational Diffusion between Social Movements: Reconceptualizing the Dissemination of the Gandhian Repertoire and the 'Coming Out' Routine", *Theory and Society*, Vol. 31, No. 6, 697–740.

Diaspora Politics: The Free Encyclopaedia, http://en.wikipedia.org/wiki/Diaspora_politics#cite_note-ShainWittes2002–0

Hoskins, Chad (1997) "Transnational Political Activity and Host State Policy: Canada's Sikh and Tamil Diaspora", A Thesis submitted in

Partial Fulfillment of the Requirements for the Degree of Master of Arts, Department of Political Science: The University of British Columbia https://circle.ubc.ca/bitstream/handle/2429/16279/ubc_2005–0054.pdf?sequence=1

Martin, Pablo San (2002) "Is Nationalism an Ideology? A Critical Exploration from the Austrian Case", UK: University of Leeds. http://www.dissidences.org/files/Microsoft_Word_-_San_Martin_Nacionalismo_Final.pdf

Ponnamblam, Satchi (1983) *Sri Lanka: The National Question and the Tamil Liberation Struggle*, London: Zed Books Ltd.

—— (1983) "Tamil Parliamentarians Attacked by Sinhala Mobs,150 Tamils Killed -1956" http://www.tamilcanadian.com/eelam/hrights/?cat=19&id=1000003

—— (1991) "Tamil Eelam Right to Self Determination" http://tamilnation.co/selfdetermination/tamileelam/9107satchi.htm

Philips, Rajan (2007) "Tamil Politics II: The Roots of LTTE's Militarism and Political Culture", http://transcurrents.com/tamiliana/archives/428

Power, Jonathan (2011) "Non-violence is New Strategy" http://www.khaleejtimes.com/DisplayArticle08.asp?xfile=data/opinion/2011/March/opinion_March1.xml&section=opinion

Sabaratnam, T. Pirabaharan, Introduction, http://www.sangam.org/Sabaratnam/PirapaharanIntro2.htm

Senthan, S. and Nirmanusan, B. (2011) "The (Re) Construction of Sri Lankan Tamil Political Identity in the UK", Berghof Peace Support and Centre for Just Peace and Democracy http://www.berghof-peacesupport.org/publicaions/SL_Diaspora_Papers_Senthan-Balasundram.pdf

Shain, Yossi and Tamara Cofman (2002) "Peace as a Three-Level Game: The Role of Diasporas in Conflict Resolution in Ambrosio", in Thomas Ambrosio (ed.), *Ethnic Identity Groups and US Foreign Policy*, Westport (Connecticut): Praeger Publishers.

South Asian Free Media Association, "Brief History of Ethnic Conflict", http://www.lankalibrary.com/pol/militancy_history.htm

Sri Kantha, Sachi (2002) "The Pirabhakaran Phenomenon, Part 44", http://www.sangam.org/PIRABAKARAN/Part44.htm

—— (2011) "Satyagraha of April 1961 in Eelam", http://www.sangam.org/2011/05/Satyagraha_1961.php?uid=4338

Tamil Guardian (2010) "99.33% of British Tamils say yes to independence 24 February 2010", http://www.tamilguardian.com/article.asp?articleid=2687

Van Dijk, T.A. (2001) *Discourse, ideology and context,* Folia Linguistica, XXX/1–2, 11–40. Available at, http://www.discourse-in-society.org/teun.html. Last checked 21/04/2005.

Wilson, A. Jeyaratnam (2000) *Sri Lankan Tamil Nationalism: Its Origins and Development in the Nineteenth and Twentieth Centuries,* Vancouver: University of British Columbia Press, March.

Section III

Reasserting Non-violence: Social Context

13

Hind Swaraj

A Historical Necessity

NAND KISHORE ACHARYA

Books have always been the inspirations of civilisations. Although it is true that a book has never been transformed into any civilisation in its entirety – for human life cannot be contained within the pages of a book, yet a book can often be seen to have been the pivotal inspiration of a civilisation. From the beginning of civilisation to medieval times religious and spiritual books like the Bible, the Quran, the Vedas and the Upanishadas have enjoyed this primacy or centrality. But after the medieval times or because the views upheld in religious literature came under question due to the evolution of modern science, although they did remain significant, they lost their position as the prime movers of civilisation. As a natural corollary to this, books that dealt with the physical or economic world, came into significance, replacing the religious books as the basis of civilisations. Charles Darwin's *Origin of the Species* may be one such book but for the present analysis we will concentrate on three works, viz., *The Wealth of Nations* by Adam Smith, *The Communist Manifesto* by Karl Marx and Fredrich Engles and *Hind Swaraj* by Mahatma Gandhi, which can be seen as inspiration for our present generations.

The first of these books *The Wealth of Nations* by Adam Smith was published in 1776. The European mind, before the publication of this book, was experiencing a sense of liberation and freedom from the shackles of superstition and the desire of the freedom of the individual as opposed to any imposed discipline was getting strengthened because of the renaissance. It was the realisation of this freedom that served as the basic metaphysical impulse and the pivotal inspiration for the development of democracy in England, the French Revolution and the American war of independence. It was being widely recognised that economic freedom was a prominent factor for individual freedom. John Locke was also of the view that the right to property was an important constituent of individual freedom. Economic freedom was considered an important dimension of individual freedom. That is why, any intervention of the state or outside agency was considered undesirable not only on moral grounds but also on economic grounds. In fact, competition was necessary to control prices and generate efficiency in the market, and availability of quality goods and services at low prices for the consumer and the society were expected to be the natural outcomes of this. An ideal market was believed to be that in which both the producer and the consumer have freedom and power to negotiate freely and that was possible in the free market economy only. It was against this backdrop that Smith proposed his theory of free market economy. He was of the view that with increase in production employment opportunities will also increase and if the state does not interfere with the market processes then *an invisible hand* will distribute this production and development to the lowest strata of the society. The logical/economic basis of the policy of liberalisation being followed and advocated all around had already been postulated by Smith in his book. Globalisation is the natural or the international or multinational kin of this liberalisation because of which interference of the state is undesirable not only in the national market, but also in the international context. Supporters of globalisation argue that subsidy, privileges or special facilities by the state to the producer in any country is a suppression of healthy market practice for which the consumer will ultimately have to bear the brunt. Hence, on both economic and moral grounds in both national and international situations a free market economy proves to be more useful. It establishes human freedom in the economic realm as well as guarantees the satisfaction of the society's needs and keeps a check on prices. But, in actuality, the free market that has evolved in the wake of Smith's formulations has given the lie to his theorisation, negating his own conclusions. The development of technology involved in the processes of production has resulted in weakening the role of labour in the production and we are now faced with what the economists call *jobless growth* which implies that though production increases employment opportunities decrease. This situation is not the result of the failure of the present system of economy but of its success. Increased production indicates development, necessitates new technologies. It is called *high rate of development* in the language of economists which implies the adoption of that technology through which the highest rate of production be achieved with the least involvement of human labour. An unavoidable outcome of this is the reduction of employment opportunities which in turn results in reduction in the purchasing power of the people and as is evident, no increase in production can be dependable without increase in purchasing power of the people. It will be hit by cycles of depression again and again.

Even if we forget the artificial demands that this blind increase in production has generated following Marshall the damage to the environmental balance, the two great and innumerable small wars that we have suffered and the dumping of ammunition in the market resulting from competition – even then – from purely economic point of view as well the present situation has given the lie to Smith's own theorisation. When Smith spoke of the free market and open economy, he had also warned that centralisation of market will not let economy remain free in the true sense, and the irony of the situation is that it is impossible to contort economic centralisation without the intervention of the state. Smith wanted to keep big competition, likely to become tyrannical, out of the market. In the liberalised globalisation the market is being strangled by monopolising faces. Mutual agreements between multinational companies do not allow the market to remain free and competitive in the true sense. This form of globalisation is being called corporate globalisation. David Korten in his study *When Corporations Rule the World* (2001) has shown that the seemingly separate multinational companies and national companies have become so interconnected and intertwined that it is no longer possible to call it competition in any clear terms. Talking of two global agricultural companies, viz., Cargill and Archer Daniels Midland and their collaborators, Korten states that while earlier out of every dollar spent on food 41 per cent went to the farmer, now only 9 per cent of it goes to him, even as the consumer is having to pay more. The famous business manager Cyrus Freidheim has come to the conclusion that soon the world economy will be governed by what may be called *relationship enterprise.* Ever the state will not be able to control this kind of monopoly for the state itself will be weaker than them – perhaps in the same manner that the native Indian states had become weaker than the East India Company!

Korten explains that the corporate world of today first creates an artificial competition. At one level the companies remain connected with each other and at another generate and promote. Competition between smaller ancillary companies connected with them peripherally as a result of which the bigger share of the capital invested comes from the smaller companies and yet the lion's share of the profit goes to the bigger companies of the corporate world. Another outcome of this is that the smaller companies are either absorbed by the larger corporations or they are reduced to functioning as agents of the latter.

Smith's free market can remain an actual possibility only in a decentralised economy which in practice is actually being routed out by the market itself. Keynes also had said that philosophy, art and literature can be seen in a universal context but products should be *homespun* only and economies are better national. The *homespun* that Keynes is talking of is possible only through *swadeshi,* for the true ideal to be sought is human freedom, for not only is it moral but it is the very basis, the only way to the social, political and economic well-being of humanity. And it is in this sense that the moral and the economic are interdependent and symbiotic.

The second book in the context is *The Communist Manifesto.* Adam Smith's economics did establish the significance of capital in accordance with his argument but the *invisible hand* that was to have distributed the production to the lowest strata of the society not only failed to deliver but the competition of capital and its contestations sowed the seeds of wars and the mad race of development that ensued poison the earth. With a remarkably astute understanding of this, Karl Marx and Fredrich Engles suggested an alternative, in the *Communist Manifesto,* they envisaged a society in which the benefits of the production could be reached to the lower strata in the real sense and nurture human freedom. The critics of communism who think that it generates oppression forget that the aim is to establish a society in which the freedom of each one to develop is the necessary precondition to the free development of all. Evidently, like Adam Smith, the pivotal value here also is freedom which is realised through the distribution of the benefits of the production to all. According to the *Manifesto*, the greatest obstacle to human freedom is the class stratification of the society due to which the class of the society in control of the means and tools of production exploits and oppresses the dispossessed, depriving them of their freedom. The *Manifesto* suggests that the deprived class should assume rule through revolution and with the ruling power develop an economy which can create a classless society. According to Marx, the state is a protector of class interests, therefore, in a classless society the state will also wither away and that will be the basis of a really free society.

The Communist Manifesto attempts through an analysis of history to establish a scientific basis for this hypothesis. Perhaps Marx's most insightful observation is that the production relations – means and tools of production-are the foundations upon which the superstructure of society is created and the change in means and tools of production, that is, the change in technology changes the production relations and therefore become the basis for the change in the superstructure of the society.

This observation of Marx is similar to the category of historians who study the development of human race from the perspective of technological advancement. These historians hold that the creation and discovery of a new technology presents new possibilities for development for humanity that not only change the means and tools of production and production processes and economy but also impacts the entire social structure and culture. Studying the history of the technological inventions of the human race historian Herald Innis had recognised that every new invention after some time, instead of remaining a mere tool, itself becomes the maker – for once invented these tools in combination with other tools start to innovate the man himself. By innovation of man Innis implies new relationships for man, for human relationship is one of the main dimensions of what we call 'culture'. If culture is the name of the structuring of the relations of the self with the other, then the changes that come into being in human relationships because of change in technology will also be perforce called cultural change and then technology can no longer be thought to be objective in terms of values. Perhaps this is what the authors of *The Communist Manifesto* and their followers failed to perceive. Analysing the processes of generating capital in a capitalist society and the class division resulting therefrom, they were unmindful of the fact that a classless society cannot be developed using the means and tools of production that generate a capitalist society even though the ruling power be in support. From this point of view the socialist revolution should have begun with a revolutionary change in the means and tools of production. After coming to power this is what should have been done in Soviet Russia. It would have been possible to change the production processes and means and tools of production with the help of the ruling power and thereby the production relationships, but the biggest blind spot not only of the Soviet socialist regime but all socialist regimes was that they undertook the unscientific attempts to change the socio-economic relationships without first bringing the concomitant change in the means and tools of production – the technology.

This inner contradiction manifest in Marx's own primary insight grows and further develops in Lenin and other policy planners and no one realises the folly of trying to create a classless society through the means and tools of production that had given rise to capitalism. It should have become evident through Marxian analysis itself that unless the means and tools of production are changed, whether it be Soviet Russia or any other so-called socialist regime or superstructure, they will be driven to adopt the economic processes of the capitalist regimes. Marx himself failed to take stock of this contradiction. The capitalist monopoly that is associated with large-scale industrialisation was what Marx had said was the basis of the abolition of private property. In *German Ideology* Marx writes that the contradiction between the means and tools of production and private property arises for the first time and this is the result of large-scale industrialisation alone. But he also states that it is important to develop large industries at a high rate, only then can private property be abolished. Here, Marx seems oblivious of the fact that the development of large industries implies the development of a technology that has produced modern capitalism in which people are replaced with corporates.

But, the presence of the practical aspects of this inherent contradiction in socialist thought that has resulted in its fall does not necessitate the acceptance of capitalism as inevitable. Another theoretical blind spot of the Soviet structure has been to have envisaged a moral order while promoting physical and material luxury. This has been the dream of capitalism as well – the only difference is that while for one the so-called freedom its basis, for the other it is the so-called equality. But when material comfort ceases to be only instrumental to life and becomes the very purpose of life, then no moral order can possibly be developed upon this foundation, that is, freedom and equality cease to be values and the only value that is left is material comfort.

Evidently then though attempts were made to create a social order on the basis of both *The Wealth of Nations* and *The Communist Manifesto* but they did not succeed because they went against the very values that these works embodied, the practical realisation of which they thought was the end that they had set out to establish, negating the very value that it stood for. So it seems only natural that humanity is seeking a new, another alternative – an alternative that is based on an alternative technology which embodies equality and freedom not as an end but also in its very process. Even modern physics has now established that the process and the product are inseparably the same. This inseparability of the process and the product can be realised in the socio-political and economic contexts only. To create a free and moral society, we should first create an economic and political technology which, not only in its outcome, but in its process also, upholds freedom, local initiative and decentralisation of power, as its pivotal force.

Hind Swaraj is a book that presents an alternative from this very perspective, or we can say that it is a book that accepts equality and freedom as the foundation of a moral order but not as a distant fruit or outcome but in the very act or process of arriving at it. It is for this reason that Gandhi seeks a change in the social order not through taking control of it but by changing its very process. In fact, a free and equal society is a non-violent society, a *satyagrahi* society, for truth and non-violence ultimately are two faces of the same coin, or we can say that non-violence is the practical or behavioural form of truth. If equality and freedom are truths, then non-violence only can be their practical realisation.

Evidently then if the dream of an exploitation/oppression-free society is to be realised, we will have to initiate an alternative technology and policy – the embryo or the blueprint of which we find in the *Hind Swaraj*. Gandhiji understood this well, which is the reason why he called the modern technology-based civilisation a satanic civilisation and parliamentary democracy a sterile woman or a prostitute. Defining *swaraj* in the *Hind Swaraj* Gandhiji emphasises its three main criterion: (1) real *swaraj* is self-rule or self-control; (2) the way to it is *satyagraha*, passive resistance, that is, soul-force and love-force; and (3) in order to exert this force, *swadeshi* in every sense is necessary.

In these postulates Mahatma Gandhi proposes a non-violent society as an alternative vis-à-vis Karl Marx and Adam Smith, the explication of which is the *Hind Swaraj.* In the field of economics, increase in production is not an end in itself for Mahatma Gandhi. As an economist he draws our attention to the fact that the aim of production is to fulfil our basic needs, not to create artificial demands for consumption, for fulfilment. Even if we forget for a moment how detrimental it is for a person or a society to be caught in the web of artificial needs morally, even then, purely from the physical point of view also, for the economy and for the physical and mental well-being, the relevance of Mahatma Gandhi's postulation cannot be refuted. It is also worth remembering that non-covetous or sacrifice tempered-consumption may in this context not be moral precepts only but even be an economic necessity, for covetousness and unbridled desire for artificial needs is the cause of uncontrollable demands. It is not the denial of basic needs because Gandhi emphasised the need not only of mental but also physical health and well-being. Not many people know about Gandhi's statement where he says that for the poor bread and butter are the manifestations of God. In fact, he even says that for the poor the economic is the spiritual. For this reason though Gandhi emphasises the need for increase in production but for basic necessities not for artificially created demands. The preferable process of this increase in production here also for him is that which creates opportunities for employment. Our modern economists hold that increase in production cannot be achieved without adopting modern technology. But, as we have already seen, this technology results in jobless growth, which is economically detrimental. There has been repeated expression of disagreement with Gandhiji's views on machinery and technology. In the essays and writings in *The Aryan Path* as well this divergence is voiced repeatedly. It has been said that freed from the capitalists they may prove to be useful for the good of the people, but the socialist experiment has given the lie to this assertion. When Gandhiji proposes *swadeshi* technology as an alternative he is also proposing employment opportunities with increase in production. In modern technology-based production, according to Schumacher, only 3½ per cent of our social time is utilised in actual production. There can be many forms of *swadeshi* technology, its prime objective is only that it gives judicious attention to human labour, locally available resources and local needs. It can also be called non-violent or *satyagrahi* technology for the emphasis is not on the words but on the vision that sees employment, production and actual need in one continuum of non-violence. For this reason the primary aim is to choose that technology which becomes the foundation of our economic processes for eventually that will be the foundation for the structuring of the society as well.

Actually *swadeshi* technology is that economic base upon which the superstructure of non-violent or free society in the real sense can be founded, which Adam Smith and Karl Marx had dreamt of. The only, though not insignificant, difference was that they were seeking it in and through processes opposed to them, which is never possible in history. When Mahatma Gandhi calls truth God and *satyagraha* the key to self-rule and advocates the adoption the *swadeshi* to test it, it becomes evident that a *swadeshi* economic order is the *satyagrahi* order or the order of divine rule. Perhaps no other spiritual or materialist thinker has ever given so much significance to the means and tools of production as the author of the *Hind Swaraj* does for he knows that for the poor the economic is the spiritual and technology is the basis of the economic, that is, the spiritual for the poor. Just as *satyagraha* is the rehabilitation of the moral in polity so is *swadeshi* the rehabilitation of the spiritual in the realm of economy. In the situation to which our modern technology has, despite the dreams of Adam Smith and Karl Marx, today brought us – we need not reiterate – there is only one way to overcome and that is the adoption of the technology that the author of *Hind Swaraj* recommends. We can have disagreements with Gandhi's other philosophical views but the need of a non-violent technology for a non-violent society is a need that we cannot ignore any longer. In this respect, *Hind Swaraj* has become a historical necessity today, if we wish to escape the vicious cycle that history has landed us in.

(Translated by **Dr Anju Dhadda Misra**)

14

Terrorism and the Gandhian Perspective

RAMJEE SINGH

Hind Swaraj was written in 1908 by Gandhiji "in answer to the Indian school of violence",[1] known as the terrorism. In reply to many criticisms, Gandhi wrote about the book in 1921: "It teaches the gospel of love in place of that of hate. It replaces violence with self-sacrifice. It pits soul-force against brute-force."[2] To the query how India can be free, it is argued that "what was possible for Mazzini and Garibaldi is possible for us."[3] However, Gandhi tries to convince the 'Reader' about the futility of fighting the Britisher with arms. From the practical standpoint, "the English are splendidly armed" and Indians were then unarmed. However, that does not frighten Gandhi. "But it is clear that to pit ourselves against them in arms, thousands of Indians must be armed. If such a thing be possible how many years will it take?" The 'Reader' without being convinced says: "All need not be armed. At first we shall assassinate a few Englishmen and strike terror, then a few men who will have been armed will fight openly. We may have to lose a million men, more or less, but we shall regain our land. We shall undertake guerilla warfare, and defeat the English."[4] Today, this objection is more relevant not only for our country but for the world at large. Science and technology have made the modern state more powerful than *Leviathan*. An armed rebellion can succeed only when there is an open military revolt, or, there is a collaboration of some equally strong foreign powers, but Gandhi's objections to the school of violence were of a deeper nature. He thought that in order to fight the then British rule, "to arm Indian on a large scale is to Europeanize it. Then her condition will be just as pitiable as that of Europe. This means that Indian must accept European civilisation."[5] We will then fight for a few rights, will get what we can and so pass our days. Gandhi thinks that European civilisation is rooted in a life-corroding competition and violence. The Indian seers and sages taught us that the mind is a restless bird; the more it gets the more it wants, and still remains unsatisfied. A man is not necessarily happy because he is rich, or unhappy because he is poor. Hence, they say, "Kings and their swords were inferior to the sword of ethics, and they, therefore, held the sovereigns of the earth to be inferior to the Rishis and the Fakirs."[6] Hence, Gandhi does not like the politics of murder or assassination. "It is a cowardly thought, that of killing others."[7] Gandhi admires the patriotism of Dhingra or Bhagat Singh but discards their methods. He says, "Those who believe that India has gained independence by Dhingra's act and other similar acts in India make a serious mistake. He was a patriot, but his love was blind. He gave his body in a wrong way; its ultimate result can only be mischievous."[8] It is further argued that sometimes terrorism pays, for example, Lord Morley might have granted reforms due to fear. But Gandhi thinks that "what is granted under fear can be retained only so long as the fear lasts."[9] But we wrongly assume that we can get men do things by force, and, therefore, we use force. It might be argued that end justifies the means and the English obtained their own freedom or imperial domination over India through brute force. But we must admit that there is a connection between the means and the end. We cannot get a rose through planting a noxious weed. The means may be likened to a seed, the end to a tree. We reap exactly as we sow.

If historical instances of bloodless non-cooperation are available so are of non-cooperation combined with violence. But "there are on record as many successes as failures in violent non-cooperation."[10] It leads to counter-violence which never ends. The so-called "revolutionary crime is intended to exert pressure. But it is the insane pressure of anger and ill-will."[11] Non-violent acts exert pressure far more effective than violent acts. They are more lasting and more convincing. Violence appears to do good but only temporarily while the evil it does is permanent.[12] Even good brought through force destroys individuality,[13] but when change is brought about through persuasion, change of heart or love, the foundation of individuality and personality is strengthened, and real, abiding progress is assured for the world. History teaches us that those who have, no doubt with honest motives, ousted the greedy by using brute force against them, have in their turn become a prey to the disease of the conquered.[14]

The "terrorism and deception are weapons not of the strong but of the weak."[15] A terrorist is not a warrior who fights openly and bravely. All their actions are secret and deceptive. They attack like thieves and kill even innocent persons. From violence done to the foreign ruler, violence to our own people whom we consider to be obstructing the country's progress is an easy natural step.[16] This we have seen during 1942 movement when many innocent people were murdered because they were charged to be agents of the government or being lack sheep. Hence, the world is sick of armed rebellions. Here, the masses have no active part to play. In a non-violent revolution, the masses not only cooperate actively in the process of revolution but also become bolder and more fearless. Then it is a misnomer to say that violence works swiftly. On the other hand, non-violence is a slow, long-drawn out process but it is the swiftest, the world has seen, for it is the surest.[17] The non-violent way will be found to be the shortest even though it may appear to be the longest to our impatient nature. The way of peace insures internal growth and stability.[18] When we take to violence, there is brutalisation of human nature, whereas those people who voluntarily undergo suffering raise themselves and the whole of humanity.[19] Violence and terrorism not only drag down themselves but mankind also. It is repugnant to invoke the beast in us.

Examples can be multiplied of killing babies, women and innocent passengers in a plane blast or through transistor bombs. It cannot be a matter of pleasure to see human nature dragged to the mire but those who take pleasure and pride in killing innocent persons are never brave but cowards of the first order. Nobody can deny the revolutionary's heroism and sacrifice. But heroism and sacrifice in a bad cause are waste of splendid energy and hurt the good cause by drawing away attention from it by the glamour of the misused heroism and sacrifice in a bad cause. The heroism and sacrifice of a non-violent satyagrahi is never inferior but is untarnished by the blood of the innocent. We must remember that the "self-sacrifice of one innocent man is a million times more potent than the sacrifice of million men who die in the act of killing others."[20] Sacrifice of self is infinitely superior to the sacrifice of others. We forget when we use force, we make it justifiable for others to do likewise.

Ahimsa is an evolutionary urge. In the case of conflict between two individuals in early times, perhaps the only vogue which prevailed was "a tooth for a tooth" and "an eye for an eye". Gradually it developed into the doctrine, "Thou shall not kill", "Thou shall not hate" and later, "Thou shall love thy neighbour as thyself". Gandhi goes one step ahead and says: "Thou shall love thy neighbour more than thyself" or "Love thy enemy". Violence is the law of the jungle and love is the law of the human species.[21] Wars, violence, hatred, destruction of various kinds and degrees have acted disastrously as obstacles and impeded the march of civilisation and culture of mankind. It is why not only the founders of various faiths like Mahavira, Buddha, Jesus and St. Francis but modern sociologists like Sorokin sees no future for humanity unless and until man becomes more altruistic.

Gandhi's name is often used in connection with the renunciation of non-violent strategy in situations of massive repression and injustice, expressed in two of the most quoted phrases: "Violence is better than cowardice,"[22] and that "Polish struggle against the Nazis was almost non-violent."[23] Gandhi no doubt sympathised with and admired those who fought bravely for justice and liberation, even with violent means, if those were the only means at their disposal, he upheld non-violence as the only desirable force to achieve liberation worthy of the human race.[24] Suffering is the badge of human race, not the sword.[25] He did not stop people to applaud the heroism of Mustafa Kamal Pasha, De Valera and Lenin but he reminded the followers of the school of violence in India that "India is not like Turkey or Ireland or Russia and that revolutionary activity is suicidal at this stage of the country's life at any rate if not for all time, in a country so vast, so hopelessly divided and with masses so deeply sunk in pauperism and so fearfully terror-stricken."[26] But ideological considerations were more important to Gandhi than pragmatic considerations. Non-violent resistance is "an all-sided sword; it can be used anyhow; it blesses him who uses it and him against whom it is used."[27] So he advises to practise non-violence even in face of criminal assaults[28] or during riots[29] or even foreign aggression.[30]

It is superstitious to think that there is valour and bravery in violence whereas non-violent resister is weak. This is gross ignorance. In fact, power of Satyagraha, that is, soul-force, is superior to the farce of arms. Physically strong men are strangers to the courage that is requisite of a Satyagarhi. Comparing a violent terrorist and non-violent Satyagrahi, Gandhi asks: "Wherein is courage required – in blowing others to pieces from behind a cannon, or with a smiling face to approach a cannon and be blown to pieces? Who is the true warrior – he who keeps death always as a bosom friend, or he who controls the death of others."[31] There is no bravery is sword. A man may be coward with a sword, whereas one who is free from hatred needs no sword. The real question is that we should adopt good means to achieve good end. Violence is a bad means and hence if we adopt it as our means, we cannot get good result. Violence ever defeats its own ends. There is a secret pride in every human heart that revolts at tyranny. Nothing good ever comes of violence (Luther). Violent delights have violent ends (Shakespeare). Nothing violent can be permanent (Marlowe).[32] If, therefore, anyone were to say: "I want to worship God; it does not matter that I do so by means of Satan," it would be set down as ignorant folly.[33] There is another proverb: "Those that take the sword shall perish by the sword," and "the professional swimmers will find a watery grave."[34] Victory of violence is short-lived, as well as counter-productive.

Hence, terrorism as a political ideology has no place in the civilised world. Generally, young men resort to terrorism because it has a sense of adventure and the young mind loves adventure and romanticism. But I say it is no fault of theirs. The young mind cannot tolerate injustice and exploitation, so they rebel against the established order or status quo. This is not bad. If a young man is worthy of the salt, he ought not to submit himself to any tyranny and injustice. Such was the case with the Indian revolutionaries. Nobody can doubt their sense of patriotism and sacrifice. They were also brave and fearless. But accepting all these qualities in them, Gandhi thought that India has not gained independence by their activities. True democracy or the Swaraj of the masses can never come through untruthful and violent means.[35] Armed risings are a remedy worse than the disease sought to be cured. They are a token of the spirit of revenge and impatience and anger. The method of violence cannot do good in the long run.[36] Through violence one may destroy one or more bad rulers but like Ravana's head, other will pop up in their places. Violence will give us a violent Swaraj. The power does not come to the people. Violent revolutions give birth to a Hitler, a Napoleon, a Cromwell, a Stalin and so on.

There is a tendency to extol one kind of terrorism and condemn the other. For example, here at present in India, there is a general trend to denounce terrorism in Kashmir, while our attitude towards terrorist violence in Sri Lanka by the Tamil activists has remained divided and lukewarm. This reveals that non-violence as a social value has not been recognised. It is viewed more or less as a *policy* and not as *creed*. Gandhi objects to this schizophrenic attitude towards violence or terrorism. To him, non-violence is an absolute value and hence there can be no compromise with it in the field of social action. To quote from the concluding portion of his autobiography: "My uniform experience has convinced me that there is no God than Truth ... (and) the only means for the realization of truth is Ahimsa."[37] In fact, God, truth and ahimsa are facets of the same reality. To disown the one is to disown the other. In Gandhian philosophy means and ends are convertible terms. That the end is high and laudable is not enough for him, the means too must be moral. Violence is immoral hence it must be eschewed. The emphasis on means is partly due to the fact that man can only strive, he cannot command results. Besides, the end grows out of the means as the tree grows out of the seed. "The opposite theory that the good end justifies all means, even violent means, is dangerous in practice and unsound ethically."[38] When we are not particular about the moral nature of the means, we easily adopt falsity and fraud, deceit and dishonesty, opportunism and violence. But these immoral means, which we adopt to achieve quick success, degrade us morally and lead us to regard *human beings as means rather than ends*. Violence deadens our finer feelings and sensitivity; makes us suspicious of everyone around us; and engenders counter-violence, revenge and counter-revenge and war.

But non-violence divorced from truth would be demoralising instead of liberating. If we let our hold of truth go, our non-violence becomes a hypocrisy. Therefore, Gandhi's non-violence always came as a rescuer of truth and justice –

Swaraj, i.e., removal of untouchability, concern for the last man and so on. He was, therefore, one with the revolutionaries, for liberating the country from the yoke of foreign rule. The revolutionaries fought the battle with the conventional weapons of violence; Gandhi discovered the "moral equivalent of war"[39] and fought with the weapons of non-violent non-cooperation, civil disobedience and other methods of Satyagraha. "There can be no Satyagraha in an unjust cause,"[40] and a Satyagrahi does not submit to injustice. But there is a virtue inherent in the method of his fight – that is, non-violence. Hence, it becomes a *dharma-yuddha* or righteous struggle conducted and campaigned through love and suffering. Hence, for Gandhi, "Ahimsa comes before Swaraj."[41] Satyagraha is neither a movement of the weak and imbecile nor "of brag, bluster, or bluff. It is test of our sincerity. It requires solid and silent sacrifice."[42] No doubt, Satyagraha is undertaken in order to remedy a wrong but is well-thought out. Thoughtless resistance will be regarded as bravado in military parlance, and violence or folly in the language of non-violence.[43] Let us all be brave enough to die the death of a martyr, but let no one have lust for martyrdom.[44] The terrorists are, no doubt, inspired by some noble cause (often misconceived), but they carry out their plan with a sense of hatred and vengeance, impatience and anger, with the result that they kill innocent people, take to other wrong methods and thus alienate public sympathy and mass support. Terrorism cannot be a mass movement or it cannot have mass involvement.

Gandhi was right in proclaiming that the millions of Indians do not desire the method of terrorism or politics of assassination. He was constrained to believe that "those who will rise to power by murder will certainly not make the nation happy."[45] The history of post-independent India has shown that terrorist movements in the country could not succeed. The brave Naxalites are now in great disarray and some of them have taken to the path of parliamentary democracy, while Vinoba's movement of land-gift *(Bhoodan Yajna)* could secure about 46 lakhs of acres of land through voluntary effort, while Jaya Prakash could successfully fight the onslaught on civil liberties and democratic freedom during 1974–77. And, as we have seen a few weeks ago how the Gandhian activist Anna Hazare through peaceful and non-violent means forced the mighty Government of India to fulfil their demand for constituting joint committee to draft Lokpal Bill.

Violence is out of date both on the global plane as well as in matters of internal social change. Arnold Toynbee rightly says: "At this supremely dangerous moment in human history, the only way of salvation for mankind is the Indian way. In the Atomic Age the whole human race has a utilitarian motive for following the Indian way. The survival of the human race is at stake … . Yet the strongest and most respectable utilitarian motive is only secondary reason … . The primary reason is that this teaching is right and is right because it flows from a true vision of spiritual reality."[46] Similarly, Martin Luther King declared: "The intellectual and moral satisfaction that I failed to gain from the utilitarianism of Bentham and Mill, the revolutionary methods of Marx and Lenin, the social contract theory of Hobbes, the 'back to nature' optimism of Rousseau, and the superman philosophy of Nietzsche, I found in the non-violent resistance philosophy of Gandhi, I came to feel that this was the only morally and practically sound method open to oppressed people in their struggle for freedom."[47]

It is a tragedy to find preparations for star wars and opening school of terrorism. We must desist to applaud acts of terrorism even when employed for a noble end, because means and end are inseparable. Instead, we should concentrate on peace research and try to perfect the science of Satyagraha. This should form part of our syllabi from the very beginning. Instead of training in NCC, we should train our youth force into Santi Sena. Peace demands a new civilisation, a new asceticism and a new attitude. Man and money power spent over terrorism, if channelised towards Satyagraha, can yield better results and create a happier society.

Notes

1. "A Word of Explanation" to *Hind Swaraj* by M.K. Gandhi, *Young India*, January 1921.
2. Gandhi wrote in (1921) "Preface to the New Edition", by M. Desai, *Hind Swaraj*, Ahmedabad, Navajivan Publishing House, Rev. New Edn., 1958, p. 14.
3. *Hind Swaraj*, p. 66.
4. Ibid., p. 69.
5. Ibid.
6. Ibid., p. 62.
7. Ibid., p. 69.

8. Ibid.
9. Ibid., p. 72.
10. *Young India*, 4.8.1920.
11. Ibid., 26.12.1924.
12. *Young India*, 21.5.1925.
13. *Harijan*, 9.3.1947.
14. *Young India*, 6.5.1926.
15. Ibid., 22.9.1920.
16. Ibid., 2.1.1930.
17. Ibid., 30.4.1925.
18. Ibid., 20.5.1926.
19. Ibid., 8.10.1925.
20. Ibid., 12.2.1925.
21. R.R. Diwakar, "Sociology of Homo-Sapiens", *Vigil*, Vol. 5, No. 34, October 3, 1953, p. 5.
22. Gandhi says, "Where there is a choice between cowardice and violence, I would advise violence. I would rather have India resort to arms in order to defend her honour than that she should, in a cowardly manner, become or remain a helpless witness to her own dishonour." *Young India*, 11 August 1920.
23. "In the same way for the Polish to stand violently against the German hordes, vastly superior in number and military equipment and strength, was *almost* non-violence." *Harijan*, 28.1.1939.
24. Devi Prasad, "Gandhi's Attitude towards Violent Struggles for Freedom", *Gandhi-Marg*, December, 1979, p. 600.
25. *Young India*, 5.11.1931.
26. *Harijan*, 12.7.1942.
27. *Hind Swaraj*, p. 82.
28. *Harijan*, 1.3.1942.
29. Ibid., 15.9.1940.
30. *Young India*, 31.12.1931, *Harijan*, 7.10.1939, 22.6.1940, 24.4.1942, 28.6.1942.
31. *Hind Swaraj*, p. 82.
32. T. Edwards and C.N. Catrevas (eds.), *The New Dictionary of Thought*, New York: Standard Book Company, 1934, p. 632.
33. *Hind Swaraj*, p. 72.
34. Ibid., p. 78.

35. *Harijan*, 27.5.1939.
36. *Young India*, 9.6.1920.
37. M.K. Gandhi, *An Autobiography*, Ahmedabad: Navajivan Publishing House, Second Edn., 1940, p. 370.
38. G.N. Dhawan, *The Political Philosophy of Mahatma Gandhi*, Ahmedabad: Navajivan Publishing House, 3rd Rev. Ed., 1957, p. 55.
39. This phrase was probably coined by William James suggesting that instead of making war itself a taboo, we should change its direction or lift up its character to a higher plane.
40. *Young India*, 27.4.1921.
41. *Harijan*, 24.6.1939.
42. *Young India*, 12.1.1921.
43. *Harijan*, 12.4.1942.
44. Ibid., 13.1.1927.
45. *Hind Swaraj*, p. 69.
46. A. Toynbee in his Foreword to Swami Ghanananda's *Sri Ram Krishna and His Unique Message*, 1970.
47. Martin Luther King, *Stride Towards Freedom*, 1959; quoted by D.S. Kothari in his keynote address to Gujarat Vidyapith, Ahmedabad on the occasion of the inauguration of Science-Ahimsa Centre on 6.4.1983, p. 3.

15

Rethinking Activism and Engendering Security

BERNEDETTE MUTHIEN

This paper will critically interrogate constructions of security generically, and human security specifically, in relation to women and notions of women's security. The constructs 'national security' and 'human security' will be critiqued, whose interests these serve, and how these constructs are specifically gendered (and class-based) and neglect issues relevant to women specifically, and other marginalised members of the international community.

Johan Galtung's triangular model of violence (1996), with its antitheses peace, will be examined, in order to explicate violence generically, which will lead to an examination of gender-based violence more specifically, premised on a deconstruction of patriarchal ideology, and drawing on the feminist anthropology of Marija Gimbutas and Riane Eisler and others.

The final section seeks to rethink activisms, employing the work of Mahatma Gandhi, Martin Luther King, Nelson Mandela and Ang San Suu Kyi.

State-centred security concerns itself with armies, guns and war, and excludes people's basic needs. This paper argues that the imperatives for peace are human security and justice.

Is Security Gendered?

At workshops in Cape Town, South Africa, grassroots women identified their needs for spouses or partners to be faithful and monogamous. Given the high rate of generic societal violence, they also requested more mortuary vans and ambulances. These women specifically called for an end to violence, an end to the gangsterism that plagues their communities, and critically, given the pandemic of gender-based violence in South Africa, an end to violence against women and children.

A study on violence against women in metropolitan South Africa found that almost 60 per cent of women felt 'very unsafe' while walking in their own neighbourhoods at night, with only 5 per cent of them feeling 'very safe' in their neighbourhoods at night (Bollen et al., 1999: 75, 78). The alarming statistics on violence against women illustrates that a lack of women's security affects the entire Southern African region. Goldblatt and Meintjes (1998: 8) discuss the effects of apartheid violence against communities, and the condition of women in the aftermath:

> The entrenchment of violence creates new daily insecurities for women – constant and overwhelming fear, exposure to abuse and obscenities, and threats of rape, kidnapping or death for themselves, their children or other relatives.

Security and Peace Studies have been dominated by men, and men's interests, particularly their emphasis on guns and war. As with most fields of study, women's interests and needs have been largely neglected and ignored.

Contesting Security

Barry Buzan (1983) recognises security as an underdeveloped and contested concept. He draws critical conceptual distinctions between defence and security, individual and national security, national and international security, violent means and peaceful ends. He applies his concept across a range of military, political, economic and social sectors. According to Buzan (ibid.: 20), the national security problem is a systemic security problem in which individuals, states and the system all play a part. Thus, Buzan (ibid.: 187) proposes the holistic notion of systemic security so that the

> national security problem defines itself as much in economic, political and social terms as in military ones.

National Security

Security has tended to be defined in terms of the nation-state. Thus, the notion of national security, emanating predominantly from the field of Strategic Studies, is dominated by the neo-realist mode of thought,[1] with its focus on power and institutions of power, especially the military. Neo-realist thought and notions of the state derive from Thomas Hobbes (1651). His infamous postulate that life in a state of nature is "nasty, brutish and short", epitomises the neo-realist hypothesis of an international state system of anarchy. Classical American neo-realist theorists, especially Carr (1939), Morgenthau (1948) and Waltz (1954, 1979), built on the Hobbesian notion of an anarchic state system. Reacting to this position, Maxi Schoeman (1998: 7, 22–23), who has extensively researched women's security in Southern Africa, criticises Waltz in particular for 'de-historicising' the international state system and assuming its

> inevitability, rather than admitting that it is a human construct and a product of a specific era and context.

The British academic, Hedley Bull (1977), tried to theorise a form of anarchy characterised by at least some interdependence and cooperation in his writings on an 'international society' of states. Bull's key contention centres on his notion of 'society' versus that of the traditional, more anarchic system, thus arguably placing his thinking between neo-liberal[2] and neo-realist thought. Issues about what constitutes cooperation, and whose interests it serves, can be derived from rudimentary studies of the world system's theory of Wallerstein (1979). More recent critical theory is fundamentally concerned with historicising the status quo, and seeking structural transformation.

This traditional notion of national security, in terms of armies, guns and war, emphasises the state as both the primary actor and level of analysis. Narrow state-centrism excludes other important actors and levels of analyses, including individuals and groups (ethnicities and religious groupings, political and ideological groups, and non-state actors like corporate mercenaries), as well as other institutions, e.g., transnational corporations (TNCs) and multi-national corporations (MNCs), international financial institutions (IFIs) such as the World Bank, as well as the global arms trade – from manufacturers to marketers to purchasers. The modern move away from inter-state war to intra-state conflict, in particular, stresses the importance of group and institutional analyses, e.g., the conflict in the Democratic Republic of Congo (DRC) involves regional, linguistic, economic group, state and international dimensions. It involves various political and military groups, especially diamond and oil TNCs, and other African states, notably Namibia, Zimbabwe, Angola, Uganda, Rwanda, as well as non-African states such as the United States, Belgium and France. It includes non-state actors such as mercenaries, arms and other suppliers – locally and internationally.

This skewed focus on the state usually excludes the worst affected, women and children, especially in rural areas, where they are the ones who have to seek fresh water and wood for fuel, which exposes them to landmines. Hence, the irony of men who plant landmines to deter other men, but which largely kill and injure women and children trying to survive during and after conflicts.

The traditional definition of security also emphasises protection from harm for citizens of a country within national boundaries. National boundaries in Africa are colonial legacies, often arbitrary, and variously disputed, e.g., the Kasikili/Sedudu Island conflict between Namibia and Botswana. Sovereignty of borders is often bestowed, with little or no consultation, and with scanty regard by the international community to the impacts on the inhabitants within the borders. Eritrea, for example, is deemed a sovereign state after its secession from Ethiopia, while Somaliland, where women contributed significantly to brokering peace, is not officially recognised.

The idea of protection from harm for citizens is narrowly defined, and effectively means protection from foreign attack, but does not preclude offensive measures deemed in the interests of citizens and state, for example, South Africa and Botswana's military intervention in Lesotho during 1998, as well as Namibia's incursions into Angola against UNITA. So too, this traditional definition of harm does not include other aspects of safety, security or well-being, including the environment, basic needs (e.g., food and housing), identity and dignity. A more holistic definition of protection from harm would mean more than the traditional protection from war and invasion by foreign armies. It would mean, to name a few examples, protection from hunger, protection from poverty, protection from sexual assault for women, children and men.

The traditional national security definition of protection from harm refers to a state-level notion of harm, and does not protect citizens from homelessness, illiteracy and unemployment. Nor does it protect citizens' fundamental human rights, as enshrined in the South African Constitution, to be free of discrimination on the grounds of race, class, gender, spirituality or sexuality. Negative peace, or the absence of war, conforms to traditional definitions of security in general, and traditional protection from harm in particular. Positive peace, on the other hand, means both negative peace, as well as the realisation of even the most basic of social justice needs.

Traditional notions of security are based on conventional (though flawed) distinctions between public and private spheres. The state has traditionally been concerned with the male-dominated public realm. Thus issues outside of the public realm, including domestic violence, job discrimination, the status of women, have not been viewed as concerns of national security.

In an interview, in January 1999, peace educator and activist, Betty Reardon[3] described the three major problems with the international security as under:

> (Firstly) it is dominantly masculine rather than human in conception; (secondly) it is designed to achieve the security of the state rather than that of persons or human groups; and (thirdly), what is most readily evident, it addresses only one of four fundamental sources of human well being. The condition of world-wide insecurity exists because the present state-centred security paradigm places a priority on protection against harm from others over all other sources of human well-being. The militarised international security system is maintained at the expense of the abuse of the natural environment. It sets limits on meeting the economic and social needs of the world's poor. It disregards and violates fundamental, universal human rights, and provides inadequate protection against the harms of ill health, poor infrastructures, and accident and disaster provision, as inordinate resources, research, human talent and human effort are squandered on the armed defence of 'national security'. The system is inadequate, indeed, dangerous because it is imbalanced. It is derived by exclusively masculine, outwardly directed standards applied by the predominantly male 'national security' establishments who have not been socialised to focus on human needs.

Human Security

A second approach that contests the national security model is proposed by Johan Galtung, who matured from radical analyses of (under)development since the 1960s to groundbreaking Peace Studies during the 1990s. Based on the work of other researchers, especially the work of Robert Johansen of the Peace Studies Programme at Notre Dame (1975–1996) over two decades, Galtung

(1996) took the debate into new realms of understanding the requirements for peace when he proposed what has come to be called the human security model. This model, Reardon asserts, focuses on environmental security, basic needs, issues of dignity and identity, and finally, protection from harm.

The human security paradigm is designed to provide a more holistic comprehensive definition of security and protection from all forms of harm. These include indirect or structural, cultural, and direct or personal, and their respective antitheses, as postulated in Galtung's (1996) model (see Illustration 1). Structural violence (with its antithesis structural peace) refers to, for example, discrimination based on class, race or gender, violence embedded in the very structure of society. Personal or direct violence implies a direct verbal or physical attack of one person on another. Cultural violence "serves to legitimise direct and structural violence" (Galtung, 1996: 31).

Illustration 1

Human Security Paradigm

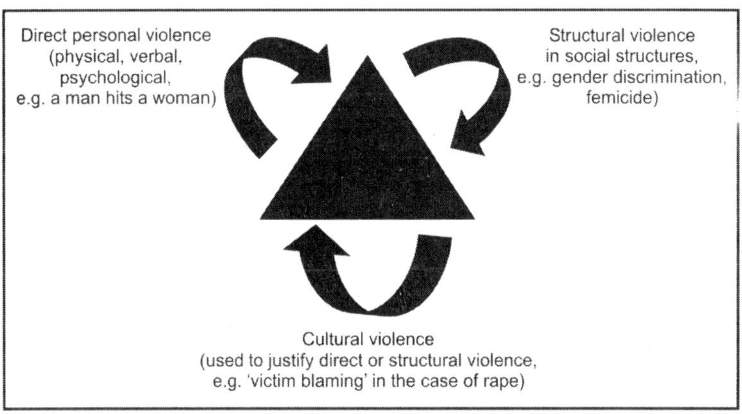

While violence against women is direct and personal (e.g., a man assaults a woman) it also embodies structural sexism and genocide, as well as cultural legitimisation which seeks its continuous replication. A subtle example of structural violence in this instance would be victim blaming which is institutionalised in law and legal practice. More pronounced forms include common practices which are sometimes codified in law, such as female genital mutilation, forced child brides, and femicide/infanticide. In relation to cultural violence, this is evident for example when survivors internalise their personal and systemic brutalisation. This relates to the sexist attitudes that keep women's opportunities limited.

The antithesis of violence, of course, is peace,[4] and the three forms of violence outlined above would also have corresponding forms of peace. If one eliminates physical assault (including physical forms of gender-based violence), he/she will experience personal/direct peace. If one eliminates structural violence (including sexism, racism and homophobia) and transform institutions appropriately, he/she will experience structural peace. And, if one eradicates cultural violence (including ways of thinking and being), he/she will experience cultural peace.

Thus, it appears that none of these forms of violence, and their respective antitheses, are entirely isolated from the other. For example, one cannot eliminate gender-based violence without transforming institutions, as well as ways of thinking and being. And if one changes cultures of violence into cultures of balance and harmony in line with a partnership model, he/she will necessarily eliminate gender-based violence since there will no longer be polar opposites, distrust and devaluation of others.

The human security paradigm, as outlined above, attempts to address critical questions about who is secure, and who not, and whose interests are served. Reactively, human security would include the absence of physical violence, or negative peace. But proactively, human security involves establishing mechanisms (policies and structures) that will ensure that individuals and communities enjoy personal, structural and cultural security, in other words positive peace.

A question that could be asked is: how is security constructed, and how does it exclude women and other marginalised groups (e.g., indigenous peoples)?

Reardon (interview, op. cit., January 1999) speaks of four sources of human security: the environment, basic needs (e.g., food and housing), identity and dignity, and finally, protection from harm. She asserts that human security of groups and individuals is essentially the expectation of well-being:

> Everything that is done in the name of security is ostensibly to fulfil that expectation. Human security derives primarily from the expectation that four fundamental conditions of security will

> be met: one, that the environment in which we live can sustain human life; two, that our basic physical survival needs for food, clothing and shelter will be met; three, that our fundamental human dignity and personal and cultural identities will be respected; and four, that we will be protected from avoidable harm. If a society can meet these conditions for most of its population it is generally a secure society; and, as it intentionally seeks to meet them for all the population, it moves toward being a just society. By these standards there are no truly secure societies in the world and probably none that are fully committed to achieving authentic human security.

In a departure from traditional practice, the new South African National Defence Force (SANDF), with assistance from civil society, drafted its security legislation in a radically new way. They redefined security in terms of development, and acknowledged the absence of an external aggressor, and the very real threat of poverty to internal stability. As chairperson of the National Conventional Arms Control Committee (NCACC)[5], Kader Asmal (1996: 33), put it:

> non-military sources of instability in the economic, social, humanitarian and ecological fields have become threats to peace and security.

Galtung's model is by far the most comprehensive in terms of inclusivity, and he painstakingly demonstrates his respect for and desire to include women in his analysis. However, it is precisely the 'phallogocentrism' of generic knowledge and thought which precludes complete transcendence of his own masculine and other subjectivities. The term 'phallogocentrism' stems from the Greek words *phallos* (phallus) and *logos* (word) or *logy* (discourse), and thus implies that traditional (male-stream) knowledge and logic, constructed by men for men, is fundamentally imbued with male bias, and will necessarily ignore the inclusion of women, or women's perspectives. It follows that universal objectivity, constructed by male theoreticians throughout history, is neither universal nor objective, but gendered, and specifically male, and hence serves particular (male) interests. Think, for example, of the founding fathers of modern democracy and social science: Greek philosophers (male) from Plato to Aristotle, and European scholars (male) from Locke to Rousseau. An example closer to home is that of African griots (male), with Senegalese griots' strategic extrusion of Senegal's part in African slavery from their oral history. Confucious, Gautama, Jesus and Muhammed were all male too.

Engendering Security

Grassroots women in Southern Africa define security as:

1. more than individual, and including families and communities;
2. more than physical, and including economics and health;
3. depending on gender justice;
4. including the quotidian or everyday (from food to sexual assault).

In South Africa a woman is raped every 26 seconds, and a woman is murdered by her male partner every four days (Medical Research Council). This can be compared with developed countries like Sweden, Belgium, Germany and the USA, where at least 30 per cent of women are battered by their male partners.

The Uncivil War against Women: Gender as Society's Battle Line

When countries are not officially at war with one another, can it justifiably be called peace when women and children are beaten and raped every few seconds in every country in the world?

To answer this question, it is necessary to examine the origins of violence. As a starting point, the following working definition of 'violence' is offered: *the harmful action or actions of one person or group against another person or group.* Looking at this definition, one can see that it speaks of one person or group, versus or against another person or group. Us and Them. Us versus Them. Polar opposites. Binary oppositions.

The construction of binary oppositions may stem from a particular identity formation, the ways in which people are taught to view themselves and the world. The conventional modern formation of identity is premised on an understanding of "I am because I am not". So one can find statements such as, "I am female because I am not male"; "I am black because I am not white"; "I am African because I am not European or North American". This construction of Self fundamentally needs an Other against which to measure itself and its value. In an intrinsically competitive environment, if the Self is to succeed and be valued, it needs to transcend or overpower the Other, and if the Self is to be valued and triumph, the Other of necessity needs to be devalued. This process can be termed 'Othering'.

Such identity construction premised on polarity[6] or 'Othering' fosters conflict over access to and control of resources. In this way power also becomes a resource, as in 'power to' and 'power over'. This belief system, based on "I am because I have and you don't", can be juxtaposed with one in which there is a more equitable distribution of resources, i.e., a more 'diffuse' form of power. Power as a relation between people became a contest over resources because it is premised on a flawed belief system centred on Othering and the devaluation of the Other.

Othering and Oppressions

The origins of Othering and oppressions centres on the explication of two fundamental belief systems. Riane Eisler (1995), based on the work of anthropologist Marija Gimbutas, posits two models – the *partnership* model and the *dominator* model. When Eisler refers to the dominator model, she means "either patriarchy or matriarchy – the ranking of one half of humanity over the other". She describes the partnership model, on the other hand, as one in which social relations are primarily based on the principle of linking rather than ranking.

> In this model – beginning with the most fundamental difference in our species, between male and female – diversity is not equated with either inferiority or superiority. (1995: xvii)

Eisler continues to argue that the dominator model is based on domination and force and the power to take life (death, killing), rather than the power to give life (birth) as in the partnership model, where actualisation and maximisation of individuals' potentials are primordial.

Western and modern thinking and beliefs are premised on the dominator model. Societies based on this paradigm are intrinsically unequal, hierarchical and oppressive. A historical precedent is found in the shift in ancient Aztec society from partnership to dominator models. More recently, modern European imperialism, which constructed the present state system in Africa, provides further examples.

Significantly, the discourse of colonisation similarly operates on a system of binary oppositions, such as female-male, black-white, infidel-believer or barbarity-civilisation. This particular way of constructing personal and group identity fosters conflict rather than cooperation, and by its very nature leads to violence. Think, for example, of the Hutu and Tutsi in the Great Lakes.[7]

However, while one bears in mind that colonisation of Africa engendered much violence, one must also not forget that some

African forebears traded in other Africans, as the histories of slavery evince. Some Africans, who operated on the construct of "I am because I am not", also oppressed and waged wars against their kinsfolk whom they felt threatened by and whose property they wished to confiscate, practices which were exploited and exacerbated by colonisation, and which continue to this day.

Partnership and 'Matriarchy'

The dominator model can be juxtaposed with the partnership model, ancient and indigenous ways of thinking that preceded colonisation, found in societies such as that of the Khoisan of Southern Africa, the Toltecs of Latin America, and almost the entire East where Buddhism was and is still widely practiced.[8]

Anne Baring and Jules Cashford (1991: 157), in their narration of the migrations and invasions into Europe by Aryans and Semites during the Bronze and Iron Ages, are effectively describing the shift from a partnership to a dominator model:

> Both invading peoples introduced the idea of an opposition between the powers of light and darkness, imposing this polarity on the older view in which the whole contained both light and darkness in an ever-changing relationship.

The partnership model is premised on harmony and balance, on mutual respect for, and interdependence of, each other and the environment, on cooperation rather than conflict. It is personified in the yin/yang symbol, which epitomises a harmonious integration of all elements into one being, all dancing fluidly together to create a dynamic organism. It perhaps embodies a different tenet like, "I am because I care; I am because I belong". This sense of caring community in ancient societies[9] is something Carol Lee Flinders has also touched on in her forthcoming book, *Reclaiming a Life of Value*. In the partnership model peace and respect are fundamental organising principles, where power is cooperatively shared.

In this model matriarchy is not necessarily the opposite of patriarchy. Ancient matriarchal societies were not hierarchical, oppressive and violent (towards men). Instead, they have been shown to be cooperative and peaceful, societies in which men and women were equal and equitably shared resources,[10] even as females were key leaders, spiritually and otherwise, of their societies.[11] Hence, the term 'matriarchy' to describe ancient cooperative societies as the antithesis of patriarchy is erroneous, and various scholars have posited alternative terms, agreeing in essence that prepatriarchal societies were both matrilineal and matrilocal (with patriarchal societies being patrilineal and patrilocal).[12]

The Origins of Gender Oppression

Ancient societies were not always patriarchal or necessarily gendered. African history records the matriarchal rule of, for example, Amanitare and other ancient Nubian queens, as well as the rule of Ashanti in North Ghana. Katarina Tomasevski refers to the civilian rule of Neber in Egypt during the Old Kingdom (c. 3100–2345 BC). She argues that indigenous Egyptian society was strongly matriarchal:

> Some historians argue that women may, in fact, have 'discovered' agriculture in prehistoric times. There are even instances of matrilineal and matriarchal societies in Malaysia, Java, the Philippines, and India. (1993: 1, 2)

In the context of gender, the dominator model presupposes a rigid distinction between the two genders. There are countless examples of modern colonisers imposing and maintaining this separation to the expense of the partnership model of thought.

In Burma, for example, British colonisers noted how 'barbaric' the native Burmese were because their genders were not rigidly separated and hierarchised. So too the Khoisan of Southern Africa. In both cases, the colonisers, aided by the requirements of capitalism, worked immensely hard at inculcating gender distinctions in these societies and communities, with horrific results. Heike Becker has shown in her studies of gender-based violence and the San that both colonisation and capitalism (as well as apartheid in Southern Africa) caused and exacerbated gender-based violence in the Khoisan communities in Southern Africa, through the introduction and fostering of rigid and controlled gender distinctions.

Especially in Africa, the impact of colonialism, grounded in monotheistic and patriarchal religious systems,[13] extended beyond the imposition of rigid gender polarities to also subvert traditional constructions of family and partnerships. The Judeo-Christian and colonial model of heterosexual, male-dominated families can be contrasted with indigenous African family practices such as woman-to-woman 'marriage'.

While studies about marriages between women have always been limited, Anthonia Uzuegbunam (2001: 3) documents this phenomenon amongst the Igbo in Nigeria, and traces documents relating cases from the 1930s. She asserts that marriages between women are common in East, Southern and West Africa, as well as Sudan. She argues that these marriages are initiated by women who are not able to bear children, who join in a (traditional) union with a younger woman who bears the family children after insemination by a carefully selected man. According to Uzuegbunam,

> ... woman – woman marriage in Igboland is portrayed as a flexible option available to women to pursue any number of interests, political, social, economic and personal. The guiding principles therefore are flexibility, heterogeneity and ambiguity. (ibid.: 11)

Uzuegbunam further asserts that these relationships are more egalitarian than conventional heterosexual ones, and that the childbearing partner enters entirely freely into the union, and continues to explain that:

> ... woman – woman marriage in Igboland is not like lesbianism where love and sexual relations are exchanged by same male sex (*sic*). Rather, woman – woman marriage has stories of love, children, companionship, commitment, sexual freedom, vulnerability and empowerment. The woman initiator invites a male with the arrangement for procreation and for pleasure. (ibid.)

This centuries-old practice of woman-woman marriage, with its intrinsic mutuality and egalitarianism, has been steadily eroded by the colonisation of indigenous African societies.

> Things are not as clear-cut as they seem. They are neither circumscribed nor separated from each other by lines. Lines are drawn in the mind. *There are no lines in nature* ... (Everything emerges) from a matrix of conditions and in turn becomes part of another matrix of conditions from which something else emerges.
>
> —Stephen Batchelor (1997: 76)

Man's fear of penetration and/or violation by the 'impure' (bisexual) Other, does seem to cast some light on the reason(s) for his rejection of her. A useful analogy can be drawn between black and white, or colonised and coloniser. The need to increase and maintain the distance between these opposites stems from the fear of the (strangeness/difference of the) Other. China Galland (1998: 117) recalls an ancient Indian story:

> Ramakrishna explained (Kali's) darkness as the result of distance. When we are far away from an object, it appears dark to us. "Go near and you will find her devoid of all color," he said. "The water of a lake appears black from a distance. Go near and take the water in your hand, and you will see it has no color at all. Similarly, the sky looks blue from a distance. But look at the atmosphere near you; it has no color.

Galland's story serves to illustrate that something only looks alien when it is not examined closely enough. Galland (ibid.: 80) cites a wise Tibetan: "'Our confusion lies in believing something to be separate from ourselves'," he begins, explaining the Buddhist view that sees mind and matter as one continuum, continually arising and falling back into itself, like waves into water." Dynamic and fluid, inseparable and one.

What is the origin of this fear of the Other? The answer could be found in dominant ideology itself. Ideology is advanced by (a group of) individuals (whether they are autonomous or form classes and/or genders) and those individuals would wish to perpetuate their own (positions of) power and privileged access to resources. If they create a new market (or dumping ground) for commodities through colonisation, they would need to subjugate the colonised Other, and the ideology of fear (and hierarchical oppositions) lends itself well to this form of exploitation. So too with the oppression of woman.

Galland (ibid.: 50) recounts the words of Wisdom Moon, the Mother of all Buddhas – known as Drolma or Mother in Tibet, Kwan Yin in Chinese, Tara (Liberator or Saviour) in Sanskrit, Wisdom or Sophia in the Old Testament, and the Goddess of Compassion everywhere:

> Nowhere can I find what is male, nowhere can I find what is female. These are simply forms, no more separate from one another than a wave is from water. But since most Buddhas have chosen to come (to earth) as a man, perhaps it would be more helpful if I became enlightened in a woman's body.

Gender-based Violence

This understanding of violence and peace now allows a more in-depth examination of the concept of 'gender-based violence'.

According to the Committee on the Elimination of Discrimination Against Women (CEDAW), gender-based violence is defined as:

> violence that is directed against a woman because she is a woman, or that affects women disproportionately. It includes acts that inflict physical, mental or sexual harm or suffering, and threats of such acts, coercion or arbitrary deprivation of liberty.

The Declaration on the Elimination of Violence Against Women notes three key spheres in which gender-based violence may occur or which may perpetrate and/or condone such violence: the family, the community and the state.[14] December Green adds one further site of gender-based violence, i.e., the economy. The concept of gender-based violence should accordingly be broadened to also include the notion of economic abuse, which has been defined in the South African Domestic Violence Act (1998) to include "the unreasonable deprivation of economic or financial resources or the unreasonable disposal of household effects in which the victim/survivor has an interest".[15]

Gender-based violence therefore occurs through the act of *being gendered*. Through the kinds of identity construction where the Self cannot exist without the Other, and where the Self cannot be valued without devaluing the Other, women are valued as less than men. (It may be useful to note that men too get raped, especially during times of conflict. This is because these more vulnerable men are made into the Other, and so feminised or turned into surrogate women. This happens in prisons throughout the world, in gangs and in other areas of conflict.)

The CEDAW definition above focuses on women as the subjects of gender-based violence; however, it should be recognised that such violence also affects men, not only as potential victims, but also when they act as *perpetrators*.

It is ironic that the dominator model, and the ways in which it articulates itself in the construction of contemporary societies, brutalises everyone, even the dominant or oppressor. If one is taught violence, control and domination as a way of life, one becomes brutalised by it, on all sides of the equation. In this way even oppressors are victimised by the system and their own violent behaviours (whether physical, institutional and/or cultural), since they cannot perceive of a more harmonious and compassionate existence. This is most readily evident in cases of family violence, especially in intensely patriarchal contexts where the role of father and provider turns on itself when the patriarch murders the entire family he is meant to protect.[16] So too when fathers rape daughters as an expression of their right of ownership over female offspring. It is also commonly known that a large proportion of perpetrators of incest are themselves survivors of such violence. The same can be said about war, where no party involved in the conflict is left unscathed by the violence, murder and carnage.[17]

Violence, murder and rape exact a toll on the psyche of both perpetrator and survivor/victim, and everyone is (re-)brutalised in the process, even spectators through vicarious trauma, as those working to combat gender-based violence will attest. As Jane Bennett puts it:

> Both women and men are vulnerable to the way dominant norms of gender relation, within their contexts, are working. Within South Africa, men are as likely to become blunt assailants of women (and often, of men), as women are to become victims of sexual abuse, domestic battery, economic abuse, and incest. Clearly, those who actively assault retain responsibility for their violence – that is a matter of principle and law. But the challenge for South Africans committed to the transformation of oppressive social norms is to untangle both 'victim' and 'perpetrator' from their terrible interlock of violence, no matter how shocking the 'perpetration' or how resonant the 'victimhood/survivorship'. (2000: 4)

Gender-based violence, as is commonly known, is not about sex or conflict. It is about control and about power, in keeping with the dominator model. Vicky Randall asserts that "if woman is associated with nature as opposed to culture, and culture is compelled to maintain itself, it follows that culture will devalue the nature it seeks to transcend, and hence man will subordinate woman" (1982: 23).

Gender-based violence is fundamentally premised on the ideology of male control over women's productive and reproductive powers, of male control over women's skills and resources, and especially of control over our power to produce future generations of producers. It is also about male control over women's sexuality, which is the key aspect of reproductive powers.

Women's productive powers include agricultural labour, wage labour in domestic service and other industries, as well as the informal sector (e.g., selling goods for small profits). Women's reproductive powers centre on our abilities to give birth and raise children, children who constitute the next generation of producers. And hence this particular function is of critical importance to patriarchy, and control of not only the present productive capacity, but that of future generations too, is very important.

As consumers, women buy and use commodities in the home. Hence women are also caught up in the endlessly repetitive task of using (if not producing) and reproducing (by baking, cooking, etc.) the commodity, and are at least equally alienated from the product. Women also support the production process, apart from their 'invaluable' roles as consumers, through their domestic work, thus freeing men for labour in the production process and the public sphere. So too women reproduce the labour force by bearing the next generation of workers (and consumers or surplus accumulators).

A critical psychological dimension of the control of women's sexuality is male insecurity about the origins of their children. Women become impregnated, and without complex and expensive medical tests, a man will never know certainly whether he is the actual father of his female partner's children. This is prominent in male anxiety over and control of female sexuality. But far more fundamental in this dominator model is the need to limit women's mobility and choice to ensure their consistent producing and reproducing (of future generations of producers, reproducers and surplus accumulators).

So too, with the kind of identity formation of Self-Other discussed earlier, with women devalued as lesser beings than men, women's sexuality is also devalued and of less consequence than that of men.

According to some writers, there are four clear indicators of gender-based violence. In societies where these circumstances prevail, gender-based violence is more likely to occur and/or in more severe forms. The indicators are:

1. economic inequality;
2. existing patterns of using physical violence to resolve conflicts;
3. male authority and control over decision-making (and excluding women from this process); and
4. restrictions on women's ability to leave the family setting.

All four indicators fit in with the dominator model, from inequality (economic and other forms); employing violence (physical, structural and cultural) as conflict resolution methods;

male control over women and others; as well as restrictions on women's (and others') mobility and freedom. In this sense, since violence generically, and gender-based violence specifically, function on the three axes of Galtung's triangle of violence/peace (personal/direct/physical, structural/institutional, and cultural), it is imperative that attention be paid to factors that exacerbate and contribute to violence, from issues of development and poverty, to HIV/AIDS. And hence even the International Monetary Fund's Structural Adjustment Programmes or SAPs (with decreased state spending on social security) contribute to gender-based violence, as Heidi Hudson (1998: 70) has shown in Zimbabwe, where the first two years of the introduction of SAPs led to health spending being cut by a third and the maternal mortality rate (a form of gender-based violence) doubled.

Rethinking Activism

Existing ways of thinking are too often premised on polarity, the kind of thinking and activism that engenders conflict rather than cooperation, and which prohibits or inhibits efforts to seek true transformative solutions for social change.

Activism can be viewed as inherently adversarial, where two sets of 'enemies' square off in battle, with neither side able to claim victory without defeat of the other; in other words, a perpetuation of the dominator model, which by its very nature perpetuates violence in a continuous cycle, as evinced by the current conflict between Israel and Palestine. Mohandas (Mahatma) Gandhi's concept of *satyagraha* (truth force[18]), in which a non-violent mass campaign of non-compliance is waged, was originally conceptualised as an alternative to the idea of 'passive resistance', which implies passivity and victimhood over agency and action. Instead, *satyagraha* is designed as not merely an alternative to violence or force, but as superior to it.[19] In the words of Geoffrey Ashe,

> The Satyagrahi – in theory – not only consents to suffer at the wrongdoer's hands, but conquers through suffering ... . Yet his [sic] victory is not the opponent's defeat. It is the opponent's conversion ... . Victory does not mean that one side triumphs at the other's expense, but that both sides are reconciled in a new harmony, with the Wrong cancelled ... . Gandhi, British-conditioned, believed in the reign of law as a moral concept. But – he insisted – some laws can and should be broken, in the name of a higher law with which they conflict. (1968: 101)

This expression of Gandhi's *satyagraha* is certainly in keeping with a partnership model. Nelson Mandela, first President of a democratic South Africa since 1994, transitioned from an adversarial position during the 1960s, with the formation of the African National Congress' (ANC) military wing, Umkhonto we Sizwe (MK), to a philosophical and political perspective perfectly typical of the partnership model more latterly during his 27 years of imprisonment by the apartheid regime. Since the 1980s Mandela consistently sought reconciliation through dialogue and negotiation with his erstwhile oppressors, eventually leading to a government of national unity, based on proportional representation, including the former apartheid leader as one of two Deputy Presidents, and senior cabinet positions for leaders of opposition parties, in the first democratic government of 1994.

Mandela's selfless desire to seek alternatives to apartheid without wreaking vengeance on perpetrators of brutality led him to a search for common ground, reconciliation and nation-building across ethnicities. Thus, both Gandhi and Mandela embody the principles of partnership, and both have proven to be formidable activists in the struggles for equity, justice and peace. Both viewed human rights through the prism of the partnership model, which allows for more creative ways of including human rights in activisms.

A key activist who embodies the principles of the partnership model in her struggle for justice and peace is Aung San Suu Kyi, who quoted her father during a speech to a mass rally during 1988: "Democracy is the only ideology which is consistent with freedom. It is also an ideology that promotes and strengthens peace. It is therefore the only ideology we should aim for" (1991: 200).

Suu Kyi's methods of resistance included several hunger strikes while unlawfully imprisoned for several years by the military dictatorship in Burma. Her struggle for human rights is firmly located in the principles of democracy, non-violence and collective discipline, as Philip Kreager summarises in Suu Kyi's book:

> These principles reflect the inspiration which Aung San Suu Kyi derived from her study and reflection on Gandhi's philosophy and practice of non-violent civil disobedience ... . Under such severe pressures (imprisoned, killed or driven into hiding), and against tremendous odds, Aung San Suu Kyi's reasoned insistence on the sole legitimacy of non-violent means and the priority

> of human rights has proven the only enduring answer: by her example, and her prevention of bloodshed, she was able to establish a real alternative for the people, who otherwise face only submission. (1991: 287, 288)

Suu Kyi also modelled her activism on the ideas espoused by Martin Luther King. Firmly rooted in the intrinsic egalitarianism of Buddhism, she noted the absence of hierarchical structures in pre-colonial Burmese society. She is a Nobel Peace Laureate (1991) along with other notable activists such as South Africa's Albert Luthuli, Desmond Tutu and Nelson Mandela.

These examples of non-violent strategies illustrate that activism does not need to be violent in order to be effective. To achieve reconciliation between conflicting parties, one needs a redistribution of power, i.e., one party has to voluntarily relinquish some of its power and resources. The dominant party often needs to be *forced* to agree to redistributive justice. However, that force does not need to be violent, as argued above.

Conclusion

The construction of identities based on polar opposites, and creation of Self versus Other, engenders oppression, inequality and violence. To get away from this, to get to the root of the violence in all societies, one needs to begin thinking of more harmonious ways of thought and living and being. And move away from domination towards partnership.[20]

While patriarchy, and the dominator model, have been around for thousands of years, evidence of societies modelled on the partnership model clearly shows that patriarchal rule is not inevitable, and that other more cooperative possibilities do exist. Historical reflections of non-patriarchal societies and periods of rule help support a belief in, and conception of, forms of existence and societies that transcend patriarchal rule.[21]

One should remind oneself that *change is possible*. Think, for example, of Chinese foot binding, which is now extinct. The practice of facial scarring of indigenous women in Sudan and some parts of South Africa, traditionally used as a form of adornment like modern-day cosmetics or make-up, is now almost extinct. As are other practices from some ethnic groups in South Africa, like the severing of a finger or part of a finger.

The key to success is to move away from the adversarial nature of the prevailing dominator system, with its inherent violence and oppression, and to move towards partnership by embracing the timeless values of *satyagraha*. In the words of Suu Kyi,

> If a people or a nation can reach their objectives by disciplined and peaceful means, it would be a most honourable and admirable achievement … . Those who have the greater strength should show restraint and tolerance towards those who have less strength … . Democracy is an ideology that allows everyone to stand up according to his beliefs. They should not be threatened or endangered … . Do not because of your greater strength be vengeful towards those who are of weaker strength. (1991: 201, 204)

> God has chosen what the world regards as foolish to shame the wise, and what the world regards as weak, God has chosen to shame the strong, and what the world regards as low, contemptible, mere nothing, God has chosen …
>
> — First Lesson, I Corinthians I: 27–28)

> Ethical integrity originates in empathy, for then we take the well-being of others to heart and are moved to be generous and caring. Our thoughts, words, and deeds are based on a sense of what we have in common rather than what divides us … . Ethical integrity requires both the intelligence to understand the present situation as the fruition of former choices, and the courage to engage with it as the arena for the creation of what is to come. It empowers us to embrace the ambiguity of a present that is simultaneously tied to an irrevocable past and free for an undetermined future. Ethical integrity is not moral certainty. A priori certainty about right and wrong is at odds with a changing and unreliable world, where the future lies open, waiting to be born from choices and acts. Such certainty may be consoling and strengthening, but it can blunt awareness of the uniqueness of each ethical moment. When we are faced with the unprecedented and unrepeatable complexities of this moment, the question is not 'What is the right thing to do?', but 'What is the compassionate thing to do?'
>
> —Stephen Batchelor, *Buddhism without Beliefs*

Notes

1. Schoeman (1998: 5) acknowledges that the literature (attempting to expand the existing narrow scope of Security Studies) is still rather thin to non-existing when it comes to broadening or exploring the agents of security.

2. Schoeman (1998: 7), citing Robert Keohane, suggests that one objective of neo-liberalism is to ensure that the state-system and the capitalist world economy function smoothly in their co-existence by diffusing any conflicts, tensions, or crises that may arise between them.

   Hence, the need to maintain the international states system, with Bull's (1977) idea of a loose society of states, cooperating to perpetuate the status quo.
3. Through e-mail communication.
4. Conflict, which is not the same as violence, is not necessarily and intrinsically bad, and may contribute to creativity if resolved peacefully. All relations, and all societies, will invariably experience conflict at least some of the time, in part due to difference(s). It is in acknowledging conflict (and differences), and dealing with it constructively and peacefully that creativity and growth can be fostered.
5. A cabinet committee charged with ratification of all sales and purchases of arms, the NCACC has, in direct contravention of its own guidelines, ratified sales of weapons to countries with dubious human rights records, such as Indonesia and Turkey.
6. According to the *Oxford English Reference Dictionary*, polarity implies two poles with contrary qualities, two opposite tendencies/opinions, while dualism implies being two-fold, duality; theory regarding two independent underlying principles, e.g., mind and matter, form and content, theological forces of good and evil equally balanced in the universe, Christ as both divine and human. So what we have is polarity and what we are striving (back) towards is duality.
7. Whether the identities of 'Hutu' and 'Tutsi' in Rwanda are based on caste or class, ethnicity, or on resources, and whether their identities preceded colonisation, is contested by Rwandans themselves, most of who argue that their ethnic identities are colonial constructs.
8. While we acknowledge that Buddhism is not entirely unproblematic, especially in the context of gender relations, the scope of this chapter precludes a more detailed exploration of this aspect.
9. It is useful to note that Gimbutas, Eisler and others, who have studied ancient Europe and the Middle East, assume time frames going back to 6000 BC at their earliest. However, more recent excavations in Africa (arguably the birthplace of humankind),

including the very recent discoveries at the Sterkfontein Caves in South Africa, show evidence of an intelligent, creative and cooperative indigenous society dating back to more than 70,000 BC.

10. As to the relations between women and men in Old Europe, the archeological evidence suggests that there was no apparent social superiority of males over females, and, generally, the distribution of goods in the cemeteries of Old Europe points to an egalitarian and clearly non-patriarchal society (Baring and Cashford, 1991: 56).
11. The National Centre for Women Development in Abuja, Nigeria, has a display of prominent women throughout recorded history, including Moremi of Ife, Mai Bintu the 'King' of Hunters, Fatima Mohammed Nur (first woman to memorise the entire Koran), Chief Mercy Eneli (the premier Ibo female in the cabinet of Igwe the Kingmaker), Maira Aisa Kili Ngirmaramma (1501–1558, who ruled Kanem-Borno for seven years, seven months and seven days), Queen Amina of Zaria, and Emotan of Benin (who ruled the old Benin Empire), as well as various female chiefs from the 19th century forward.
12. To more accurately describe patriarchy, Eisler proposes the term *androcracy* (Greek *andros* = man; *cratos* = rule), and she depicts the pre-patriarchal non-hierarchical social constructions as *gylany* (Greek *gynę* = woman; *an* from *andros* and *l* as a linking of the two genders) (1995: 105).
13. Tomasevski emphasises that the subjugation of women did not begin "until the advent of the religions, and became more intense as the centuries rolled on".
14. Article 2(a)–(c) of the Declaration on the Elimination of Violence against Women UN General Assembly Resolution 48/104, 20 December 1993.
15. Section 1(ix) (b) of the Domestic Violence Act 116 of 1998.
16. South Africa is an example of a particularly patriarchal society where family murder by a patriarch is routine, especially amongst sectors of society that are highly militarised and/or hierarchised, e.g., the police force.
17. The excessively high levels of generic societal violence in South Africa, as well as the pandemic of gender-based violence in the country, is said to be one legacy of apartheid, where white boy-soldiers were systematically brutalised in a similar way to the liberation movements' (largely black) youthful combatants. The Vietnam war is said to have had similar effects in both the USA and Vietnam.

18. The Hindi word *satya* means truth.
19. C.f., e.g., *Gandhi* by Ashe (1968). And one of many of Gandhi's own writings, including "Civil Disobedience and Non-Violence".
20. It may be appropriate to acknowledge that both models, when used in this contrasting way, are in themselves binary oppositions.
21. Think also of times when patriarchy did not exist, for example, the time of Amanitare of ancient Nubia (Northern Ethiopia/Southern Sudan). She was one of several ancient African queens who ruled but was eventually deposed by others hungrier for power (and more violent).

References

Ashe, Geoffrey (1968) *Gandhi*, New York: Stein and Day.

Ashrawi, Hanan (1995) *This Side of Peace*, New York: Simon & Schuster.

Aung San Suu Kyi (1991) *Freedom from Fear and Other Writings*, New York: Penguin.

Baring, Anne and Jules Cashford (1991) *The Myth of the Goddess: Evolution of an Image*, London: Arkana.

Batchelor, Stephen (1997) *Buddhism without Beliefs: A Contemporary Guide to Awakening*, London: Bloomsbury.

Bennett, Jane (2000) "Gender-based Violence in South Africa", *The African Gender Institute Newsletter*, Cape Town: University of Cape Town, Vol. 6, May.

Bollen, S., L. Artz, L. Vetten and A. Louw (1999) *Violence against Women in Metropolitan South Africa: A Study on Impact and Service Delivery*, Monograph 41, September, Institute for Security Studies.

Bull, Hedley (1977) *The Anarchical Society: A Study of Order in World Politics*, New York: Columbia University Press.

Buzan, Barry (1983) *People, States and Fear: The National Security Problem in International Relations*, Sussex: Wheatsheaf.

Carr, E.H. (1939) *The Twenty Years' Crisis 1919–1939: An Introduction to the Study of International Relations*, London: Macmillan.

Eisler, Riane (1995) *The Chalice and the Blade: Our History, Our Future*, San Francisco: Harper Collins.

Flinders, Carol Lee (2002) *Reclaiming a Life of Value*, Publication forthcoming.

Galland, China (1998) *The Bond between Women: A Journey to Fierce Compassion*, New York: Riverhead.

Galtung, Johan (1996) *Peace by Peaceful Means*, London: Sage.

Gandhi, Mohandas (Nd.) "Civil Disobedience and Non-Violence", *The International University Society Reading Course: The Commonwealth Story*, Vol. 9, Edinburgh: International University Society.

Green, December (1999) *Gender Violence in Africa: African Women's Responses*, London: Macmillan.

Hobbes, Thomas (1952) (1651) *Leviathan*, Oxford: Oxford University Press.

Hudson, Heidi (1998) "A Feminist Reading of Security in Africa", *Caring' Security in Africa*, Monograph 20, February, Institute for Security Studies.

Morgenthau, Hans J. (1948) *Politics among Nations: The Struggle for Power and Peace*, New York: Alfred A. Knopf.

Muthien, B. and H. Combrinck (2003) "When Rights are Wronged: Gender-based Violence and Human Rights in Africa", in B. Kuumba and M. White (eds.), *Transnational Transgressions: African Women, Struggle and Transformation in Global Perspective*, Lawrenceville, NJ: Africa World Press.

Muthien, B. and I. Taylor (2002) "Executive Outcomes: The Return of Mercenaries and Private Armies", in T.J. Biersteker, R.B. Hall and C.N. Murphy (eds.), *Private Authority and Global Governance*, New York: Alfred A. Knopf.

Muthien, B. (2000) "The Privatisation of War in Southern Africa", paper at Demilitarisation and Peace building in Southern Africa Conference, Pretoria, Bonn International Centre for Conversion (BICC) and Centre for Conflict Resolution (CCR), publication forthcoming.

Pech, K., W. Boot and A. Eveleth (1998) "South African Dogs of War in Congo", *Mail & Guardian*, August 28, 6–7.

Randall, Vicky (1982) *Women and Politics*, New York: St Martin's.

Schoeman, M. (1998) "An Exploration of the Link between Security and Development", in H. Solomon and M. Schoeman (eds.), *Security, Development and Gender in Africa*, Halfway House: Institute for Security Studies.

Tomasevski, Katarina (1993) *Women and Human Rights*, London and New Jersey: Zed Books.

Turshen, M. and C. Twagiramariya (eds.) (1998) *What Women do in Wartime: Gender and Conflict in Africa*, London: Zed Books.

Uzuegbunam, Anthonia (2001) "Conflict Management Implications of Woman: Woman Marriage among the Igbos of Nigeria", WAAD 3rd International Conference, Antananarivo, Madagascar, October 8–17.

Vickers, J. (1993) *Women and War*, London and New Jersey: Zed Books.

Wallerstein, I. (1979) *The Capitalist World Economy*, Cambridge: Cambridge University Press.

Waltz, K. (1954) *Man, the State and War*, New York: Columbia University Press.

—— (1979) *Theory of International Politics*, New York: Random House.

16

The Apotheosis of Mohandas Gandhi

Is Going Global Going Too Far? And How Can Peace Education Respond?

JOHN SYNOTT

A New Gandhi Monument in Australia

It is a strange phenomenon when the image of Mohandas Gandhi who died as a result of a violent assault against him by a stranger in 1948 can be invoked to promote a sense of security for Indian students in Australia in 2010. Yet this is exactly what happened recently at the University of New South Wales, Sydney. The India Consul-General to Sydney, Mr Amit Dasgupta, donated a large cast-iron bust of Gandhi to UNSW and it was recently unveiled in a prominent corner of the university's library lawn. As reported in *The Australian* newspaper's Higher Education section on September 1 (Rowbotham, 2010: 23) the Consul-General Gupta stated that the bust is for "peace, it's for tolerance, it's for multiculturalism" and will become a meeting point for students. Perhaps I also can dream that the monument will become a place to teach informally Gandhi's philosophies, politics and non-violent tactics, for there are none of them offered within the university's thousand courses. Yet this university is one of the most prominent in chemical and technological research in Australia and the region, including areas such as robotics, quantum computing and biomedical research. One would expect Gandhi, if he were alive, to see the irony of his image being used to promote studies in such areas rather than the paths he followed.

The background to this quite unprecedented installation of Gandhi represents a coming together of important concerns and representations of both India and Australia, as well as the particular university. These interests are specific and general, national and global. The placement of Gandhi at a focus of these matters says something further important about contemporary cultural change and interaction, as the following discussion briefly will examine.

At the core of concerns is certainly the trade value of Indian students to the current economy of Australia and to the future economy of India. The students are here principally to improve their education so they can pursue high-level careers and be specialists in India and so continue to build the developing economy. In spite of occasional political rhetoric about students mostly arriving in Australia with plans to obtain permanent residency visas and remain here, the vast majority of international students return to their home countries. However, the education market is highly remunerative to the host country – Australia. So, both nations have a big stake in the presence and success of the students. India, in particular, provides a high proportion of post-graduate students to Australia at the current time and this is anticipated to increase.

Over the past couple of years there have been a number of incidents in Australia where Indian students have been the victims of physical assaults by small groups of Australian young men and, indeed, there has been at least one death associated with an apparently racially-based attack. After the murder of an Indian student in Melbourne and a number of other assaults where the victims were Indian students, such attacks became, briefly, the centre of attention in many Indian newspapers, bringing condemnation of anti-Indian sentiment in Australia, calls for people not to send their children to Australia to study and also for Indians to retaliate by attacking Australian tourists in India. The print media in both countries profited by publishing provocative – and opposing – articles on the issue.

The situation became so inflamed that Australian universities sent high-level delegations to India to assure officials and the public that Australia is indeed a very safe country and that students are very welcome in Australia. This was certainly a strategy behind the Gandhi monument at UNSW. *The Australian* article reported that "Pro-Vice Chancellor (International) Jennie

Lang says that while there haven't been any attacks on UNSW's 390 Indian students, the university is conscious of their safety and that of all its students" (ibid.).

The need to remove any concerns about student safety has been heightened by a national downturn in Indian student visas for the current year by 54.6 per cent compared to the previous year. This general trend of falling student numbers extends across the international student sector which is down 60.4 per cent in 2010 when compared to 2009 enrolments (ibid.).

The reason for this trend is the global financial crisis and, given that education exports are the fourth largest export and the largest non-commodities export from Australia, it is easy to recognise the efforts that are made to shore up Australia's largest knowledge-based industry.

The Legacy of Gandhi in the Contemporary World

Issues of national interest aside, this incident raises for me another concern more directly related to the meaning and legacy of Gandhi in the contemporary world. Somehow there has been distributed around the globe a symbolism and myth about Gandhi that is far removed from the contexts and issues of the times in which Gandhi emerged as an independence leader in India. The installation of a statue of Gandhi at UNSW is just one instance of many such statues of Gandhi being constructed around the world in the contemporary times. This apotheosis of Gandhi that began in the peace movement of the West over the past three decades or so gradually has been co-opted by commercial and institutional interests, such that his views, personality, and association with non-violent political strategies have resulted in the formulation of a Gandhi brand, whereby the mere image of Gandhi can be presumed to promote peace and tolerance through its symbolic significance. The Hollywood movie of Gandhi romanticised the Gandhi story while selling it to the English-speaking world, and institutions have now seized on the image. One can imagine a Gandhi perfume not too far in the future, whose fragrance is associated with sensations of peacefulness!

The West, of course, has a historical strength in icon-making, as seen in the history, architecture and artefacts of Christianity, so people in these cultures readily receive such symbolism when it is promoted by dominant institutions. The spread of Christianity around the world has been accompanied by the dispersion and local renewal of images representing the iconic figures in Christianity. Perhaps the best known of these is the statue of the Madonna overlooking Rio de Janeiro, but churches, public places and homes around the world engage in this practice. Also, this tradition was arguably part of the cultural rationale and acceptance behind the public imagery of the 'saints' of communism in previously Christian countries ranging from Russia to Cuba. Just as the statues of Christian icons in St Peter's Square in Rome replaced earlier idols of the Roman Empire, the statues of Lenin, Tito or Castro displaced the statues of Virgin and saints in countries that turned to communist governments and societies.

However, in the case of Gandhi, this public myth-making began in India and not the West. The Hindu tradition also is famous for its production of religious icons and the mythological stories that are identified with them, so it was relatively easy to assimilate Gandhi into the pantheon. Recording his impressions of India in the early decades of post-colonialism, the celebrated writer V.S. Naipaul, from Trinidad with an Indian family background, observed ways in which the significance of Gandhi had been appropriated away from the masses and become owned by the powerful. In 1967, Naipul wrote, as example:

> There is a whole department of the Central Government at work on *The Complete Works of Mahatma Gandhi*; they have an entry, under that name, in the Delhi telephone directory. But *The Hindu* newspaper of Madras reported in March that 90 per cent of high-school students in one district knew nothing of Gandhi except that he was a good man who fought for independence. (Naipaul, 2002, 27)

In this essay Naipul wrote of the widespread belief in the 'magical intervention' of Gandhi and other persons raised to the level of sacredness in India and how this simplifying of the world acted to disempower people from engaging in rational analysis of their own conditions and from setting their own goals and actions. Such attachments, he suggests, capture individuals and whole sections of society in dependent and accommodating dispositions that prevent them from seizing the possibilities of a different future.

Within peace studies it may be time to examine the ways in which Gandhi has been elevated as the standard-bearer of non-violent philosophy and tactics. Are teachers and students of peace studies paying too much attention to Gandhi and not enough to themselves? Knowing about Gandhi – his life, philosophy, writings and cultural leadership – is objectively interesting but can such knowledge be sufficient in strengthening and growing the transformative power to actually change society – which is what Gandhi was on about. Gandhi certainly was a student of the writings of Tolstoy, Ruskin and Thoreau and from them he acquired important insights into civil disobedience and non-violent resistance. However, it was the existential conditions of his existence and the socio-political repressions against which he rebelled, specifically racist repression of Indians in South Africa and the British colonial tyranny over India and Gandhi's own people. Moreover, Gandhi regarded his approach as distinctively Indian and rooted in Indian culture. In his excellent study of Gandhi's role as a social change agent, Richard Fox (1989) paid particular attention to Gandhi's pursuit of tactical experiments in pursuit of his political goal, which was Indian independence. At the core of this was Gandhi's pursuit of a spiritual modernisation whose roots he found deep in Indian culture as opposed to the material modernisation of the West. His principal weapons became a series of experiments in confrontation and alternative social practices that he regarded as inherent in the core of Indian spiritual civilisation as against the material core of the hegemonic British society that had effectively enslaved India. Such notions included *ahimsa* and *satyagraha* (Kumar, 2010). They were for him experiments that had elements of risk and sometimes failure, but he was willing to adapt the lessons learned from his models into his current circumstances and explore their possibilities for successful political actions.

Anthologist R.G. Fox commented that, by the time of Gandhi's death, the cultural principles he espoused such as *ahimsa* and *satyagraha* had become so central to the Indian post-independence identity that "there was a real struggle over what it should become thereafter" (Fox, 1989: 171). History in India has shown that soon after Gandhi's death the *satyagraha* movement became divided along different paths, either towards a mild social reconstructionism (Vinoba) or a dynamic and confrontationist non-violent socialism (Lohia) (ibid.: 170). In adopting some aspects of Gandhi's *satyagraha* the respective heirs each claimed to have inherited essential features but actually they had lost the essence of the utopian movement. With the facts of such diversions in India, so soon after Gandhi's departure, and by those who were his contemporaries and close to him, we must realise that Gandhi's vision finished with him. Others could seek to emulate him but such efforts ultimately proved fruitless. Fox (ibid.: 171) commented that the Nehru government "succeeded in hijacking Gandhian utopia: it carted it around like ideological baggage". Similarly, Fox claimed that Vinoba's Gandhian utopia "became a daydream" because it lacked any struggle or way to experiment on existing society with utopian intentions. Such trends emphasise the incapacity of a great innovator or leader to exercise authority from the grave. In fact, Fox shows how even before independence "there were attempts to make Gandhi a figurehead without authority, a saint without substance" (ibid.: 172). Fox (ibid.: 151) observed that "Gandhi disliked his Mahatma reputation, not least of all perhaps because he found the trappings of sainthood inconsistent with a social revolutionary's mantle".

Reclaiming the Gandhi Spirit

These facts and general discussion of Gandhi's impacts in India at the time of independence bring us back to the Gandhi statue in Sydney. I find the tokenism of this gesture an affront to the very principles and confrontationist tactics employed by Gandhi against oppression and for utopian social change on behalf of the masses of Indian people. This monument has been established specifically to convey some message to Indian students and the society at large that they are safe and welcome, as articulated by the Indian Consul-General at the unveiling. The intentions may appear superficially attractive and present an image of Indian and Australian authorities working together. But, the real intent of the monument at this university is to induce students to keep coming here and bring their money with them. The sudden interest in Gandhi at UNSW leaves me uncomfortable.

An experimental act with more of Gandhi's radical and confrontationist spirit might be a statement by the university to refuse to engage in research that can lead to weapons productions or creating scholarships for poor Indians to experience university in Australia, or even the promotion of peace and non-violence studies and skills among its Aussie students. However, they will never do these experiments for fear of losing money and reputation. The hijacking of Gandhi continues, it seems, and is being associated with 'brand India' as it becomes more global. This needs to be resisted if the authentic soul of Gandhi's social experiments is to be rediscovered outside India and applied creatively to the socio-cultural conditions of the place and time. This brings a conclusion that Gandhi followers may do well to look inwards more often than outwards. Gandhi's achievement was built on rigorous self-discipline. From introversion and personal practice those inspired by Gandhi's examples might build their own skills and abilities through experiments in non-violent social transformation, and with a willingness to accept the sanctions and punishments that disobedience against oppressive laws, values and institutions will inevitably bring.

Gandhi in Peace Education

The above case illustrates some further considerations that can bring new energy and direction as to how Gandhi and his work are treated in the broad field of peace education. If it is the case, as I have suggested in this chapter that Gandhi is becoming a symbol of 'Brand India' in its push towards a stronger internationalised economy and worldwide influence, then peace education offers a field where a balanced understanding of Gandhi can be promoted. Just as Gandhi himself undertook campaigns to challenge dominant discourses regarding Indian identity as a colonial subject, peace educators can challenge the emerging appropriation of Gandhi as an iconic brand of the nation in its global capitalistic development. Peace education offers the ideal site for critically analysing the appropriation of Gandhi by the very forces he opposed and for promoting alternative discourses centred on the critical politics of Gandhi and the paths he advocated towards the achievement of humanistic, non-violent egalitarian societies in India specifically and the world at large.

A brief survey of some prominent peace education publications of recent decades shows that while Gandhi's ideals, personal examples and principles (e.g., *satyagraha*) shape the terrain of much contemporary peace education research and exposition, there have not been many publications centred on Gandhi. I refer here particularly to publications in the West, for there is certainly a richer repertoire of Gandhian studies published in India (e.g., Dadhich, 2003, 2004; Kumar, 2010). The international Taylor and Francis Group journal *The Journal of Peace Education*, for instance, during the period 2004–2010 published just one article with a focus on Gandhi's work (Tamatea, 2005), but at the same time Gandhian principles such as non-violence informed many of the articles in the journal during that time. Similarly, prominent books in peace education such as Burns and Aspeslagh (1996), Wintersteiner, (1999), Harris and Morrison (2003), which are all terrific books in peace education, deal sparely with Gandhi and his work.

One excellent analysis of Gandhi's work in the context of peace education is that of D. Allen. From a careful analysis of Gandhi's writings this author identified many areas where Gandhi offers valuable insights into peace education and also weaknesses in the Gandhian perspective on peace education. Allen concluded that the Gandhian perspective "has great value in critiquing other models of education, in serving as a catalyst that allows us to re-think our normal assumptions and dominant concepts and positions, and in offering new creative positive alternatives" (Allen, 2007: 306). However, this author cautions that practitioners in peace education must be selective especially "in revalorizing and reformulating basic Gandhian values in new more relevant ways and in integrating Gandhian and other compatible insights and contributions" (ibid.).

While Allen's discussion is focussed on identifying how Gandhi's writings can contribute to peace education, my proposal here is that, reciprocally, peace education can fulfil an important role in ensuring that the public understanding of Gandhi's life and work maintains its integrity. Such a position will reiterate the non-violent, liberationist and critical positions identified with Gandhi, as against the branding of Gandhi as an essentialist Indian product to be exported around the world for the purpose of marketing India Inc. Therefore, there is a need to systematically undertake some additional research and analysis of Gandhi to produce a comprehensive publication in peace education centred on Gandhi and his work. Such a project could include the following areas of focus in respect to Gandhi's achievements and experience:

- social and historical contexts
- personal journey and biography
- responses to hegemonic and oppressive political and economic power
- views on personal responsibility and the development of discipline
- social vision, equality and emancipation
- non-violence and its ways of practice

- knowledge, truth and wisdom
- community and social relations

These are some areas out of many that peace educators can develop within organised learning frameworks both in India and internationally, so that there is a well-articulated and credible alternative discourse promoted that critiques the appropriation of Mohandas Gandhi as a vehicle for Indian national expansion in the competition for brand prominence in the global marketplace.

References

Allen, D. (2007) "Mahatma Gandhi on Non-violence and Peace Education", *Philosophy East and West*, Vol. 57, No. 3, 290–310. Available online at: http://muse.jhu.edu/journals/philosophy_east_and_west/v057/57.3allen.pdf.

Burns, R. and R. Aspeslagh (eds.) (1996) *Three Decades of Peace Education around the World*, New York: Garland Publishing.

Dadhich, N. (ed.) (2003) *Non-violence, Peace and Politics: Understanding Gandhi*, Jaipur: Aavishkar Publishers.

—— (ed.) (2004) *Towards a More Peaceful World: International and Indian Perspectives*, Jaipur: Aalekh Publishers.

Fox, R.G. (1989) *Gandhian Utopia: Experiments with Culture*, Boston: Beacon Press.

Harris, I. and M.L. Morrison (2003) *Peace Education*, Jefferson NC: McFarland & Co.

Kumar, Ravindra (2010) *India and Mahatma Gandhi*, New Delhi: Kalpaz Publications.

Rowbotham, Jill (2010) "Gandhi Takes a Stand at UNSW", *The Australian*, Higher Education, September 1, 23.

Naipaul, V.S. (2002) "A Second Visit (orig. 1967)", in Pankaj Mishra (ed.) *The Writer and the World*, London: Picador, 15–34.

Tamatea, L. (2005) "The Uses of Gandhi in Education in Bali: Different Responses to Globalisation: Implications for Social Justice", *Journal of Peace Education*, Vol. 2, No. 2, 139–160.

17

Problematising Modernity

Gandhi and Ecologism

NISHIKANT KOLGE AND N. SREEKUMAR

Incredulity towards modernity can be considered as a common launching point of Gandhi's mission (Gandhian project) and ecologism. Gandhi believes that the exploitation of one's fellow men and nature is built into the very structure of modern society. Today, most of the ecologists have come to an agreement that solutions for contemporary ecological problems cannot be found from within the existing modern institutional structures and it is necessary to rethink about the basic organisation of modern society that generates such problems. Here, the word 'ecologists' is used to refer some of the green political thinkers like Andrew Dodson, Baxter Brian, Jake Kosek, James Connelly and W.M. Adams and as the *International Encyclopaedia of Environmental Politics* says political ecologists find inspiration in deep ecology (Connelly and Adams, 2002: 185) Some of the deep ecologists like Arne Naess and Eric Katz are also referred to as ecologists. Both Gandhi and the ecologists believe that the root cause of today's problems lies in the way modern man understands and relates himself with other men and nature. Therefore, Gandhi and the ecologists problematise some of the fundamental assumptions of modernity, on which both the social and political lives of men and their relationship with the non-human world are organised in the contemporary world.

Problematising modernity does not amount to be its complete rejection and neither Gandhi nor ecologism does it. As observed by Ronald Terchek, even though Gandhi finds the enlightenment project encumbered with pretentious claims to know the truth, he sees no need to completely reject modernity out of hand (Terchek, 2001: 3). And, his appreciation of some aspects of modernity is also well known. The ecologists too share a similar approach. Andrew Dodson, a leading ecologist, writes:

> So while radical green politics ought to be characterized as a challenge to the contemporary consensus over norms and practices that have its most immediate sources in the early enlightenment, it would be a mistake to think it pays no mind whatever to those norms and practices. (Dodson, 2002: 11–12)

Hence problematising modernity simply means to challenge some promises of modernity proclaimed by dominant modern Europe, which ultimately bring hopes of human emancipation by presenting over all transformation of traditional or pre-modern social structures. The traditional and pre-modern societies are predominantly characterised as social structures of inequalities based on kinship, hereditary privileges and established authority and modernity is projected as an age of reason, equality, freedom and justice. Modernity indeed brings such notions into prominence. But Gandhi and the ecologists try to demonstrate that modernity as it is understood by dominant modern Europe is not all about equality, freedom and justice but it also carries its own forms of inequality, domination and normalisation. This paper attempts to draw a parallel between the Gandhian and the ecologist critiques of this dominant modern European understanding of modernity, in order to highlight the basic axioms of this understanding which are responsible for the creation of the modern structures of exploitation and tyranny. It will also try to resolve the apparent tension between the positions of Gandhi and the ecologists, which appear when we attempt drawing a parallel between their critiques of the above mentioned dominant European understanding of modernity.

Understanding the Dominant European Project of Modernity

As it is mentioned above, Gandhi's and the ecologists' rejection of modernity is not a complete denial of the latter. They recognise the importance of modern virtues like, equality, justice and order in organising human societies. They also appreciate modern notions like autonomy and freedom. Indeed their disagreement is not with modernity as such, but with the way in which it is predominantly understood in Europe. Modernity need not essentially be linked with westernisation, industrialisation and urbanisation. It brings forth virtues like reason, universality, order, autonomy, equality, freedom and justice. But, the European project of modernity, which Gandhi and the ecologists oppose, emerges as an industrial and urban project and is projected as a universal phenomenon. This claim of universality of the European project of modernity is constructed by establishing the paradigmatic status of its understanding of science, technology and the concepts of growth and development.

Gandhi and the ecologists challenge this claim of universality and attempt to demonstrate that it is a specific project of a particular group of people. As Ashis Nandy says, for Gandhi, the choice was not between modernity and tradition but between different traditions.[1] Furthermore, they both discard the European myth which projects modernity as facilitating human enlightenment and emancipation, and attempt to show how domination and exploitation work in the modern social, economic and political structures, in spite of modernity's idealising virtues like equality and justice. As Thomas Pantham says, for Gandhi, the basic error of the project of Western post-enlightenment modernity is its exploitation of, or violence to, its other (Pantham, 1995: 1010–2). Many ecologists here agree with Gandhi. For instance, Jake Kosek observes that modernity and its trappings polluted both nature and the human soul (Kosek, 1996: 127).

Dominant Modern European Understanding of Science

European concept of science – a principal agent of carrying out the European project of modernity – is one of the central focuses of criticism of both the Gandhian project as well as ecologism. But their critiques of modern European sciences should not be considered as "anti-science" or "anti-rational", which was a sign of romanticism or conservatism. They do indeed acknowledge the importance of science and rationality in human life on many other occasions. As Arne Naess says, it was only as a professor that he became aware of the difficulties of suppressing the significance of the development of feeling in human affairs while at the same time worshipping reason. He affirms that both are constantly needed.[2] Gandhi must have had the same idea while writing, "I plead not for the suppression of reason, but for a due recognition of that in us which sanctifies reason itself" (Gandhi, 1969, 31: 498).

They are also not as such against the claim of science as an autonomous system of knowledge aiming at arriving objective truth. They are against the modern European attitude which hesitates to evaluate science and its uses and importance in terms of its impact on human society and nature. They believe that science needs to be judged not only in terms of certain specific ethical issues relevant in any particular field of science, but also from a more comprehensive ethical and moral perspective. They believe that conceiving science as a system of knowledge free from any external standards of judgment will make it a mere tool to exploit others. As observed by W.M. Adams, rationalisation is the process by which human reason frames and allows ordering and control of both nature and society (Adams, 2009: 46). Gandhi also shares this view and his rejection of modern civilisation is based on the conviction that it reduces wisdom to knowledge and the latter to a form of power only useful as an instrument of control over nature and other men (Parekh, 1989: 22). Therefore, both Gandhi and the ecologists believe that this modern European attitude of looking at science and its uses in isolation from its impact on human society has to be rejected because it not only makes possible but also legitimises man's exploitation of his fellow beings and nature.

Apart from this, both Gandhi and the ecologists are against modern European attribution of omnipotence to science and rationality, according to which science is not only accepted as *a priori* knowledge but is also regarded as superior to other modes of knowing. It leads to the belief that every human belief and truth claim has to be justified through rational analysis. Both Gandhi and the ecologists reject this and they believe in the legitimacy of other human modes of responding to the world like faith, emotions, arts, ethics, and many other modes of knowing. As observed by Terchek, for Gandhi, modern science's greatest danger comes from its mode of thinking; sweeping aside alternative ways of understanding the cosmos, morality and oneself (Terchek, 2000: 89). They believe that these alternate modes of knowing are not only helpful for human beings for coping up with the world but also very important in determining their legitimate place in the world and their relationship with nature. In short, their aim is not as such to reject or diminish the importance of rationality in human life but to complete it by demonstrating the importance of faith, emotions and many other alternate modes of enquiries to comprehend the complexity of human life and its relation with nature.

Dominant Modern European Understanding of Technology

Technology is not a specific European or modern phenomenon. It is found in one or other ways in every known human civilisation at every time. Gandhi and the ecologists are not as such against technology, but they oppose its excessive use, which is a very specific Modern European phenomenon. Gandhi emphatically says that he is not opposed to machinery. He adds that the opposition is to its misuse, or its excessive use (Gandhi, 1969, 37: 158). Both Gandhi and the ecologists acknowledge the importance of technology in human life. But they caution that an element of instrumentality is inevitably associated with the very idea of technology. They affirm that technology proved to be an effective instrument to those who possess it for exploiting others.

Most of the ecologists are concerned about constructed hierarchies and exploitation within human society as well as between man and the non-human world. Arne Neass asserts the need for limiting the impacts of this modern European attitude towards technology on the non-industrial countries and defending the Fourth World against foreign domination (Naess, 2005, 10: 41). James Connelly and Graham Smith write:

> There is however a widespread recognition that technology tends to shape contemporary society, creating new wants and desires; its social and ethical impact often leading to a sharp separation of humanity form natural world. Strong anthropocentric, Promethean attitudes of control and domination abound. For greens this attitude and relation too technology must be reversed. (Connelly and Smith, 2003: 76)

Like most of the ecologists, for Gandhi too man's relationship with his fellow beings and the rest of the world are at risk due to the excessive use of technology. But he argues that the excessive use of technology should be rejected primarily because it poses threat to the dignity and autonomy of the individual. As Ashis Nandy says:

> Gandhi was against technologies which replaced the uniquely human aspects of men. Not only because such replacement turned a person into a mechanical part of the production machine, but also because it turned him into a mechanical, 'dead' consumer of utilities. (Nandy, 1987: 138)

Gandhi was ready to accept those technologies which do not pose a threat to human dignity and autonomy. For instance, he was in favour of using the *charkha* or spinning wheel, sewing machine and the bicycle because he believed that they do not replace human being and respect human dignity and autonomy. He was once asked where would these exceptions end if he made them for the Singer sewing machine and his spindle and Gandhi replied by saying that they end where they cease to help the individual and encroach upon his individuality (Gandhi, 1969, 70: 242).

Ecologists too reject excessive use to technology with due acceptance of its importance in human life. But the focus of their concern is to find out a way to establish an equilibrium between human beings and the rest of nature rather than safeguarding human dignity and autonomy. As asserted by Brain Baxter, "... we may begin to employ our scientific and technological ingenuity ... in a way which does not threaten the integrity of the biosphere."[3]

Dominant Modern European Understanding of Progress/Development

Gandhi and the ecologists were also opposing the idea of development that has been excessively used by the dominant modern Europe in order to justify its exploitation and domination. The latter understood development as more or less consisting in reaching an acceptable standard of living for all people. This standard of leaving is largely defined in terms of material or economic progress. As it is mentioned in UNDP's *Human Development Report 1996*, human development is the end – economic growth a means.[4] Gandhi and the ecologists are against such a reductionist understanding of progress/development.

Form the very outset it is important to mention that their criticism of this concept of progress/development is not the result of a longing for an utopian past, like the one exhibited by the European romantic tradition. Andrew Dodson writes that this would be an especially big mistake if we were to jump to the conclusion that modern green politics is only a form of reincarnated romanticism (Dodson, 2000: 12). Gandhi too affirms that his criticism of modernity is not an attempt to go back to the so-called ignorant, dark ages (Gandhi, 1969, 70: 242). For both the ecologists and Gandhi this concept of progress/development is never built with the primary aim of meeting human needs; rather its very existence is based on creating artificial mad desires and an indefinite multiplication of wants.

Most of the ecologists argue that in this relentless pursuit of material wealth modern man fails to comprehend the interdependence between humans and their environment. The non-human world is separated from man and is looked upon as something which fosters the satisfaction of his needs. Due to this ignorance modern man is not able to recognise and assign any legitimate value to the non-human world and nature and continues to exploit it in vain hope of satisfying his chimeral desires of accumulating material wealth. They are of the view that many of the contemporary crises related to the environment like global warming, erosion of ozone layer and acid rain are the logical culmination of this ignorance. They believe that this senseless pursuance of economic growth makes modern man blind towards the consequence of the reckless consumption of natural resources.

To put it apocalyptically, they articulate this negligence as jeopardise, not only to human life but also to life as such in the planet. They argue that there are physical limits to the demand which man can impose on the planet because earth is finite and its resources are finite too. This concern is well articulated in the report 'The Limits to Growth' published in 1972 by "The Club of Rome" – a group of prominent scientists, educators, economists, industrialists, civil servants. It says:

> If the present growth trends in world population, industrialization, pollution, and food production and resource depletion continue unchanged then the limits to growth on the planet will be reached sometime within the next one hundred years. The most probable result will be a rather sudden and uncontrollable decline in both population and industrial capacity.[5]

Since 1972 onwards, this "limits to growth" has been used by the ecologists to undermine the justification for reckless consumption of natural resources.

Although assigning legitimate value to the non-human world is the central concern for the ecologists for criticising the dominant modern European understanding of development, there are many ecologists who wish to emphasise the social problems arising as a consequence of this understanding. Many of them mount a socio-economic critique of the inequalities in human societies. Irvine and Porton, in this context, observe that, limiting differentials between people is as essential as limiting economic growth and technological innovations (Irvine and Ponton, 1998: 80).

Gandhi too rejects this view of development because like many ecologists, he believes that it coalesces with the mad desire of an indefinite multiplication of wants. But he mounts his opposition from a different ground. He finds these mad desires obnoxious because he believes that they disturb the true nature of human civilisation by emphasising only one expect of human life – economic or material growth – and by undermining other very important aspects of human life. He affirms that civilisation in the real sense of the term consists not in the multiplication, but in the deliberate and voluntary reduction of wants (Gandhi, 1969, 44: 103). He argues that human problems cannot be overcome with more goods or even a more equitable distribution of goods, no matter how desirable the latter goal may be for him.[6] He therefore appreciates the traditional ways of living in which, according to him, people find beauty and meaning of life in voluntary simplicity, poverty and slowness. In *Hind Swaraj*, he writes:

> Observing all this, our ancestors dissuaded us from luxuries and pleasures. We have managed with the same kind of plough as existed thousands of year ago. We have retained the same kind of cottages that we had in former times and our indigenous education remains the same as before. (Gandhi, 2006: 53)

Gandhi strongly favours this traditional idea of deliberate checks on economic growth. He believes it is very essential to maintain an equilibrium in life, as human civilisation according to him provides better scope for flourishing human life with all its potentials. Indeed his concern for ancient civilisation was a concern for dignity and the autonomy of the individual because he holds that individual is the one supreme consideration (Gandhi, 1969, 24: 251). He further believes that when abstract principles, such as economic growth, become central, human beings are lost, mealy expendable means to some bright, elusive end.[7]

Gandhi and the Ecologists: Apparent Tensions

Both Gandhi and the ecologists, in their respective criticism of the European project of modernity, though identify similar problems, yet differ in their basic concerns. It seems that for Gandhi this project has to be rejected for the sake of respecting individual dignity and autonomy. Indeed, as we have seen, Gandhi was not as such against modernity; he was only against the exploitation and oppression in its name, which squeeze individual's dignity and autonomy. He was ready to accept many modern virtues, provided they respect individual dignity and help realising autonomy. Apart from this, he was also ready to denounce tradition wherever he found it was degrading the individual dignity and suppressing his or her autonomy. In short, his fight against modernity was a struggle to safeguard the individual.

On the other hand, the ecologists are attempting to develop an environmental philosophy that explains man's relationship to the natural world with an emphasis on the value of nature and natural processes (Katz, 2000: 21). This seems to be varying from the fundamental Gandhian concerns. There are indeed many ecologists who also raise concerns over the spread of inequality within human society across the globe. Yet safeguarding the dignity and autonomy of individuals was not their central concern. Instead, they were emphatic about acknowledging the legitimate value of the non-human world. From Gandhi's point of view there may not necessarily be a contradiction between these two views. As observed by Thomas Pantham, for Gandhi, the autonomy of the *moral* self is linked with the well-being of the 'other' (Pantham, 1995: 104). The 'other', for Gandhi, includes the non-human world as well.

It thus appears that the ecologists' point of view is not only different from Gandhi's, but also contradicts his position as he sounds overtly anthropocentric when he argues for the dignity and autonomy of the individual. One of the important objectives of the ecologists consists in transcending anthropocentrism and adopting a perspective of egocentrism (Katz, 2000: 18). In this sense, their respective positions cannot be seen as complementary to each other.

Discussion on Anthropocentrism: An Effort to Resolve Seeming Differences

Most of the ecologists agree that replacing anthropocentrism with ecocentrism is fundamental to ecologism. But they believe that it is not an easy task. Since only humans are moral agents, and only they are capable of developing theories, norms and perspectives, then to what extent can any of these can escape human centredness? Is it really possible to develop any non-anthropocentric perspective at all? Questions like these have been haunting scholars since long. Many ecologists were even prepared to accept 'human centredness' as unavoidable. They distinguish between what is an unavoidable 'human-centred' perspective from anthropocentrism and, seek to establish a harmonious equilibrium between man and the non-human world with such a perspective, where 'human centeredness' is really unavoidable. Andrew Dodson in *Green Political Thought* uses the expressions 'weak' and 'strong' anthropocentrisms to refer respectively to approaches that are 'unavoidably human-centred' and that conceives non-human world purely as a means to human ends. Further, he argues that "anthropocentrism in the weak sense is an unavoidable feature of the human condition" (Dodson, 2000: 51).

Tim Hayward uses the terms 'human 'speciesism' and 'human chauvinism' to make similar kinds of differences (Hayward, 1998: 46–49). Naess too adopts such a distinction. He says that in criticising the homocentrism or anthropocentrism we are pointing to an image of man as an immature being with crude, narrow, short-sighted interests (Naess, 2005, 10: 1886).

Even though, Gandhi emphasises the dignity and autonomy of the individual, it would be erroneous to see it as an effort to place man at the centre of the world with supreme authority over the non-human world. As Bhikhu Parekh observes, man for Gandhi was not the centre of the universe and he did not see the need radically to mark him off from the rest of the universe and lay excessive stress on his uniqueness (Parekh, 1989: 86–87). Gandhi indeed completely rejects the European Enlightenment and Judo-Christian idea that man is a master and a possessor of nature. On the contrary, he believes in essential interdependence and oneness of all living beings and non-living beings. "I believe", he says "… that if one man gains spirituality the whole world gains with him and if one man falls the world falls to that extent."[8] As it is mentioned above, Thomas Pantham observes that for Gandhi, the autonomy of the *moral* self is linked with the well-being of the 'other' Thus, his emphasis on dignity and autonomy of the individual is not a kind of 'strong anthropocentrism' or 'human chauvinism'. It is nothing more than a mere acceptance of what Arne Naess says, "it is specifically human both to see and formulate the limitations for the role of human beings in the ecosphere and to experience their identification with the whole" (Naess, 2005, 10: 86). It is also just an echo of Hayward's idea of 'enlightened self-interest' – a kind of realisation that self's personal capacities cannot be fully developed in isolation from others (Hayward, 1998: 113). As observed by Dodson, Hayward's belief is that an 'enlightened self-interest' is the best way forward, since it is more conceptually coherent than biocentrism or ecocentrism, and because it accords better with basic human motivations (Dodson, 2000: 102). At this stance, when most of the ecologists believe that a perspective of human-centred value is an unavoidable feature of the human condition and they also agree that ideas like 'enlightened self-interest' or 'self-realisation' can do more justice to their core doctrines than ideas like 'biocentrism' or 'ecocentrism', Gandhi's emphasis on the dignity and autonomy of individual does not seem to be contradicting these ecologists' positions. Here, both the concerns of the Gandhian project and of ecologism are not in contradistinction to each other, but on the contrary they emerge as complementing each other.

Notes

1. Roger Garaudy writes, For Gandhi ... Nandy writes, "The choice is not between a traditional technique and a modern technique; it is between different traditions of technology." In Foreword, Ashis Nandy (1987) *Traditions, Tyranny and Utopias: Essays in the Politics of Awareness*, Delhi: Oxford University Press, p. vii.
2. Cited in series editor's introduction of *The Selected Works of Arne Naess*, Alan Drengson (ed.) (2005), in Cooperation with the Author and with Assistance from Bill Devall and George Sessions, Dordrecht, The Netherlands: Springer, p. 50.
3. Cited in James Connelly and Graham Smith (2003) *Politics and the Environment: From Theory to Practice*, Second Edition, London and New York: Routledge, p. 50.
4. Cited in Tatyana P. Soubbotina (2004) *Beyond Economic Growth: An Introduction to Sustainable Development*, Second Edition, Washington, DC: The World Bank, p. 8.
5. Cited in James Connelly and Graham Smith, op. cit.
6. See J. Ronald Terchek (2000) *Gandhi's Struggle for Autonomy*, New Delhi: Vistaar Publications, p. 111.
7. Ibid., p. 114.
8. Cited in Thomas Weber (May, 1999) "Gandhi, Deep Ecology, Peace Research and Buddhist Economics", *Journal of Peace Research*, Vol. 36, No. 3, p. 352.

References

Adams, W.M. (2009) *Green Development: Environment and Sustainability in a Developing World*, Third Edition, London and New York: Routledge.

Barry, John and E. Gene Frankland (2002) *International Encyclopaedia of Environmental Politics*, London: Routledge.

Brian, Baxter (1999) *Ecologism: An Introduction*, Edinburgh: Edinburgh University Press.

Connelly, James and Graham Smith (2003) *Politics and the Environment: From Theory to Practice*, Second Edition, London and New York: Routledge, 50.

Dodson, Andrew (2000) *Green Political Thought*, Third Edition, London: Routledge.

Drengson, Alan (ed.) (2005) *The Selected Works of Arne Naess*, in Cooperation with the Author and with Assistance from Bill Devall and George Sessions, Dordrecht, The Netherlands: Springer, 50.

Gandhi, M.K. (1996) *The Collected Works of Mahatma Gandhi (hereafter CWMG)*, New Delhi: The Publication Division, Ministry of Information and Broadcasting, Government of India.

—— (2006) *Hindi Swaraj*, Ahmedabad: Navajivan Publishing House.

Hayward, Tim (1998) *Political Theory and Ecological Values*, New York: St. Martin's Press.

Irvine, S. and A. Ponton (1998) *A Green Manifesto: Policies for a Green Future*, London: Macdonald Optima.

Katz, Eric (2000) "Against the Inevitability of Anthropocentrism", in Eric Katz, Andrew Light and David Rothenberg (eds.), *Beneath the Surface: Critical Essays in the Philosophy of Deep Ecology*, Cambridge, Massachusetts and London: The MIT Press.

Kosek, Jake (1996) "Purity and Pollution: Racial Degradation and Environmental Anxieties", in Richard Peet and Michael Watts (eds.), *Liberation Ecologies: Environment, Development, Social Movements*, Second Edition, London and New York: Routledge.

Nandy, Ashis (1987) *Traditions, Tyranny and Utopias: Essays in the Politics of Awareness*, Delhi: Oxford University Press, vii.

Pantham, Thomas (1995) "Gandhi, Nehru and Modernity", in Upendra Baxi and Bhikhu Parekh (eds.), *Crisis and Change in Contemporary India*, New Delhi: Sage Publications.

Parekh, Bhikhu (1998) *Gandhi's Political Philosophy: A Critical Examination*, London: Macmillan Press.

Soubbotina, Tatyana P. (2004) *Beyond Economic Growth: An Introduction to Sustainable Development*, Second Edition, Washington, DC: The World Bank, 8.

Terchek, J. Ronald (2000) *Gandhi's Struggle for Autonomy*, New Delhi: Vistaar Publications.

—— (April-June 2001), "Problematizing Modernity: Gandhi's Decentering Impulse", *Gandhi Marg*, Vol. XX, 5–20.

Weber, Thomas (May, 1999) "Gandhi, Deep Ecology, Peace Research and Buddhist Economics", *Journal of Peace Research*, Vol. 36, No. 3, 352.

Index